PRAISE FOR *INTO THE ABYSS*

Winner of the Edna Staebler Award for Creative Nonfiction

"With INTO THE ABYSS Carol Shaben gives us an astonishing true story of catastrophe and redemption. Shaben writes from the inside out, as in the best nonfiction, creating a nuanced and tightly braided portrait of four men and their shared trauma that is by turns terrifying and deeply humane. Every line in this story rings true."

—John Vaillant, author of *The Tiger*

"Well-written...[This] work casts troubling light on the enormous challenges faced by pilots at these smaller airlines and the harsh realities of travel in Canada's unforgiving northern regions."

—*Library Journal*

"[Shaben] vividly recreates how these four total strangers managed to survive the tragedy."

—*New York Post*

"Absorbing...Shaben's gripping narrative seizes the reader from the first chapter."

—*Toronto Star*

"The gripping account...is ultimately about the survivors, telling the story in scouring yet respectful detail of the four men who limped away from the fatal crash."

—*Edmonton Journal* (Canada)

INTO THE ABYSS

AN EXTRAORDINARY TRUE STORY

CAROL SHABEN

GRAND CENTRAL
PUBLISHING

NEW YORK   BOSTON

First published in Canada in 2012 by Random House Canada.

Text and maps by Andrew Roberts.

Grand Central Publishing
Hachette Book Group
1290 Avenue of the Americas
New York, NY 10104

www.HachetteBookGroup.com

Printed in the United States of America

LSC-H

Originally published in hardcover by Hachette Book Group.

First trade edition: May 2014

Printing 13, 2021

Grand Central Publishing is a division of Hachette Book Group, Inc.
The Grand Central Publishing name and logo are trademarks of Hachette Book Group, Inc.

The Hachette Speakers Bureau provides a wide range of authors for speaking events.
To find out more, go to www.hachettespeakersbureau.com or call (866) 376-6591.

The publisher is not responsible for websites (or their content)
that are not owned by the publisher.

Library of Congress Catalog Number: 2012949751

ISBN 978-1-4555-0196-0 (pbk.)

For Riyad

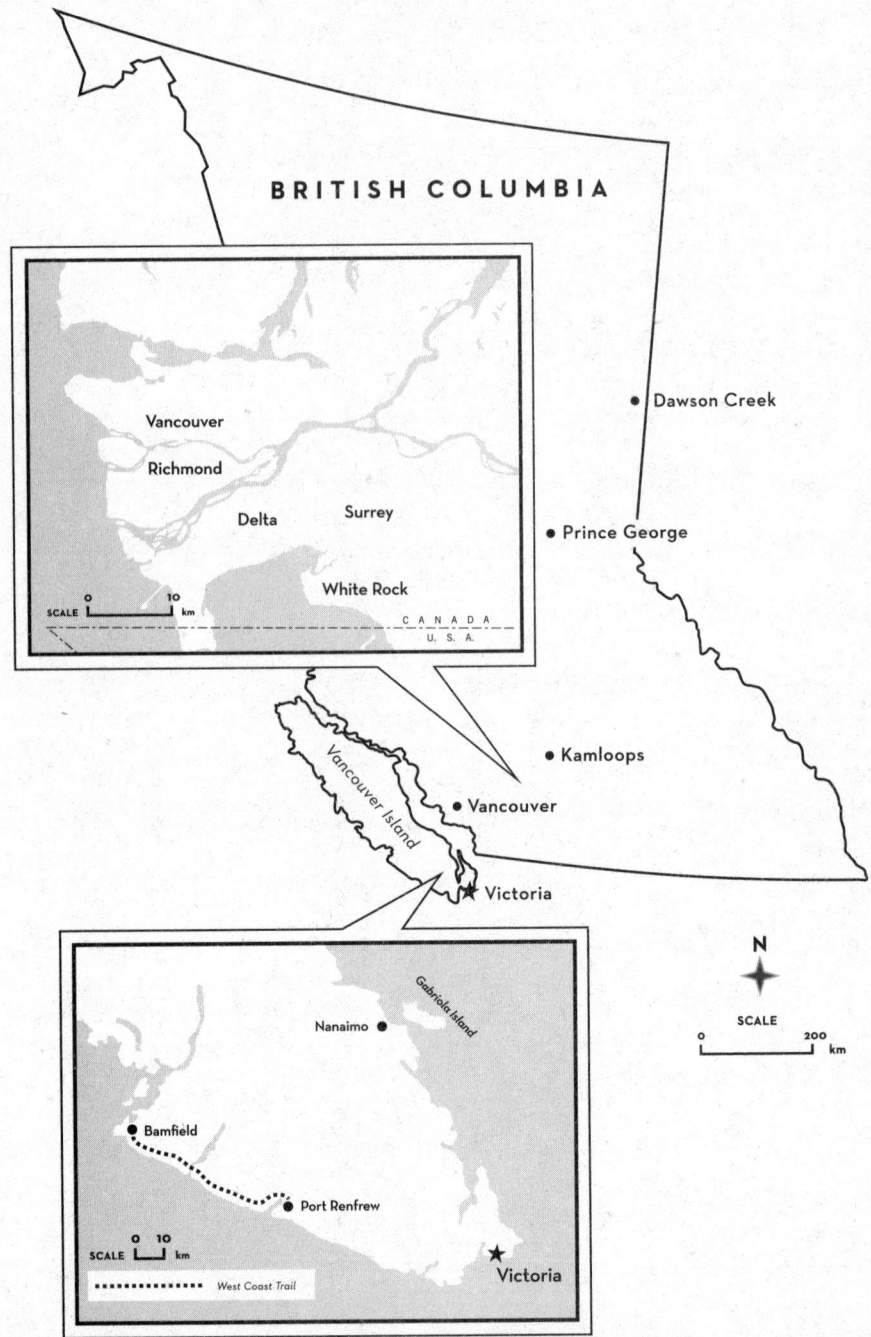

SOUTHERN BRITISH COLUMBIA COAST

BRITISH COLUMBIA

Vancouver

Richmond

Delta

Surrey

White Rock

SCALE 0 10 km

CANADA
U. S. A.

Dawson Creek

Prince George

Kamloops

Vancouver

Vancouver Island

Victoria

N

SCALE 0 200 km

Gabriola Island

Nanaimo

Bamfield

Port Renfrew

SCALE 0 10 km

West Coast Trail

Victoria

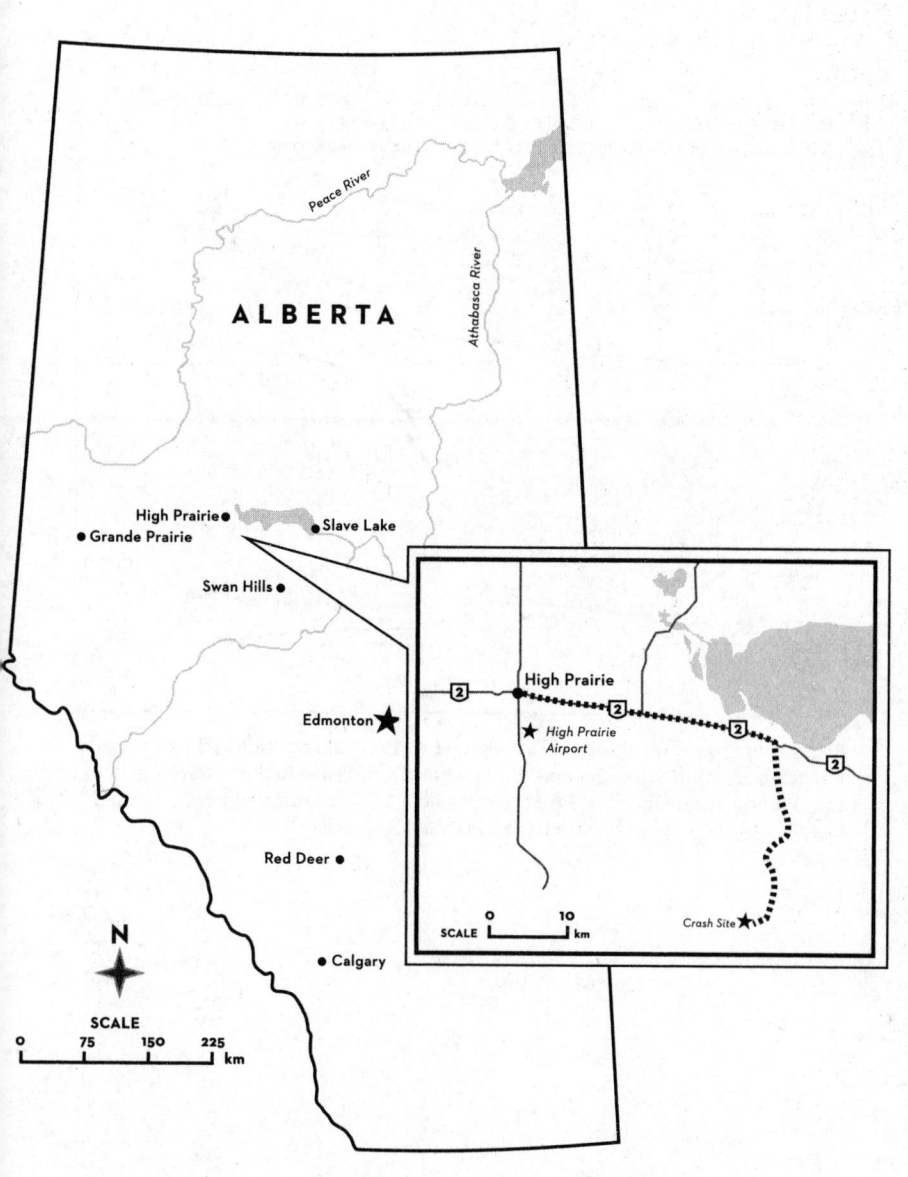

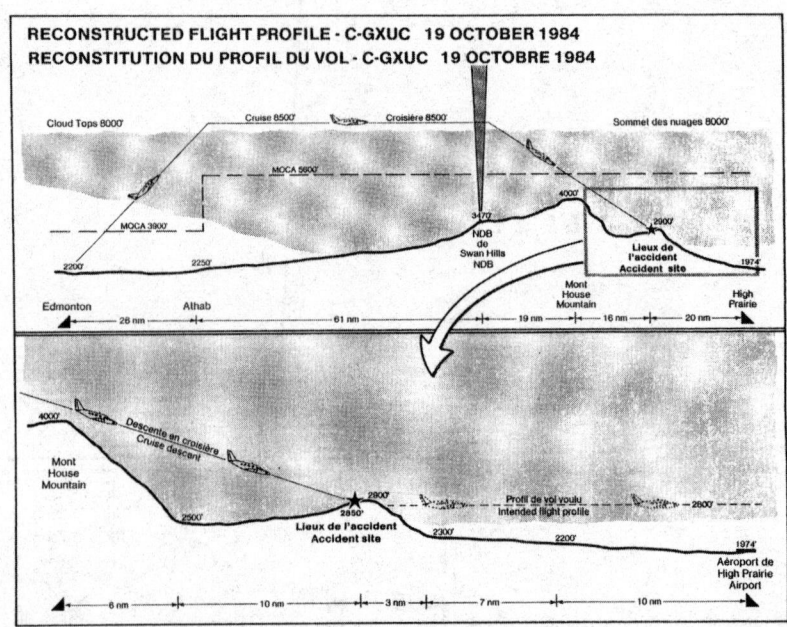

Flight route based on an original, copyright © 1984 Library and Archives Canada. Canadian Aviation Safety Board Civil Aviation Occurrence Report, Wapiti Aviation Ltd. Piper Navajo Chieftain PA-31-350 C-GXUC, High Prairie, Alberta, 20 mi SE, October 19, 1984. Report Number 84-H40006, Appendix B.

It is by going down into the abyss that we recover the treasures of life.
Where you stumble, there lies your treasure.

JOSEPH CAMPBELL

CONTENTS

INTRODUCTION

I first learned of my father's plane crash from the *Jerusalem Post*. I was twenty-two and working as a journalist in the Middle East. The crash happened on October 19, 1984, but I didn't find out about it until two days later. I was sitting at my old metal desk with a cup of mint tea and the morning paper. That day it wasn't regional conflict or politics that caught my attention, but the headline of a short news item buried at the bottom of an inside page: *Party Leader Killed in Alberta Plane Crash.*

The article was tiny—fewer than fifty words—but its impact was staggering. "Grant Notley, leader of the New Democratic Party in Alberta, and five other people were killed in the crash of their twin-engine plane," the Associated Press reported in the opening line. I read on in disbelief. Four survivors had spent the night and much of the next day huddled in deep snow and sub-zero temperatures before being rescued. Among them was the provincial housing minister, Larry Shaben: my father.

I dropped the paper, grabbed the phone. My brother James picked up.

"Dad's fine," he assured me, but for some reason I didn't believe him.

"Put Mom on," I practically yelled.

"He's okay," my mother told me. "We were going to call, but it's been crazy and, well . . . we didn't want to worry you."

I was crying, feeling very far away. "I'm coming home," I said.

It was Christmas before I could get time off work to return to Canada. Two months had passed and my father's physical wounds had healed. Inside, however, something elemental had changed. He was subdued, quietly haunted, in a way I had never seen before. He'd lost a close colleague that night and had seen others from our town and the surrounding communities die.

My family had experienced the event firsthand and assimilated its extraordinary details. The survivors of the crash—a rookie pilot, an accused criminal, a cop taking him to face charges, and my dad, a prominent politician—had boarded the plane as total strangers. Men from wildly different backgrounds, they had helped one another survive a long, bitter night in the Canadian wilderness. The story had a mythical quality that tested the bounds of reality.

Distance, the crash's impact on my father, and the unlikely friendships that formed between the survivors lodged the event firmly in my psyche. Who were these men? What had they experienced on that snowy, fog-drenched night as they struggled together to cheat death? How had it altered them? If I faced a similar near-death experience, would it change me? Would I continue to live my life as I had been living it?

My curiosity was insatiable. Though I peppered my dad with questions, his answers were disappointingly vague or simply not forthcoming. The crash had affected him deeply, but *how* remained a mystery he kept largely to himself. He refused to discuss the people who had died or what he had shared with the men who had survived.

"It was a long, cold night," the *Edmonton Journal* quoted him as saying shortly after the crash. "We talked about things, private things I'd rather not discuss."

"He has nightmares," was all my mother would say.

In the months and years following the crash, my father forged extraordinary bonds with his fellow survivors, especially Paul Archambault, the twenty-seven-year-old criminal on the plane. Every so often, the scruffy drifter would arrive unannounced. No matter how busy my father's schedule was, he always had time for Paul. My dad would talk about these meetings with delight and obvious affection. Their relationship was important to him in a way I never fully understood. He cared deeply about how Paul's life was progressing and worried during his long absences, as a father would for an itinerant son. After one visit, my dad spoke enthusiastically about a dog-eared sheaf of papers that Paul had brought with him, a manuscript he was writing about his experience that night.

My dad also kept in touch with Erik Vogel, the young pilot who had flown the plane. Every year on the anniversary of the crash, Dad would call him to talk about how lucky they were to be alive. Erik had been just twenty-four—two years older than I was at the time—when the crash occurred. Years later, though juggling the demands of parenthood and my own business, I felt compelled to seek him out. I found him working in a nearby city as a firefighter and living with his family on a quiet tract of land less than an hour's drive from my home.

I arranged a meeting and drove out to Erik's farm. The former pilot's first words to me were "I've been waiting years for you." Over coffee in his kitchen, within sight of a solid wood butcher-block table on loan from Scott Deschamps, the fourth crash survivor, Erik shared his story. Though almost twenty years had passed since the ordeal, he cried as he recounted the events of that night. They had never left him. Nor had his burden of guilt over the deaths of six passengers.

When I drove away hours later, I carried his dust-covered leather flight bag—a tote the size of a small suitcase in which he had filed away his pilot logbook, years of airline rejection letters, court documents, photos and every newspaper clipping he had seen about the tragedy or those involved. Sifting through the contents of Erik's flight bag was like opening the door to a lost world. All of a sudden an event that had seemed surreal came into sharp, dramatic focus. My dad, it turned out, was not the only one to have been transfigured by what happened that long-ago night.

Joseph Campbell, the American mythologist who coined the phrase "follow your bliss," wrote extensively about man's quest for meaning. According to Campbell, all heroic journeys, from the time of the ancients to the present day, begin with a call to adventure—a challenge or opportunity to face the unknown and gain something of physical or spiritual value. This call often comes in the form of a transformative crisis, an event that kicks out our foundations of complacency and makes us examine universal questions of existence: Why was I born? What happens when I die? How can I overcome my fears and weaknesses and be happy?

Few of us will ever face the kind of life-and-death trauma experienced by the men in this story. Their ordeal forced them to confront the precious and limited nature of their existence on earth. In the words of Campbell, they entered the forest "at the darkest point where there is no path." How these four men found their way forward that night and in the years that followed is both remarkable and inspirational.

Scott Deschamps—the rookie RCMP officer who had boarded the flight handcuffed to Paul Archambault—was no exception. Unlike Erik, however, it took me three years to persuade Scott to be interviewed.

Perhaps more than any of the survivors, he had deliberately, painstakingly, rebuilt his life as a result of his experience. His resistance to share his story, Scott told me, was rooted in its deeply personal nature. He had spent more than a decade trying to understand what had happened to him the night of the crash. He eventually agreed to be interviewed only because of my family connection to the story.

Researching Paul Archambault's life was far more difficult. How does one go about unearthing details about a vagabond who'd been drifting since he was fifteen? Thinking it was a long shot, I placed ads in newspapers on either side of the country—one in the city where Paul was living at the time of the crash and the other in the town where he'd grown up some 3,800 kilometres away. To my amazement, my phone started ringing almost immediately. Those who called not only remembered Paul, they told me that he had made a lasting impression on them. Though Paul's parents were dead, an aunt in his hometown of Aylmer, Quebec, contacted me. When I met her, I soon realized that she and her husband hadn't been close to Paul since he was a child. Nor were they in touch with other members of his family, with the exception of a younger brother who had been institutionalized for much of his early life. They didn't know the brother's whereabouts, but told me that he called from time to time.

"When he does, could you give him my number?" I asked without hope. Months later Paul's brother called. Miraculously, in his possession was the tattered sixty-page manuscript my father had spoken of a quarter century earlier.

By that point, the story had sunk its hooks into me. At its underbelly was a compelling and dangerous truth about the commuter airline industry. Across the globe, barely a week passes without news of a small plane crash. Contrary to public perception, commuter airlines represent the largest sector of commercial aviation in North America and perhaps the world, accounting for more than half of all domestic flights. In Canada, a country characterized by its sparse population and rugged, remote terrain, small planes are a lifeline for residents in isolated, northern communities like the one in Alberta where I grew up. Commuter operations are the workhorse carriers that connect thousands of people to larger population centres and provide a vital source of supplies and medical support.

Bush flying, as it is still known in Canada's north, has always been a dangerous business—a hard-driving, high-risk profession ranked as one of the deadliest in North America. The pilots are often young and idealistic, driven by a desire for freedom and adventure. With few exceptions they are trying to work their way toward careers with major airlines. First, however, they must pay their dues by building logbook hours flying for small airlines. Some pay with their lives. Inside Erik's battered flight bag, he'd kept a file thick with articles on dozens of small plane crashes that had occurred in the years since his tragedy. "It's frustrating to see it happen over and over again," he told me.

The more I read about the commuter airline industry, or heard about yet another small plane crash, the more shocked I became. A major investigative report on Canadian aviation incidents between 2000 and 2005—before the federal government reduced public access to its aviation occurrence reports—noted that during that five-year period there were literally thousands of reported incidents involving danger or potential danger to aircraft passengers. How was it that the flying public wasn't in an uproar?

Typically it's only when large jets fall from the sky that people take notice. Outraged by the body count, they demand government investigations and seek ironclad assurances that the airline at fault addresses safety concerns. Meanwhile, small passenger planes continue to crash with frightening regularity. But apart from the loved ones of those who die, few sound the alarm. When they do, it's a faint cry in the wilderness that goes unheeded. Even fewer consider the pilots in these crashes—often young and frequently scared—who battle fatigue, terrain, weather or mechanical malfunction on a daily basis.

As is sadly the case when one tries to apportion blame for the vagaries of fate and circumstance, I came to see Dale Wells, the owner of the airline involved in my father's crash, as the villain in this tragedy. It took me years to summon the courage to talk to Dale. Our eventual rendezvous at an Edmonton restaurant completely reversed my opinion. Dale was both humble and forthright. Like Erik, he had also kept meticulous records. After our meeting he walked me to his car in the parking lot and handed over a massive box filled with files and documents.

"Say hello to your father," he said as we parted. "I always thought he was a wonderful man."

My father didn't live to see me finish this book. In April 2008 he was diagnosed with cancer. He died less than five months later. As I was preparing to board the flight home to Alberta to be at his bedside, I asked him if there was anything he wanted me to bring.

"Your manuscript," he said.

I'd written only a few rough chapters, but it didn't matter. He insisted.

I spent two days at the hospital. And during those two days I read to him. It was the last time we were together.

This book is my tribute to my father, Larry Shaben, and to Erik Vogel, Scott Deschamps and Paul Archambault. Their strength, courage and dignity are an inspiring example of how individuals can journey from the depths of tragedy and loss to the riches of lives begun anew.

PART I

Fate rules the affairs of mankind with no recognizable order.

LUCIUS ANNAEUS SENECA

DEPARTURE

Erik Vogel was in over his head and didn't know how to get out. There were half a dozen reasons why the twenty-four-year-old rookie pilot didn't feel comfortable flying tonight, but with his job at Wapiti Aviation on the line—or so it seemed to him—none of them counted. Erik had been in and out of cloud for most of his outbound flight from the small northern Canadian city of Grande Prairie, Alberta, and had watched wet snow continue to fall. The wheels of his ten-seater plane had touched down at the municipal airport in Edmonton, Canada's most northerly provincial capital, just as the last light of day was leaving the murky sky. He was running behind schedule and working hard to make up time. Standing 6'3"with a lean, athletic build, warm brown eyes and a wavy crop of dark hair, Erik appeared every inch a young, attractive and confident aviator. Inside, however, he was scared.

After unloading his passengers and their luggage, he'd crossed the tarmac to the terminal building to collect his outgoing passengers. He glanced at his watch: 6:40 p.m. That gave him only twenty minutes for ticketing and check-in, refuelling, and loading the luggage and passengers for the return flight north. There was no way he'd be off the ground by his scheduled departure time of 7:00.

His only hope was that tonight would be a repeat of last night and that there wouldn't be passengers bound for the small communities of High Prairie and Fairview, which had tiny airports with no air traffic control. He also prayed that by some miracle he'd pick up a co-pilot. As he approached the check-in counter Erik was overjoyed to see Linda Gayle, Wapiti's Fort McMurray agent, already selling tickets. Wapiti retained Linda on a part-time basis for the Fort McMurray flights and she wasn't obliged to help out pilots flying other routes, but tonight she'd decided to do him this favour.

"What have we got?"

"We're fully booked," she replied.

"So no chance of a co-pilot?"

Linda shook her head. That seat had been sold to accommodate another passenger.

His stomach churning, Erik asked the question that had been plaguing him ever since he'd talked to the pilot who'd flown the morning schedule. "Any passengers bound for High Prairie?"

"Four," Linda told him. "Plus two on standby."

A town of 2,500 people 365 kilometres northwest of Edmonton, High Prairie was on the other side of a high ridge of rugged and densely wooded terrain known as Swan Hills. Because the airport had no control tower, regulations dictated that pilots could fly into High Prairie only in visual conditions, meaning when the weather was clear. The pilot on the a.m. sked had warned Erik that there was a lot of snow on the runway and he'd had a hard time taking off.

As Erik stood wondering how the hell he was going to manage the flight, two men approached. One, about 5′10″, bull-chested and casually dressed with a hedgehog coat of close-cropped auburn hair, dropped his shackled left hand heavily on the counter. Handcuffed to him was another man. Of similar height, he had a brawny build with an unkempt mop of frizzy brown hair, and deep blue eyes that softened the strong angles of his face. Sideburns stretched like woolly carpets down either side of his cheekbones and above his upper lip, a generous arch of moustache curved over small, even teeth.

"Where do you want me to sit?" the first man asked. Below a prominent brow, green eyes regarded Erik intently as he explained that he was an RCMP officer escorting a prisoner to face charges in Grande Prairie.

Erik swallowed hard. He remembered the story of a prisoner getting loose on a charter flight out of Vancouver and trying to attack the pilot.

"At the very back," he said, regarding the prisoner warily. The man exuded a nervous energy like a charged circuit, and wore only jeans, a wool-lined jean jacket and an open-collared shirt: not exactly appropriate for the weather.

"I'd like to board him first," the cop said.

Erik nodded, then asked Linda to finish ticketing the passengers while he went to the nearby weather office to see if Luella Wood, High Prairie's airport manager, had filed her customary 6 p.m. weather report. She had, and the news wasn't good: the cloud deck was broken at 500 feet and overcast at 900. A visual approach required a 1000-foot ceiling and 3 miles' visibility.

As he walked back to the counter, Erik surveyed the other passengers in the departure area: four men and two women heading home on a Friday night. He stepped behind the counter and grabbed the PA system mic.

"Attention, passengers on Wapiti Flight 402," he announced. "I'm not sure whether we're going to be able to land in High Prairie because the ceiling is so low. If we can't, we'll have to go on to Peace River because they have a controlled approach. If there are any passengers headed for High Prairie who don't want to take the flight, please let me know."

Erik scanned the faces of the passengers in front of him. Regardless of the weather, they expected him to get them home. They weren't going to give him an out. He ran a hand wearily across his forehead, trying to erase the tension that had settled there. He'd done what he could. At least if he overflew High Prairie, it wouldn't come as a surprise.

As he walked outside to load the luggage, an icy wind whipped along the tarmac, wet flakes dampening his face. The airport—a dark triangle of land slashed out of the bald northern prairie—was shrouded in fog and beyond its muted southeastern border, the lights of downtown cast a dull violet glow. A collection of squat buildings flanked the airport's southwestern perimeter and beside them silhouettes of airplanes perched like frozen birds, wings outstretched as if already in flight.

Erik took a deep, shuddering breath to calm his nerves and tried to focus on the positives. He'd warned his passengers about the flight, so there wouldn't be any flak if he ended up taking High Prairie passengers on to Peace River. Linda had done the ticketing, so he'd been able to check the weather—a luxury he seldom had time for. He'd even had a dinner of sorts, eating the untouched half of a sandwich left by a Wapiti pilot who hadn't had time to finish it.

Erik's efforts to stay upbeat didn't last. When he got to the plane, the fuelling service hadn't yet arrived and he had to scramble to get the tanks filled. By the time they finished, he was behind schedule. He hastily piled some of the luggage into the plane's nose compartment and then crammed the rest into the rear hold behind the seats. Though regulations required that he calculate the weight and balance for the aircraft, he didn't bother. What difference would it make? Erik didn't feel he could leave passengers or their luggage behind, and in winter conditions like tonight it would be foolish to skimp on fuel when he didn't know whether he'd be able to get into the uncontrolled airports on his route. He estimated the fully fuelled, nine-passenger flight would be overweight to the tune of about 200 kilograms, and there wasn't a damn thing he could do about it. The queasy feeling in his stomach grew as he walked back to the terminal to escort the cop and his prisoner outside.

When they arrived at the aircraft he watched uneasily as the constable unlocked the handcuff from his shackled wrist and snapped it closed around the prisoner's free one. Erik pulled open the hatch and gave the go-ahead to climb aboard.

Behind the terminal doors, Larry Shaben squinted through thick wire-rimmed glasses at the snow falling in white waves across the tarmac. Forty-nine, with a broad, balding forehead, olive skin and enormous brown eyes, Larry was immaculately dressed in a navy suit and brown ultra-suede topcoat. A second-generation Canadian of Arab descent, Larry was an elected member of the Alberta government and the country's first Muslim Cabinet minister. His executive assistant had driven him to the airport directly from his office at the Alberta Legislature just in time to catch his flight home for the weekend. Now he waited impatiently to board.

The doors opened and the pilot entered, bringing a blast of frigid air with him. It blew the thinning strands of dark curly hair from the crown of Larry's head and he quickly smoothed them back into place. The politician had watched the pilot frantically working to prepare everything for the flight. He was young and seemed on edge. Larry had detected strain in his voice when he'd made the announcement about possibly not being able to land in High Prairie, and had immediately called home to let his wife, Alma, know.

"I'll tell you what . . . if we can't land and you have to pick me up in Peace River, I'll buy you dinner."

Though he hated the thought of Alma driving on the highway in these conditions, there wasn't another option. And it was only 130 kilometres. Larry would drive the two of them home after dinner and let her sleep in the car.

It had been a gruelling week at the Ledge, as he and his colleagues often called the Alberta Legislature. That morning the government's fall session had begun. For the next six weeks Larry would spend his days sitting in chambers debating and voting on bills and motions. In preparation for the time away from his office, he had spent the past week working twelve- to fourteen-hour days to get on top of the mountain of paperwork he had to deal with as the Minister for Housing and Utilities.

As he typically did every Monday morning, Larry had flown south from his home in High Prairie to Edmonton, where he rented an apartment five minutes' walk from the Legislature. By Friday, he was so tired that he couldn't imagine driving the twenty minutes across the city to the municipal airport, let alone the four hours north to High Prairie. Now that the weather had turned, the thought was even less appealing.

As he'd dashed out to his aide's car, Larry could feel the chill weight of moisture in the air—unusual for Edmonton, which was prone to brittle cold and clear skies. The city roads had been thick with slushy new snow and Friday night traffic crawled.

When he'd arrived at the terminal Larry had little energy for conversation, but among the cluster of passengers at the check-in counter were some he knew well. One, Gordon Peever, a next-door neighbour whose kids had grown up with Larry's own, was director of finance at a vocational college near High Prairie. Gordon often travelled to Edmonton for work and that morning he'd caught a ride to the city with a friend to attend a meeting. Gordon had planned to take the bus home that afternoon, but for some reason decided to catch a cab to the airport in hopes of getting a flight. He'd worried he'd be on standby, Gordon told Larry, but had been lucky enough to get a seat after a passenger cancelled. Larry also greeted another local resident, Christopher Vince. The young British-born man had recently moved from Calgary, a city three hours' drive south of Edmonton in the foothills of the Rocky Mountains, to take a government job training social workers. His wife, Francis, a schoolteacher, had just started teaching at the local junior high school, and the two seemed to be settling well into small-town life. Larry didn't recognize the other two men and women in the departure area, but had said hello. As a high-profile elected official, people often recognized him and he prided himself on being friendly and engaging, even at times like this when he felt utterly drained. Fortunately tonight the passengers' attention was elsewhere. They were abuzz with gossip about the rakish man in handcuffs who had just boarded the plane.

Scott Deschamps stiffly stood guard beside the ten-seat Piper Navajo Chieftain, the only departing plane on a barren stretch of tarmac. Snow had thickened the night, and an icy wind sent shivers through him. His prisoner and all but one passenger and the pilot were already aboard. Scott watched a trim, suit-clad man in his mid-forties hurry across the tarmac, briefcase in hand, and climb the few steps to the cabin. When he'd disappeared inside, the pilot motioned Scott to follow. He ducked through the open door and stood near the rear aisle seat next to the exit. The pilot entered soon after, his tall frame bent almost double as he pulled the hatch closed. He turned the handle and looked over his shoulder at Scott.

"Watch me." The pilot's voice was just above a whisper as he inserted the safety pin. "You need to know how to open this door in case of an emergency."

Dale Wells discouraged his pilots from giving safety briefings to passengers because he felt they frightened them unnecessarily, but Erik wasn't taking any chances.

Scott leaned forward to watch and listen. If there was one thing he was confident about, it was his ability to handle himself in an emergency. He gave the pilot a nod when he finished and watched him move up the aisle and settle in the cockpit next to the well-dressed passenger who had arrived late. Scott dropped into the empty seat, buckled his seatbelt and glanced at his prisoner. He was holding his handcuffed wrists in the air in front of him.

"Can't you take these off?"

Scott studied the man beside him. The constable hadn't known what to expect when he'd arrived in the city of Kamloops in British Columbia's southern interior that morning to pick up Paul Richard Archambault, who had a long rap sheet of B and E's and robberies dating back to 1976. As the day had progressed, however, Scott had been surprised to find himself enjoying the company of his prisoner, who had proven to be quick-witted and likable, with a ready if off-colour sense of humor.

He and Paul had been together since early morning and Scott felt like he had a pretty good read on the guy. He wasn't likely to be a danger. Scott fingered the key inside his jacket pocket. It was against RCMP regulations to remove his prisoner's handcuffs, but he felt comfortable with the risk. He fixed Paul with a stern look.

"Okay," he said, "but let there be an understanding: if there is any trouble, the full force of the RCMP will be on you."

Paul nodded solemnly and then a smile cracked the rugged lines of his face.

Scott slipped the key into the lock of the handcuffs, unfastened them, and tucked them into the briefcase at his feet. He turned to gaze out the small cabin window. Falling snow and a veil of cloud muted the city lights. Beyond their glow, the world was darkly smudged. Scott exhaled heavily. It had been an exhausting day. Ten hours had passed from the time he first picked up his human cargo. Since then they'd been bounced unceremoniously from flight to flight. Scott had a confirmed booking for the two of them that morning on a flight out of Kamloops. However, when Scott arrived at the RCMP detachment, the staff hadn't done the paperwork for Paul's release and the men had missed their flight.

Finally, they were on the last leg. Scott had managed to snag two seats on one of the few planes flying north from Edmonton to Grande Prairie that night. The flight was a milk run with three en route stops, which meant it was going to be another couple of hours before he arrived in Grande Prairie. Scott was sick of take-offs, landings, and the confined space of airplane cabins. He laid his head back and felt something jut into the back of his neck from the rear cargo hold directly behind his seat. He turned to adjust the baggage so he could get comfortable. Above his head, he could see briefcases, small suitcases and a computer monitor piled precariously at a 45-degree angle to the ceiling of the cabin. The compact luggage compartment was completely full and there appeared to be nothing separating him from the cargo in the rear hold. Spotting his garment bag, Scott pulled it out and rolled it into a makeshift pillow. The fabric scratched the back of his neck, but at least it was soft. He wanted to close his eyes and sleep. But sleep wasn't an option. Not yet.

He'd sleep when he got home. The thought carried an edge of melancholy. Grande Prairie didn't seem much like home without Mary. Two months earlier his wife had moved back to the west coast to take a job. He supposed he couldn't blame her. After all, they'd had an agreement. She'd promised to give Grande Prairie three years. She'd stayed nearly five.

In contrast to the breathtaking stretch of southern coastal British Columbia where Scott had grown up, Grande Prairie was a rough-edged, northern prairie city attracting more than its share of transients and troublemakers. Just north of the 55th parallel, it was the largest and final urban centre between Edmonton, Alberta, and Fairbanks, Alaska. The city served as a provisioning stop for people travelling north, as well as a hub for the region's two economic power-houses: agriculture, and oil and gas. In the midst of the oil boom, Grande Prairie had also been one of Canada's fastest-growing cities with its population nearly doubling from 13,000 in 1971 to its current size of 25,000.

The place had its own beauty. The open vistas and bright skies were a stunning contrast to the often grey and rainy coastal climate of British Columbia. Grande Prairie summers were pleasantly warm and the days languorously long. Bear Creek, a verdant belt of treed parkland, bisected the city from north to south. Beyond the city limits, the landscape, though relatively flat, was not featureless. Farm fields rolled out to the north, east and west in a golden patchwork of barley, wheat, canola and oats. To the south was a vast boreal forest extending to the foothills of the Canadian Rockies.

In many ways his first posting had been good for Scott. An avid outdoorsman, he'd loved being able to get into the bush to hunt and fish. He also enjoyed the steady income and the stature his job gave him in a small city where the locals treated you like family, and over time he'd built a circle of friends.

Winters, however, had been challenging. The days were short and bitingly cold, and temperatures frequently plummeted to -20°C. At times an unbearably fierce wind would barrel across the prairie, pushing the wind chill as low as -50°C. At that temperature, exposed skin would freeze almost instantly and locals would rush to plug in their vehicles' block heaters to keep the engine oil warm so their cars would start. The snow often flew in late October and stayed until May. This year it had arrived even sooner. Yesterday, the first winter storm had swept across the region, bringing heavy snowfall. But Scott hadn't been in Grande Prairie to see it. Earlier that week the head of his detachment had asked for a volunteer to fly to Kamloops and bring in an accused criminal arrested on an outstanding warrant. Scott had jumped at the chance, hoping to tie in a brief layover in Vancouver to visit Mary.

It had been wonderful to see her, yet so much felt unresolved. Scott had put in for a transfer to the coast so they could be together, but there was no telling when or if it would happen. To make matters worse, she had recently begun talking about starting a family. Scott wasn't sure he was ready. He was only twenty-eight and just beginning to hit his stride as a cop. After five years he was making decent money. He'd recently banked enough to buy a BMW—the envy of the detachment. There would be plenty of time to have kids. Even as he thought this, Scott's confidence wavered. In this one area, he felt completely out of his depth.

Erik was running almost half an hour late and somehow he'd have to make up time. He clipped his lap belt and his eyes darted uneasily to the passenger in the co-pilot's seat—a last-minute arrival for the flight. Erik offered a clipped hello, wondering nervously whether the official-looking gentleman next to him might be a government air safety inspector. Transport Canada occasionally had inspectors ride along anonymously to check on airline operations, and recently Wapiti Aviation seemed to have had more than its fair share of scrutiny.

Erik tried to put the man beside him out of his mind, and reached forward to grab his headset. He was stopped short by his shoulder strap's broken recoil mechanism. It was just one of the small maintenance issues that irritated him. He flicked the useless strap from his shoulder, pulled on his headset, and radioed for clearance. Edmonton Departure gave him the go-ahead, and he taxied to runway 34. Above him the sky was black. Wet snow smacked the windshield and Erik felt his heartbeat marking time amid the roar of the engine. He checked his watch: 7:13.

"Wapiti 402," a voice squawked into his headset. "Runway three-four cleared for takeoff."

"Four-oh-two rolling, three-four," Erik replied.

Within minutes, they were off the ground, climbing toward a bank of thick cloud.

As the plane flew north from Edmonton, Erik brooded. He needed to get a handle on what he was going to do. He had filed an instrument flight plan to Peace River, an airport 385 kilometres northwest of Edmonton that had an instrument approach. That meant that even if Erik could see only a few hundred feet in front of him, he could still get in safely. But Erik had to get in and out of the airport at High Prairie first. The runway there was a short, dimly lit strip of asphalt equipped with only a single non-directional beacon—a simple radio ground transmitter that did little more than help Erik pick out the airport amid a vast swath of snowy terrain. The only way he would be able to land was to drop below the clouds and try for a visual approach, a tall order considering the cloud ceiling there was 500 feet off the deck and broken, and completely overcast at 900 feet.

Erik was in the untenable position of trying to obey two masters. The first was Dale Wells, his boss at Wapiti Aviation. Erik felt pressured to get into his destinations even if it meant pushing the weather, though Dale never came right out and said it. Many bush pilots face direct pressure from management: "Do whatever's required to get the job done, and if you have to bust the weather to land, don't get caught."

The second master was the Ministry of Transport, whose regulations stipulated that a visual approach wasn't even legal on a night like tonight. In short, Erik needed to follow one set of rules without getting violated for breaking the other.

He felt like a condemned man. If he didn't get in he could lose his job; if he did, he could lose his licence. Nervously, Erik shot another look at the man beside him.

The Piper Navajo's flight path was Alpha 7, a low-level controlled airway passing just east of High Prairie. Erik's plan was to stay on the airway, flying on instruments, until he was beyond the high terrain of Swan Hills. Then he'd alter course slightly west, transit into uncontrolled airspace near High Prairie and drop down to see if he could spot the airport.

Flying on instruments—also known as IFR or Instrument Flight Rules—is akin to flying blind to the world outside the cockpit windows. Much more complex than flying visually, it's a skill vital to pilots who fly at night or in bad weather, requiring them to navigate solely by reference to cockpit instruments.

The land below was invisible, obscured beneath a blanket of cloud and darkness. Erik raised himself in his seat and looked for any sign of lights, but the earth was lost to him. He had been so preoccupied he'd paid little attention to the windshield. Now he noticed a delicate trace of rime blossoming along its edges. Ice was the last thing he needed. He continued to ascend, keeping a close eye on its slow advance. He reached his clearance altitude of 8,000 feet and the plane was still in cloud, rime closing like a lace curtain across the windshield. He flipped the switch to activate the de-icing boots and turned on the landing lights to get a better look at the wings. A thin crust of ice had begun to layer their leading edges. Erik strained to see the movement of the de-icers, rubber membranes covering the wings that expand to break the ice. Nothing was happening. His palms were slick with sweat as he clutched the yoke. He needed to get above the cloud, and fast.

"Departure, 402," Erik radioed Edmonton Departure Air Traffic Control. "Level eight requesting ten thousand."

"Wapiti 402, cleared to ten thousand."

Erik nosed the plane skyward and at 8500 feet it broke clear. He exhaled. Holding altitude, he turned his attention to what lay ahead.

First, he had to make up time. It was already 7:30 and he was due into High Prairie at 8:00. He throttled forward and increased his airspeed to 175 knots. Now he needed to acquire his bearing. Edmonton's distance-measuring equipment extended only 120 kilometres from the airport. Without a distance readout, Erik was forced to use dead reckoning, a skill he'd learned but far from perfected as a bush pilot. He tuned his automatic direction finder to a ground transmitter near the town of Whitecourt, which was directly along his flight path to High Prairie. The automatic direction finder or ADF is a simple navigation tool that, when tuned to the radio frequency of a fixed ground beacon, causes a directional needle to swing toward the beacon. The pilot adjusts his heading so the needle points to the nose of the plane, indicating the aircraft is tracking directly toward the beacon. The problem with this rudimentary navigation system is that it doesn't tell the pilot how far away the plane is from the beacon.

Typically, Erik would have used a second ADF to help him determine this distance by tuning it to a non-directional beacon located in the high ridge of rugged terrain further along his flight path to High Prairie. As his plane flew past that beacon, the needle on the second ADF would swing around 90 degrees and point off the wingtip, giving Erik a cross bearing or intersection point. Then, using dead reckoning—a complex series of calculations involving speed, elapsed time and course—he could figure out his distance from his destination.

Unfortunately, only one of the plane's two ADFs was serviceable. That meant he would have to toggle his single working ADF back and forth between the frequencies of two different ground transmitters. The thought of doing this to determine his location, as well as dealing with everything else, all without the help of a co-pilot, made Erik stiff with apprehension.

After a moment he homed in on the Whitecourt beacon and adjusted his course so that the needle of his ADF swung to point toward the nose of the plane.

Good, Erik thought. At least he was heading in the right direction.

Time passed. His head ached from the pressure of pounding blood. Suddenly, the ADF needle swung 180 degrees to point off his tail, indicating that he'd passed the Whitecourt beacon. Erik tuned the dial once more, this time to the frequency of the High Prairie beacon. Again, he adjusted his heading so the compass needle pointed toward the plane's nose. Now he needed to home in on the Swan Hills beacon, approximately two-thirds of the distance to High Prairie.

Having flown the route fewer than a dozen times in clear weather, Erik was under the impression that the Swan Hills beacon was on the summit. That meant when the needle swung to point directly off his left wingtip he would be abeam of the high point of land on his flight path and could safely begin his descent into High Prairie.

In reality, however, the terrain didn't drop off after the Swan Hills beacon, but continued to rise for 30 kilometres beyond it to the 4,000-foot summit of House Mountain. Only then did the land slope downward, though not steadily. Thirty-two kilometres southeast of the High Prairie airport the terrain rose again to the 2900-foot crest of a densely wooded hill.

Inside the cockpit, the loud hum of the engine vibrated in Erik's ears. He was feeling utterly cut off from the world when a voice crackled in his headset.

"Wapiti 402, if you read Edmonton, contact Centre now, one three two decimal zero five." He'd been on Edmonton Departure traffic frequency 119.5 and was now being asked to transfer over to 132.05—Edmonton Air Traffic Control Centre.

Erik adjusted his radio. "Wapiti 402."

"Wapiti 402, good evening," a voice said. "You're radar identified . . . what's your altitude now?"

"Eight five zero zero. We were given a block eight to ten," Erik said. "Ah, sir, I don't . . . I wasn't told to go over to Centre."

"You can remain on this frequency," the voice told him.

Erik was thinking fast now that he had ATC on the radio. He needed to let them know his plans.

"It looks like we're gonna have to go into High Prairie," Erik said, "so I'll be requesting a descent to MEA and then out of controlled airspace probably at 19:45, 50 sometime."

The High Prairie airport lay within a mile-wide strip of uncontrolled airspace between two ATC-monitored flight paths: Alpha 7—the one Erik was on—and Bravo 3, a flight path to the west. That allowed Erik to exploit a loophole in the system. He'd requested a descent to MEA, or minimum en route altitude, in this case, 7,000 feet above sea level. However, once he'd passed Swan Hills he'd begin veering west out of controlled airspace. Then he'd drop down below that to see if he could get a visual on the High Prairie Airport. Air Traffic Control knew it wasn't legal, but when it wasn't in their controlled airspace they turned a blind eye.

Erik had first seen the technique—known among pilots as a *bullshit approach*—flying in the Arctic, but he wasn't sure what his plan should be for High Prairie. He'd only flown into the town in poor weather on one other occasion, as a co-pilot on a route check a month after he'd joined Wapiti. On that flight, the plane had broken through the clouds 2000 feet above the airport. The thought of attempting such an approach tonight unnerved Erik, but he felt he had to try. If he couldn't spot the runway, he'd climb back up and into controlled airspace. Then he'd reestablish radio contact with Edmonton ATC to let them know he'd overflown High Prairie, and could carry on direct to Peace River.

"Wapiti 402, I check that you'll be landing at High Prairie."

Okay. But how low should he go before he bailed out on landing? He thought for a moment, and decided on 2800 feet. The High Prairie airport was at an altitude of 1974 feet. That would give Erik an 800-foot safety margin, as low as he dared go on a bullshit approach on a night like this. Erik worried that if the plane didn't land, Dale would ask what altitude he had tried. Erik could then tell his boss he'd attempted at 800. Even Dale couldn't fault him for that.

"Wapiti 402, you're re-cleared present position direct High Prairie."

"We check that," Erik said. "The signal's not too strong so I may not pick it up for awhile. I'll just stay on the airway and after Swan Hills abeam looking for descent."

"Wapiti 402. Roger."

Erik had covered his bases. He scanned his instruments. His speed over ground was 189 knots, his altitude holding at 8500 feet. After a few moments, the needle of his ADF swung around and pointed off his left wing, indicating the plane had passed Swan Hills. Erik tuned the ADF back to High Prairie's frequency and adjusted his course several degrees west until the needle was again pointing straight off the plane's nose. Then he began to descend.

The Navajo reentered cloud at 8,000 feet, dropping steadily at 300 feet per minute. It was a rate Erik came up with after factoring in his time, distance, heading and rate of travel. He checked the windshield for ice. It was advancing once more along the margins, though not alarmingly. What he couldn't see were the crusts of ice building on the leading edges of each wing. What he did not realize was that ice, his overloaded plane and an error in his dead reckoning calculations had put him at least 20 nautical miles, almost 40 kilometres, behind where he thought he was.

Erik watched the needle on his altimeter dial continue to whirl counterclockwise: 7,000 feet, 6,500, 6,000, and then 5,600—the minimum obstruction clearance altitude. He estimated he was now no more than ten minutes from the High Prairie airport. He'd hold at 5,600 until he passed over the airport's beacon and his ADF needle swung behind him, indicating he'd flown over the runway. In aviation terms this is referred to as *station passage*. Then he'd circle down to 2800 feet to see if he could make an approach. He knew that the small snow-covered airstrip would be difficult if not impossible to see in this weather, but if he could get under the clouds and spot the runway, he'd be okay.

In the meantime, he decided to radio the airport to get an update on the weather. Luella Wood, the airport's sole employee, was expected to be in contact around the time Wapiti flights were due to arrive. However, he couldn't raise her on the radio and that distressed him. If Luella told him the cloud deck was below 800 feet, then he wouldn't even attempt to land.

Suddenly, from the blackness below Erik saw a flash of orange flame—a flare pot from an oil well burn-off. For a few seconds it illuminated the trees below like a blowtorch. Though he couldn't yet see the lights of the town, it seemed the cloud ceiling might be higher than forecast. The thought occurred to Erik that he might *actually* make it into High Prairie after all. He checked his watch: 7:55. According to his calculations he should be passing the High Prairie beacon any minute. *I'll just start creeping down,* he thought.

Larry had been hoping they wouldn't have to fly into Peace River and now it seemed he was getting his wish. The pilot had just told the passengers to turn off all cabin lights and to fasten their seat belts. It was dim inside except for the warm amber glow of the *Fasten Seat Belt/No Smoking* lights. Larry couldn't wait to be home. His stomach growled and he longed for one of Alma's hearty Lebanese meals. He was craving a cigarette and looking forward to lying down on the comfortable couch in their family room after dinner to watch TV. Often, he didn't watch long before he fell asleep, and Alma would be gently shaking him awake, encouraging him to come upstairs to bed.

He felt the plane descending and checked his watch. Just after 8:00. Though they had departed late, it appeared they'd arrive pretty much on time. Larry had been one of the first passengers to board and had noted both the police officer standing alone outside the door and his prisoner already settled in the rear right-side window seat. Larry had shuffled up the narrow aisle and when he'd reached the front of the cabin, had laid a hand on the back of the co-pilot's seat. Then he'd hesitated. Typically, this was where Larry liked to sit, enjoying the view and chatting with the pilot. Tonight, however, he hadn't felt like talking, and simply wanted to put his head back and rest. He'd taken off his coat and slid into the seat directly behind the pilot. Gordon had taken the seat across the aisle from Larry. After a delay, Larry heard footsteps advancing hurriedly up the aisle and was surprised to see Grant Notley sweep past him and settle into the co-pilot's seat. The leader of the New Democratic Party, Alberta's official opposition, had planned to drive home to Fairview that afternoon with his wife, Sandra, but had instead remained in Edmonton for a meeting. He thought he'd have to stay overnight, but the meeting had wrapped up earlier than expected.

"I just got the call that Wapiti had room for me," he told Larry.

He was happy for Grant. Larry wouldn't wish the long drive north on anyone tonight, especially him. Two months ago on the highway home, he'd hit an elk. The collision had totalled his car and Grant had had to crawl through the shattered windshield to get free of the wreck.

"I am lucky to be alive," Notley had said the next day.

As the plane continued its descent, Larry peered out the window. Flashing pulses from the wing lights punctuated the murky soup of night. He craned around the pilot's seat to watch the altimeter steadily falling—4,300 feet one minute, 4,000 the next. Suddenly he heard something bang against the side of the plane—one reverberating clang then another.

"What was that?" he asked

"Ice," the pilot replied, a note of alarm in his voice. "It must be coming off the propellers."

Larry squinted into the night, and saw nothing but a thick veil of cloud. He heard the pilot speak into his headset: "Traffic advisory High Prairie, Wapiti four zero two is inbound from the southeast on descent."

Larry looked at the altimeter once more: 3,000 feet. He knew the airport's elevation was just under 2,000. They *had* to be close. He turned to the window and pressed his forehead against it, cupping his hands around his glasses to blot out the light from the instrument panel. His lenses were inches from the window as he strained to see the lights of home. *Where were they?*

Erik radioed High Prairie, but once again received no answer. *Where the hell was Luella?* He didn't pause to consider that an error in his calculations had put him further back than he thought and that distance as well as the rising terrain he was rapidly approaching were obscuring radio transmission. He had other things on his mind. He'd been so preoccupied with his dead reckoning calculations that he'd paid scant attention to the windshield. It had become opaque and the world outside blurred behind a frosty film. He could hear ice breaking off the props and banging against the plane as if someone was hurling rocks at the fuselage.

Erik sucked at his moustache with his bottom lip.

Jesus, there must be a hell of a lot for it to be doing that, he thought. Still his exhausted brain didn't register that that amount of ice would have slowed the plane's speed, and that he was 20 nautical miles short of his destination. Instead, his concentration was focused on the task ahead. When he flew past the High Prairie non-directional beacon the needle of his ADF would swing behind him. At that point, he'd look for the airstrip and if he didn't see it, he'd throttle the power back up and be gone. First, though, he had to pass the beacon.

The needle should swing any second now, Erik thought. *It's going to swing by. I'm right there. Why isn't the needle swinging?*

Then the thought occurred to him that he'd been fixated on getting into High Prairie. How the hell was he going to get *off* the runway if it was snowed over, his plane was overweight and his wings iced up?

The Navajo was moving fast now, lashing through cloud, making up time. The power was right up and Erik was sweating. He glanced at the altimeter: 2850 feet.

Holy shit, he thought. *I'm going to hit my 2800-foot minimum and the needle hasn't swung yet. I'd better level out.*

Erik started pulling back on the controls just as snow-covered treetops, invisible behind his frosted windshield, loomed suddenly out of the blackness.

IMPACT

Wapiti Aviation Flight 402 hit the treetops 75 feet above ground at 175 nautical miles per hour. The plane screamed forward another 104 feet before its right wing slammed into a bank of trees. The trees sheared 8 feet from the wing and took off part of the plane's right aileron. With the wing gone, the plane rolled to the right, crippled wing down, hitting a large clump of poplars. They clawed off another 30-inch piece of the right wing along with 18 inches of the vertical stabilizer. Banking sharply, the plane crossed an open swath of cutline, and then entered a second stand of trees, which tore off an engine cowling, the right-side fuselage windows and frames, and additional portions of the wings. Finally, at the end of a wreckage trail 538 feet long, the plane hit ground. By then it had rotated a full 90 degrees.

The fuselage plowed nose down through three feet of snow. Ground impact caused the final separation of engines, nacelles and remaining portions of the wings. Cold air gushed into the cabin, chased by snow and debris, which smashed through the damaged aircraft like a tsunami, snapping off seats in the plane's mid section. Broken trees and airplane parts followed, slashing seats and shaving back the roof like the lid from a sardine can. The fuselage bounced and skidded another 146 feet, ripping metal from the plane's right side. Cargo stowed in the obliterated nose cone broke loose, careening through the cabin and blowing out the rear of the aircraft where it was strewn along a wide wreckage path. The plane finally came to rest upside down 684 feet from where it had first hit the trees.

Paul Archambault had been rolling his second cigarette, planning to stash a series of them on his body before he was again taken into custody, when the plane's wing clipped the trees. The second he felt the violent shake of the plane, he dropped his pouch of tobacco and papers. *Jesus Christ*, he thought, *I'm going to die.*

Paul had been in several serious accidents in his life and recognized the sensation of time slowing down. He wasn't going to wait for death to grab hold of him. As the plane shuddered violently through the trees, he heard the sound of ripping metal all around him. He was jolted forward and an excruciating pain gripped his stomach. By the time the plane hit the ground, he was already fumbling for his seatbelt. Luggage and briefcases flew toward him through the cabin, and cargo and bodies tumbled crazily. Something hard smashed the side of his face. Clawing madly, he found the buckle release and pulled it. Paul sailed through the air as the plane flipped upside down. He circled his arms wildly, swimming above the onslaught of snow and debris like a skier caught in an avalanche. When everything stopped, Paul was lying on top of a jumble of luggage and broken wreckage. He was only still for a heartbeat. The smell of fuel overwhelmed him and he thought: *This thing is going to explode!*

In his past dozen years of nomadic, on-the-edge existence, Paul had learned when it was time to get the hell out. He lurched blindly toward the cool air cascading from a broken window and quickly pulled himself through it and out into the frigid wilderness, immediately sinking up to his thighs in deep snow. The sickening stench of fuel filled his nostrils and he waded, as if through quicksand, away from the wreckage. Only then did he turn to look at the plane. *Holy shit*, he thought, as he stared at what was left. The plane was upside down and both of its wings had been ripped completely off. His next thought was disbelief, followed by anger. The pilot had crashed.

"You dumb, fucking asshole!" His words rang into the night as he put distance between himself and the wreckage, his legs punching deep into the snowpack. "What the fuck were you doing, you stupid son of a bitch?"

His fear sailed skyward with every word. Pain ripped through his stomach and he felt blood, warm and wet, flowing from a gash on his forehead as he stumbled through a void of darkness. Dense walls of gnarled, leafless trees pressed in from all sides, and above them was nothing but an oppressive cloak of weather. Paul turned his face to the sky and gulped the sharp night air. His heartbeat hammered in his ears as he began to search for a way forward.

A single word pulsed through Paul's frightened brain: *escape.* His immediate thought was to put distance between himself and the plane. It was bitingly cold, but he was oblivious. He'd slept on the street so often he was accustomed to the bitter chill of night. He had also spent his fair share of time in the bush, both during his training as a naval cadet when he was a teenager, and in his ten years kicking across the country. He scanned the dense brush that surrounded him for a clearing. The terrain was rugged, and the snow was shockingly deep. Still, he was a survivor. He thought briefly of his duffle bag somewhere in the wreckage. In it were his wallet, five changes of clothes and a few personal effects—his life's possessions. He pushed the thought of losing them to the back of his mind. It wouldn't be the first time he'd headed out with nothing but the clothes on his back. He also thought about the pouch of tobacco and the rolling papers he'd had on his lap; gone, too. Stopping in the thigh-deep snow, Paul shoved his hand into his jean jacket pocket and fished out the single cigarette he'd rolled before the plane had crashed. One end was wet, so he tore it off and, pulling out the lighter he'd stashed in the front pocket of his jeans, he lit the other end.

Paul stood still for a moment, inhaling deeply. As smoke snaked into his lungs, he tried to settle his raw-edged nerves. He'd head in the direction the plane had been travelling. He reasoned that the town they were bound for couldn't be that far away if they were coming in for a landing. Once there, he'd hit the road, hitchhiking, as he always did to put distance between himself and his troubles. If he left now, no one would miss him.

PART II

Once you have tasted flight, you will forever walk the earth with your eyes turned skyward, for there you have been, and there you will always long to return.

LEONARDO DA VINCI

FLIGHT

Erik Vogel came to his passion for flying honestly. Vogel means "bird" in German, and Erik grew up in the slipstream of flight. His father, William Vogel, was a senior pilot with Air Canada, Canada's largest commercial airline. From an early age, Erik had watched his dad don a crisp white shirt, navy blazer and captain's hat, shoulder his enormous leather flight bag, and head off for work. While most of his friends' fathers were bound for nearby offices, stores or work sites, Erik's dad was winging across the country or around the world.

William Vogel, however, was more than a pilot—he was a prominent political figure. In 1973, when Erik was thirteen, his dad successfully ran for public office and became a civic counsellor in Surrey, a growing municipality forty minutes' drive southeast of Vancouver. By the time Erik graduated from high school in 1978, his dad was mayor. Bill Vogel had a reputation for scheduling his flights around council meetings and the multi-tasking mayor's expectation that his oldest son would make something of his life was high.

Though Bill had urged his son to pursue flight training with the military as he had, Erik chose a different route. Two months after he graduated from high school, the eighteen-year-old began his pilot's education at Trinity Western College, a nearby small Christian liberal arts school. Erik selected Trinity not because of any religious devotion, but because its two-year aviation program was considered more prestigious than many of the smaller private flying schools in the area. Largely owner-operated, most local flight schools provided little more than the requisite forty-five hours of instruction required to certify for a private pilot's licence. Trinity, by contrast, offered a five-semester program from which graduates emerged with a commercial pilot's licence. For Erik, this was to be his fast track to becoming a pilot for a major commercial airline.

After a discouraging desk-bound semester studying avionics and the principles of flight, Erik was allowed to take to the sky. His training took place in a Cessna 150—a trim two-seater with dual controls. Unlike the jetliners his father flew, the cockpit of the Cessna was like a steamer trunk with windows. The top of the console was level with Erik's eyes, making him feel like a small child who couldn't quite see over the dashboard.

Erik folded his lanky frame into the tight cockpit and stared nervously at the controls—an unsettling array of dials, levers, switches and knobs. Though he'd studied avionics on paper, the instruments crowded in front of him seemed like confusing clock faces in a surreal Dali painting. He was practically thigh to thigh with his instructor, a squat nugget of a man with a weathered face and thick meaty hands, which he jabbed toward the instruments, asking Erik to identify them in turn.

Airspeed indicator. Artificial horizon. Altimeter. Turn and bank indicator. Heading indicator. Vertical speed indicator. Compass.

Then Erik was nervously ticking his way down the pre-takeoff checklist and run-up procedures.

Priming engine. Fuel mixture: full rich. Fuel selector: on. Carburetor head: cold. Throttle: one-quarter.

His instructor, seemingly satisfied, hit the ignition switch and after a few creaky turns, the propeller blurred into motion. The heavy hum of the engine filled the cockpit while Erik sat stiffly, awkward and over-sized in the small space. He felt compressed, surrounded by a flimsy bubble of metal and Plexiglas, and held the control yoke in a death grip.

"Lightly on the controls," the instructor counselled, inviting Erik to follow his movements. "Same with your feet. Lightly on the pedals."

The instructor punched a button on the NAV/COM panel and requested clearance. His communication with the control tower, clipped and precise, sounded like a rapid-fire exchange in a foreign language. As soon as the tower cleared them, the instructor throttled forward and the plane began to taxi toward the runway. "Hardest thing to master, taxiing," Erik remembers him saying.

Beneath the soles of his running shoes Erik could feel the pedals gently moving, first one, then the other. The instructor deftly aligned the plane with the centre line of the runway awaiting final clearance. When he got it, he opened up the throttle in a smooth practiced move-ment. The engine roared and the plane accelerated down the runway. The control yoke eased back beneath Erik's hands. Then, without effort or warning, the small craft was airborne. It climbed steadily, and as it rose, the buildings of the airport appeared below, grey and brick-like, and the sound of the engine seemed deafening despite Erik's headset. The plane steadily gained altitude and in the co-pilot's seat, Erik let the instructor's movements at the controls radiate through his hands and feet. Exhilaration surged through him.

"Great, isn't it?" the instructor asked. "Think you can keep her level?"

Erik's hands tightened nervously on the controls, and then remem-bering, he eased his grip. He nodded. As the plane hummed toward the Pacific Ocean, Erik found himself grinning.

He was flying.

In the following weeks, his instructor taught him straight-and-level flight, climbs and descents, and turns and slips. Then Erik was on to bigger challenges: takeoffs and landings and recovery from stalls and spins. Each session was a revelation. From the second he climbed into the small cockpit, Erik was in another world, one of magic and possibility.

His first solo flight came unexpectedly. It was the morning of a clear fall day and Erik had spent forty-five minutes flying circuits around the Langley airfield with his instructor in the right-hand seat. At the end of each circuit Erik would do a touch-and-go—landing the plane, then immediately taking off again while the plane's wheels were still rolling.

His instructor had been hard on him, putting him through the paces without giving him pause to think, only react. Finally, Erik landed the plane and brought it to a full stop. Instead of telling him to taxi to the terminal, his instructor opened the door and climbed out.

"Don't dive at the runway when you're bringing her in," he said, reaching back into the cockpit to re-clip his safety belt. "And if you're in doubt about landing, just go around again."

The instructor leaned forward and adjusted the elevator-trim control to compensate for his missing weight. With a nod, he closed the cockpit door.

Erik felt a momentary panic, his mind suddenly devoid of all he had learned. Then, with the ringing *whap* of the instructor's palm against the thin metal fuselage, it came rushing back. Erik throttled forward, turned and taxied back to the end of the runway. He radioed for clearance and when he got it, released the brakes and opened up the throttle to full power. Without the weight of his instructor in the tandem seat, the plane surged forward as if it *wanted* to take flight.

Erik's hands were light on the controls, his pulse quickening as he picked up speed. He pulled gently back on the controls to raise the nose. He was in the air. As he climbed steadily skyward he felt his heart leap as if freed from his chest. The clean lines of the land grew fuzzy and the vibrations of the engine rang through his bones. To the north, the Coast Mountains rose with their craggy peaks, and westward he saw the blue-grey ocean, its surface frosted with tiny whitecaps.

Erik felt a rush of pure elation. For the first time, he was absolutely certain that it was his destiny to fly.

But destiny had a caveat. When Erik graduated from Trinity Western College, local flying jobs were non-existent. Though he had a commercial multi-engine pilot's licence and 250 hours in the cockpit, he was still on the bottom rung of the ladder when it came to a professional flying career. To achieve his dream of becoming an airline jet pilot, Erik needed to build flying hours, and lots of them.

In Canada, rookie pilots must log 1,500 hours before they can apply for an Airline Transport Pilot Licence. An ATPL allows pilots to captain large multi-crew airplanes the world over. The highest level of certification, it is also the minimum requirement for pilots hoping to land a coveted job with a major commercial airline.

Determined to build the flight time he needed to make it to the majors, Erik headed north in search of work. With his parents' help, he purchased a one-way ticket to Yellowknife, the gateway to one of the continent's last true frontiers: the Canadian north. He was twenty years old.

Winter still clung to the land when Erik arrived in early May 1980. From above, Yellowknife appeared like an ancient outpost of pale, low-slung buildings dwarfed by the massive expanse of Great Slave Lake and limitless treed and rocky plains. The land looked bruised, and long stretches of tarnished snow mottled the earth. Situated on the 62nd parallel, Yellowknife was the last major population centre before the end of the treeline and the beginning of the Barren Lands, a vast sub-Arctic prairie also known as the tundra. Though the city of 9,000 seemed small and desolate to Erik, it was home to almost one-tenth of the entire population of northern Canada—a vast and rugged landscape covering almost 4 million square kilometres. *The North*, as Canadians colloquially call it, comprises almost 40 percent of the country's land area and stretches from the 60th parallel all the way to the North Pole. It is a land of harsh temperatures and hardy inhabitants, fewer than 3 per 100 square kilometres. Erik was excited to be among them, making his living as a pilot. He felt that his life was finally beginning.

Erik had learned from a former college buddy that a small northern cargo carrier by the name of La Ronge Aviation was looking for co-pilots. *Just come*, his friend had urged. The day after his arrival, Erik paid a visit to the airline, confident that with his aviation college training and recently acquired IFR rating, he'd be a shoo-in for a job. To his disappointment, the owner informed him that the company wouldn't be hiring until after Victoria Day, three weeks away. Erik must have looked stricken, as the man then suggested that he try The Range.

"They looking for co-pilots?" Erik asked hopefully.

"Nope," he told Erik. "Waiters."

The tavern at The Gold Range Hotel was exactly the kind of drinking establishment you might expect to find in a northern mining town. It was dim and the stench of beer and cigarette smoke was steeped into its walls and threadbare carpet. A hefty bar ran its length and behind it were shelves stocked with an assortment of whiskey, rum and other spirits. The tabletops were worn smooth by the elbows and forearms of big-boned miners and oil patch workers who made The Range their second home, and the carpet was pocked black with cigarette burns.

Erik had frequented the Scottsdale Pub back in his hometown of Surrey where many of the male waiters did double duty as bouncers. He assumed the same code applied in a tough northern mining town. He was wrong. In Yellowknife waiting tables was women's work, but after a good word from the folks at La Ronge, Erik became the first male server ever hired at The Range.

He took the ribbing that accompanied his new job in stride. The way he saw it, he had no choice but to stick it out until La Ronge was hiring again at the end of May. A few days into the job, Erik served a group of young men who rattled his resolve. They were clean-cut and self-assured, different from the regular crowd. One man, wearing a white shirt and sporting a close-cropped haircut, remarked on The *Strange*'s new waiter. He asked Erik his name and then took to derisively calling him *Enrico* for the night. Erik soon discovered that the men were pilots who had also come north to build flying time. Two more weeks as a barmaid suddenly seemed far too long.

The next day, Erik dropped in on Ptarmigan Airways, one of the larger carriers providing scheduled passenger service out of Yellowknife.

"Enrico," a voice yelled as he entered the office. It was the pilot who'd ribbed Erik the night before. "What are you doing here?"

"Looking for a flying job," Erik said.

The pilot looked sheepish and introduced himself as Duncan Bell. When Erik asked about a job with Ptarmigan, Bell shook his head. The airline had no jobs, he said, but reassured him that La Ronge always needed co-pilots for their summer season.

"Just don't expect too much," Bell had warned him.

———

A few days into his new job, Erik understood what Bell had meant. Being hired at La Ronge as a "co-pilot" was little better than being a rampie—a heavy labourer who loaded, unloaded and fuelled planes. Erik began his shifts hauling drills, drill rods and other cargo bound for remote oil camps, as well as 450-pound fuel barrels to power the return flights. Then he'd climb aboard for the ride. Because there were no runways where the planes were bound, aircraft were equipped with oversized tires—called tundra tires—for landing on rough terrain or with floats to land on water. When the pilot reached his destination, the co-pilot would unload the cargo and manually refuel the aircraft using a hand pump—a tedious, arm-numbing task. It didn't take Erik long to realize that he'd been hired more for his size than for his flying skills. Where the other new hires were referred to as grunts, Erik was called Supergrunt. All were licenced pilots looking to build flying time, but in contrast to the pilots at La Ronge, who earned $8,000 a month, co-pilots earned $1,000.

Erik's first flight took place on May 21 and lasted seven-and-a-half hours—a far cry from the one-hour training circuits of his college days. Vast distances separated the remote camps and Erik soon found himself at the controls across hundreds of kilometres of tundra. Summer days north of the 60th parallel—the "land of the midnight sun"—were almost endless. With the pilot and co-pilot taking turns at the helm, La Ronge's planes could literally fly around the clock. Typically, the pilot handled takeoffs and landings, and flew until he was tired. Then he would clamber into the back of the plane to sleep and Erik would take over, waking the pilot when it was time to land. The problem was that Erik couldn't claim any of his flying hours until La Ronge gave him a Pilot Proficiency Check or PPC—an evaluation by an approved check pilot certifying Erik as competent to fly a particular aircraft. Though Erik and the other co-pilots reminded their bosses about the required PPC, they didn't do so vociferously. Young eager pilots willing to take their places were plentiful and flying time, even if not officially sanctioned, was better than no time at all. Still, without a PPC, Erik was little more than a phantom flyer, taking the controls during the deep crease of still-light night when the world slept, and sliding back into his rampie role when morning or civilization arrived.

The long summer days steamrolled into fall and the promised check ride never came. Winter freeze-up edged closer and at the end of September 1980, the company relocated its planes to its northern Saskatchewan headquarters to switch their landing gear from floats to skis for the winter. Erik caught a ride, expecting that he'd be first in line for a pilot's job. But when he landed in the town of La Ronge, he joined a long line of equally experienced co-pilots hoping for the same break. Erik took stock. With more men than machines and a logbook filled with 700 hours he couldn't claim, he decided to head home.

He wasn't back in BC long before the North came calling in the form of Len Robinson, a former La Ronge pilot with whom Erik had frequently teamed up during the summer.

"I've got a real co-pilot's job for you," he said. The airline was called Shirley Air and based out of Edmonton. "It's short term," Robinson cautioned, "but you'd be flying a Twin Otter." Twin Otters are the Cadillacs of small commuter planes—turboprops that carry up to nineteen passengers.

"What do I have to do to get the job?" Erik asked.

"Get yourself to Edmonton."

When Erik thanked Robinson, he shrugged it off. "After last summer," he said, "let's just call it even."

Less than a week later, Erik was in Edmonton. The city of half a million people had long been the jumping off point for bush pilots ferrying workers and supplies to the North. Erik's contract lasted little more than six weeks, but it gave him enough logbook hours to land him a co-pilot's job at Ptarmigan Airways back in Yellowknife. Duncan Bell was still with the carrier when Erik returned in late May 1981.

"Hey, Enrico!" Bell greeted him warmly. "I'm looking forward to finally flying together."

The two men never got the chance. Soon after joining Ptarmigan, Erik learned that a company called Simpson Air based in the trading post of Fort Simpson several hundred kilometres west was looking for pilots. Erik didn't think twice about leaving Ptarmigan and seizing the opportunity to finally fly in the captain's seat.

Paul Jones, one of the airline's co-owners, picked Erik up in Yellowknife.

"As far as I'm concerned," Jones told him, "if you survived a summer at La Ronge, then you must be okay."

Erik's second stint in the North was an entirely different experience from his first. He was pilot-in-command and the hours in his logbook grew steadily. The flying was breathtaking and he loved being alone in the cockpit and watching the rugged beauty of the land stretch out beneath him. The Canadian Shield, a massive expanse of low-lying rock, lay across much of the North's southern reaches. In winter it was an unending white wasteland, but in summer it was pocked and aglitter with rivers and thousands of lakes. Patches of muskeg— swampy basins of moss-covered water and decaying vegetation—were cradled between jagged outcrops of limestone and shale. In the east, the low-lying glaciated plain gave rise to mountains that reached heights of nearly 10,000 feet. Glaciers hugged the cols of these white giants and sheer, spectacular cliffs plummeted into deep fjords.

Though seemingly barren, the North was alive with wildlife ranging from bears and wolves to caribou and countless bird species. On one flight Erik spotted a lone grizzly bear running, its powerful muscles undulating under a rich coat of fur. On another he came upon a herd of caribou. Erik was 1,000 feet up when the landscape suddenly transformed into a moving mass with no beginning or end in sight. As far as his eyes could see forward, back, and to either side, there was only an ocean of caribou, their antlers bobbing like a briar of nude branches and their mottled beige bodies spread like a dappled fleece over the land.

That summer Erik flew almost every day as pilot-in-command, progressing from a 300-horsepower Cherokee Six to a Cessna 185, a big-tailed, six-seater—known as a "taildragger" for the small wheel affixed to the underside of the tail. He was twenty-one and literally and figuratively on top of the world. He had manoeuvred his way into the upper echelons of northern bush flying.

Bush flying originated in Canada. One of the first recorded commercial passenger bush flights took place in October 1920 after a fur buyer walked into the Canadian Aircraft Company in Winnipeg, Manitoba, and asked to be flown hundreds of miles north to his home in the settlement of The Pas. By land, the journey across bush, muskeg and bountiful lakes would typically have taken the man several weeks. He arrived in a day. Within a year bush planes were exploring the North to within a hundred miles of the Arctic Circle, opening up isolated areas of the continent.

Early northern bush pilots battled bitter temperatures, blinding snowstorms and the unknown perils of uncharted terrain. They were larger-than-life men with names like Wop May, Punch Dickens and Doc Oaks, and their exploits became the stuff of legends.

Wilfred Reid "Wop" May, one of the most famous, was credited with helping bring down the Red Baron during World War I. May was only eighteen and on his first patrol of the western front when the feared fighter pilot, Baron Manfred von Richthofen, suddenly dropped in on him. May's guns jammed and the German strafed his wings with machine gun fire, yet the young pilot managed to elude the Red Baron. So intent was the German ace on finishing the fight that he broke his own rule and followed May's plane across Allied lines where another countryman, Roy Brown, helped bring the Baron down.

Like many veterans who wanted to continue flying after the war, May gravitated to the North where pilots faced different, but no less formidable foes. In January 1929, May was asked to deliver serum to a remote community battling a diphtheria outbreak. He flew for two straight days in the open cockpit of an Avro Avian biplane, the serum wrapped in a blanket at his feet with a charcoal heater. He arrived with his hands virtually frozen to the controls.

Today's bush pilots maintain their vaulted position as courageous, self-reliant adventurers, providing a crucial lifeline to many isolated communities in the Canadian and Alaskan wilderness. While the planes may have changed, the pilots who fly them haven't. Far from help if anything goes awry, they must often fend for themselves in inhospitable environments where the penalty for a mistake can be death. Bush pilots have the highest mortality rate of any commercial pilots and bush flying consistently ranks in the top three of the world's most dangerous professions, after commercial fishermen and loggers.

Erik soon came to understand that the special cachet bush pilots carried still existed among the remote, tight-knit communities of the North. Pilots were like freewheeling saviours buzzing in from afar to deliver precious supplies or to transport the ill to hospital. Part of a handful of high-status outsiders—including RCMP officers, doctors, nurses and teachers—pilots in the North were akin to dignitaries. Erik enjoyed his newfound stature, and by the end of his second northern summer felt like he was finally building the experience and confidence needed to face the challenges of winter bush flying.

During freeze-up in late October 1981, while Simpson Air switched its planes' landing gear from floats to skis, Erik flew south to visit his family. His trip to Surrey coincided with a special occasion—his father's fiftieth birthday celebration. The night of the party, relatives and friends gathered at the Vogel home where the festivities carried on past midnight. It was not until the early hours of the morning, when the hosts were bidding their last guests goodbye, that events took a terrible turn. A family friend noticed that her convertible sports car was no longer parked in the driveway. Mortified, the Vogels had immediately contacted the police to report the car missing and called a cab to take her home.

Early the next morning someone banged on the door. Erik answered it to find a young police officer standing on the porch.

"Are you here about the stolen car?" Erik asked. The cop didn't answer immediately and Erik recalls being taken aback by his expression. "He had a terrible look on his face."

Erik remembers the officer then asking to speak to the parents of Reginald Vogel. Reginald was the given name of Brodie, Erik's sixteen-year-old brother, but no one in the family *ever* called him that. Erik reluctantly climbed the stairs to his parents' bedroom and knocked on their door. His mother's reaction surprised him.

"I don't want to talk with him," she'd said. "Tell him to go away."

A moment later Joan Vogel descended from the bedroom. Erik remembers hearing the officer stammer the words: *son* and *Reginald*. Erik's mother yelled: "I don't have a son named Reginald! His name is Brodie!"

The colour drained completely from the officer's face and he shifted his weight uncomfortably from one foot to another. He tried again: "Your son . . . Reggie?"

By that time, Bill Vogel had appeared on the stairs, his face ghostly white.

Later that morning Erik accompanied his father to the morgue. By then they had learned that Brodie had borrowed the sports car to take his girlfriend home. Driving back along the highway from Vancouver, perhaps speeding to get home before the owner missed her vehicle, Brodie had slammed into a cement overpass.

"It was terrible," is all Erik could say of the moment they pulled the sheet off his little brother's body so that he and his father could identify the corpse.

Erik took a two-month leave after his brother's death to help his parents cope with the loss. Something intangible had shifted inside him when he returned to his job with Simpson Air in January 1982. Though never a risk-taker, he began to be unnerved by the dangers of bush flying. The echo of his mother's plea not to return to the North reverberated in his head: "Please. I can't bear to lose another child."

Meanwhile, Simpson Air was flourishing, expanding its reach north into the High Arctic. It purchased an old airline base 300 kilometres above the Arctic Circle in Cambridge Bay—an outpost on the southeast shore of Victoria Island servicing passenger and research vessels travelling the Northwest Passage. The company offered Erik a captain's position on their six-seat twin-engine Piper Aztec, their sole plane stationed in the community at the time. Logging pilot-in-command hours on a multi-engine aircraft was gold to a rookie pilot, so Erik migrated further north to the frozen forehead of the continent.

The High Arctic during winter is one of the harshest environments on the planet. Darkness drapes the days and blizzards frequently strafe the landscape, erasing the margin between earth and sky. With no visual reference to the land or guiding hand from air traffic controllers, Erik had to rely on his fledgling dead reckoning skills. Flying was often perilous and he had several close calls to prove it. One occurred during an emergency medical evacuation or medivac to Gjoa Haven, a tiny Inuit community 370 kilometres east of Cambridge Bay. Erik was to pick up a pregnant fourteen-year-old in distress and transport her more than 1,000 kilometres south to the hospital in Yellowknife. Ted Grant, Simpson Air's co-owner, came along as co-pilot. A long-time northern RCMP officer, Grant had recently quit the force to turn his part-time passion for flying into a second career. Though he'd held a pilot's licence for years, Grant had just acquired his IFR rating and was relatively inexperienced flying on instruments.

Erik had a terrible cold the night of the medivac, his sinus pain unbearable as the plane carrying him, Grant, the patient, and a nurse ascended out of Gjoa Haven. Rather than climbing to 10,000 feet, Erik elected to give his aching sinuses a break by flying at 7,000, though it would make it more difficult to pick up signals from any en route ground beacons. With seven hours of fuel on board, Erik filed a flight plan directly to Yellowknife, just under five hours away over barren terrain with few navigational aids. When the plane reached altitude, he contacted the nearby Distant Early Warning radar station for help with his bearing, and then set a course southwest.

"I'll take over this leg," Grant offered, urging Erik to go to sleep. Knowing he'd have to fly another charter later that night, Erik didn't argue. He tipped his head back and closed his eyes for what seemed like only a minute. When he opened them, Grant had an IFR chart spread in front of him and told Erik that he hadn't picked up the en route navigational beacon at Contwoyto Lake. Erik was instantly wide awake.

It was ink black outside and snow buffeted the cockpit windows. Terror gripped Erik and he immediately thought of Martin Hartwell.

Hartwell was a Canadian bush pilot who, ten years earlier, had flown an evening medivac from Cambridge Bay to Yellowknife carrying a nurse and two patients: a pregnant Inuit woman and a fourteen-year-old Inuit boy with appendicitis. The plane left during a storm, became lost, and smashed into a hillside, killing the pregnant woman and the nurse. Hartwell broke his knee and both ankles in the crash, but he and the Inuit boy, David Pisurayak Kootook, survived. For weeks the two huddled near the wreckage, enduring brutally cold temperatures. The boy constructed a lean-to gathered wood, and built a fire. Hartwell, a vegetarian, eventually resorted to eating pieces of flesh from the nurse's body to stay alive, but Kootook refused to consume human remains. It took thirty-one days before rescue teams found the crash site. Hartwell was alive, but the Inuit boy who had cared for him had died the week before.

Erik's insides turned liquid as he took the controls and flew blindly into the night. His eyes moved frantically across his cockpit instruments, but they offered little comfort. He had no choice but to keep flying, though he had no idea of what lay ahead. It was only by sheer luck that Erik eventually picked up the signal from the Yellowknife navigational beacon more than 150 kilometres away. By the time Erik landed he felt totally spent. Refusing to fly the second charter, he checked himself into a Yellowknife hotel room for the night.

Erik had barely recovered from the unnerving experience of his medivac when he heard news from a fellow pilot that Duncan Bell had crashed his plane. Bell, who was flying a medivac to the small Inuit community of Coppermine, had been lucky. He'd flown into the tundra at cruise speed on approach to the airfield. His plane had torpedoed into the snow, bounced and then careened along the surface until it eventually came to a stop. But the fuselage had remained intact and all three people aboard—Bell, his co-pilot and a nurse—had survived.

Why would Bell do something so stupid? The opportunity for Erik to ask him never arose. Bell lost his job with Ptarmigan after the crash and disappeared from the North.

Erik put Duncan Bell out of his mind. There were other things to worry about. Until his brother's death, Erik had accepted that a certain degree of danger was part of his job. Now it seemed that bush flying was demanding too much of him. Bush operations often require pilots to overlook minor but potentially costly maintenance issues, and to push the weather.

"If we never pushed the weather," Erik recalls his boss, Paul Jones, telling him, "we'd never stay in business."

Erik remembers another occasion when the company asked him to fly from Fort Simpson to Fort Liard despite a severe thunderstorm warning. Erik could see enormous thunderheads rising like dark gargoyles from the horizon—a definite no-go scenario.

"Just fly around them," he remembers Paul Jones telling him, before ushering the passengers onto the aircraft. Erik skirted the black wall for a time, flying parallel to the front, but eventually his heading led him straight into it. A gaping crevasse appeared ahead and Erik entered it. For a moment his plane seemed to hang, dreamlike, in a void of atmosphere. On either side of him clouds towered like grimy fortress walls and far, far above, he glimpsed blue sky. Light rain began to speckle the windshield, building until it ran in rivulets along the cockpit windows. Then hell erupted. The aircraft pitched violently for a moment before smashing into a seemingly solid wall of obstruction. Erik wrestled with the controls and the artificial horizon gauge oscillated as the plane shuddered violently. He heard a passenger vomiting and the smell filled the small cabin, heightening the sour taste already in Erik's mouth. Lightning split the clouds and the sky hummed hot and electric around him. Seconds later the air cracked with a deafening boom of thunder. Erik felt his insides churn, and a clammy wetness glossed his palms where they gripped the yoke.

As he neared his destination and began his approach, a fierce cross-wind pushed him off course and Erik struggled to crab back onto the glide slope path. His wheels touched down, but the runway was slick with water and the plane skidded off the end and onto the grass. For several minutes Erik sat limply in the cockpit. In the cabin no one moved. No one uttered a word. Finally, Erik mustered the energy to deplane his passengers and unload their baggage. He was scheduled to fly a return flight, but refused.

"I'm not going anywhere," Erik told Jones. "We just got the shit kicked out of us."

In the ensuing weeks, Erik's relationship with the company further deteriorated. He began refusing flights and insisting on immediate repairs. Tensions reached a breaking point on April 21, 1982, the day before his twenty-second birthday. Erik's former high school sweetheart, Lee-Ann Rydeen, had come north for the occasion. She arrived in Fort Simpson the day Erik was to fly the company's new engineer to Cambridge Bay, and was going to come along for the ride.

As Erik was preparing for takeoff, Jones radioed him from his incoming flight. "Shut her down," Jones told him. Within moments Jones was on the ground and striding toward Erik's plane.

"What's she doing here?" Jones asked, nodding toward the young woman in the co-pilot's seat.

Erik explained that Ted Grant had given him permission for Lee-Ann to accompany him and the engineer to Cambridge Bay.

"We'll see about that," Jones said. He headed toward the hangar and disappeared inside, only to return moments later.

"Get out of my plane," Jones told Erik. "You're done."

Erik didn't argue. The truth was, he *was* done. The risks had simply become too great. With hundreds of hours of flight time under his belt, Erik figured he'd have little trouble finding a job at another airline. He figured wrong. He wouldn't fly again until two years later, when word came to him that a small northern Alberta airline called Wapiti Aviation was looking for pilots.

WAPITI

Erik was ecstatic to sign on with Wapiti Aviation on August 30, 1984. Dale Wells, its thirty-six-year-old chief pilot, maintenance engineer and flight instructor, seemed competent and straightforward, and Erik quickly grew to know Dale's dad, Delbert, the company president and director of operations, and Dale's mother. The Wells family even hosted Erik in their home for a couple of nights until he found a place to live. Erik recalled the pilot proficiency check that Dale gave him in his first week as one of the most thorough he'd ever received. He'd been impressed.

By September 6, Erik had completed his route check and been assigned captain on a twin-engine ten-seat Piper Navajo. But the challenges of flying with Wapiti Aviation far exceeded anything he'd faced in the Arctic, testing the bounds of his abilities. In comparison to flying in the far north, where the skies were uncontrolled and pilots crossing Canada's vast expanses had room to manoeuvre, Wapiti's passenger flights between Grande Prairie and Edmonton were complex. In short order, Erik had to learn approach procedures for six different airports, the locations and workings of eighteen navigational beacons, and the nuances of the weather and terrain in between. The airline maintained a fleet of fourteen single- and twin-engine commuter airplanes flying a loop of tightly timed stops to small communities in northern Alberta. Erik flew two to four flights a day, six days a week. When he wasn't flying, he was on call for medivacs.

During one of his first flights, he'd connected by VHF radio with a former bush pilot he'd met four years earlier when they'd both worked in the Arctic. Shortly into the chat, the pilot asked Erik to switch over to a private frequency, then asked, "What the hell are you doing at Wapiti?"

Erik told him that he'd been desperate for work. He'd applied to dozens of airlines, but no one was hiring. When he'd learned about Wapiti, he'd been driving a transit bus for the handicapped in the Vancouver bedroom community of Surrey.

"That company's bad news," the pilot told him. "Get out of there."

Soon after that exchange, Erik had a second chance encounter with another former Arctic bush pilot. Erik had just landed his plane in Edmonton and was waiting to be refuelled. The fuel truck finally arrived and a tall, familiar-looking man in a rampie's jumpsuit got out. Erik's eyes widened. It was Duncan Bell.

Erik had heard nothing of Bell since the pilot had crashed his plane. The two men shook hands awkwardly. There was no light banter, no *Hey, Enrico!* Erik had wanted to ask him what had happened on the day he crashed. He still couldn't understand how Bell could have made such a careless mistake, but considering how the tables had turned for the two pilots, Erik said nothing.

The meeting with Bell reinforced Erik's feeling that he was lucky to be aloft, even if there were rumblings about Wapiti. September unfurled mild and clear, the landscape aglow with vivid fall colours— brilliant reds and oranges against enormous blue prairie sky. In the fields, combine harvesters worked overtime and from above Erik watched them moving like small bugs across the prairie, consuming golden oceans of wheat and depositing neat bales like pats of butter upon the earth. The flying had been surreal, the air so crisp and clear that Erik half expected to look back to see clean sharp lines where the wings of his plane had sliced through it.

The pace was punishing, but at twenty-four, Erik figured he could handle it. He was banking flying hours like bonus points in a pinball game. But the job took a toll and by mid-October Erik was down to 180 pounds from the 205 he'd weighed when he'd signed on. He often ate poorly and hadn't had more than a few decent nights' sleep in weeks. He missed his family and friends back on the coast, and Lee-Ann, to whom he'd become engaged after returning from the Arctic.

Erik quickly learned why the bush pilot who'd radioed had warned him. Wapiti was a busy airline and the pressure on pilots to maintain their passenger schedules, regardless of the weather, was high. He had recently overheard a fellow Wapiti pilot, Mark Poppleton, on the radio during a flight in poor weather.

"I can't get through," Poppleton had said, fear in his voice as he circled the airport. He didn't want to return to Grande Prairie, he later told Erik, because he worried that Dale Wells would get in the airplane and make him do the flight again. Wapiti's chief pilot was known to take planes back up after a pilot had aborted a flight, bringing the terrified pilot along to show him how it was done. If a pilot declined to take a flight a second time, he might just find himself grounded and working in the hangar. Two weeks later he could be gone. Fourteen pilots had quit or been fired from the airline in the previous six months.

Transport Canada had frequently cited Wapiti for safety violations, including landing when the weather was below allowable limits, flying with one pilot when conditions required two, and unsatisfactory aircraft maintenance. In recent weeks, the government had grounded eight of the company's planes because it had failed to conduct the mandatory airworthiness inspections.

"It didn't strike me as a place I wanted to stay a long time," Erik would later say of his time at Wapiti Aviation. The ace up his sleeve was that he didn't think he'd have to. Erik had an inside line on a better flying job with a Calgary-based cargo carrier. He needed only thirty-five more hours on a multi-engine plane and the job was as good as his. The way Erik figured, he would say goodbye to Wapiti by the end of the month. All he had to do was keep from getting fired.

Unfortunately, yesterday's fiasco hadn't helped. Tuesday, October 16 had been the last in a six-day flying stint on the morning schedule and Erik had been looking forward to a day off. As usual, he was at the Wapiti hangar at 4:45 a.m., which gave him just enough time to prep for his 6:00 a.m. departure. It was a milk run—outbound, a yo-yo of takeoffs and landings arcing north then east from Grande Prairie to the towns of Fairview, Peace River and High Prairie, and then south to Edmonton. Inbound, a direct flight back to Grande Prairie, arriving by mid-morning. Then Erik spent several hours helping out around the hangar. Watching the weather move in, he was grateful that he wasn't scheduled to fly the following day, and in the early afternoon he went home to bed. He'd slept less than an hour when his pager went off—a series of shrill beeps cutting through his fog of exhaustion. It was Dale Wells.

"I need you back here now," Dale told Erik. "We've got a medivac to Edmonton."

Erik dragged himself out of bed and back to the airport. In the short time he'd been asleep, winter had arrived with shocking suddenness, blue sky wiped away by a rag of grey. Snow had also started to fall, swirling like tiny dervishes along the road to the airport.

Erik was on the phone getting a weather briefing when Delbert Wells entered the hangar. Dale's father was a compact, wiry man in his early seventies with a bowlegged gait; a farmer his entire life who, as far as Erik could see, didn't know the first thing about flying. Twelve years earlier Del had sold the farm to support his son's dream of starting an airline. Now he was president and head of flight operations.

"So I'll need a co-pilot," Erik said aloud into the phone, confirming the conditions he'd just received from the weather office and hoping Del would take the hint.

The cloud ceiling had dropped to less than the legal minimum for a single pilot and Erik wanted to make sure his boss understood that today wasn't a day for flying solo. Del muttered loudly and though Erik couldn't make out the exact words, the gist of it was clear: take this flight or you won't be taking any. Crestfallen, Erik hung up the phone and headed outside.

A paramedic, Neil Godwin, was waiting beside an ambulance when Erik taxied over to the terminal. By the time the two men had loaded the patient and were airborne, it was dusk. The temperature had dropped noticeably since Erik's morning flight and fat flakes spun around his cockpit windows. It wasn't until he descended into Edmonton that he broke through the clouds. At 500 feet above the deck the runway suddenly appeared, a grey belt of asphalt barely distinct from the cloud and surrounding snow-swept fields.

It was dark when Godwin finally got back to the terminal, apologetically explaining that the emergency department had been backed up. Erik waved off the apology, anxious to be airborne. Stepping outside, white tufts of his breath floated upward like pale ghosts. Erik and Godwin loaded the empty gurney and climbed into the cockpit. Moving quickly through his checklist, Erik cracked the throttle to half open and then flipped the starter switch. A series of rapid-fire sounds erupted and the prop spun into motion, but the engine would not fire. After a few seconds, he stopped then hit the starter switch back over and tried once more. Again the prop spun into motion and the engine strained to engage. No luck. Erik tried several more times, and on the last, instead of the familiar *chk-chk-chk-chk-chk* of the engine turning over, the pilot heard only a weak murmur followed by a sickening clicking sound. The starter had burned out. Erik's stomach flipped like some great slug rolling over. He'd have to call Dale and let him know. Erik knew how much his boss hated having his planes out of service and if the airline lost revenue on Erik's account, there'd be hell to pay. He walked with Godwin back into the terminal, got him a seat on Wapiti's evening flight back to Grande Prairie, and then called Dale.

"I'm stopping in Edmonton tonight on my way down to Calgary," Dale told him. "We'll try to hand prop it."

Bone tired, Erik sat down to wait. He dared not close his eyes, fearing that if he did, he wouldn't wake up until Dale was standing over him. Dale's plane didn't arrive until after eleven and Erik rushed outside to meet it.

For nearly twenty minutes, the two tried to hand prop the plane— a technique where one person sits at the controls while the other cranks the propeller. Finally Dale called it quits, saying that he would have to fly in a new starter on Wednesday's morning flight. Without further instructions for Erik, Dale strode away toward his plane.

The young pilot was at a loss. By the time he mustered the courage to ask Dale about a hotel room, he was already 30 feet away and out of earshot. Erik stood beside his disabled plane, frozen fingers tucked into the armpits of his parka, until he saw Dale's aircraft taxi down the runway, take off, and disappear into a low bank of cloud.

Inside the deserted terminal, fluorescent lights cast an antiseptic glow. Erik was numb with anxiety, and a raw ache churned the pit of his stomach. It was almost midnight and the agents and baggage handlers were shutting things down. He felt tears burning as he stepped back outside into the cold. He looked around helplessly. Down the service road a lone light shone in the trailer of the Shell refuelling depot. He vaguely knew the attendant who worked there, and walked toward the trailer. The attendant was just closing up when Erik reached the door.

"I'm grounded for the night," Erik told him. "I need a place to sleep." The attendant nodded in the direction of a battered old couch pushed up against the wall. It wasn't much, he said, but Erik was welcome to it.

Erik shifted his weight on the sagging couch. He'd curled into a C on the matted upholstery, long legs accordioned into his torso, and had lain awake shivering through the night. Outside, snow fell hard and steady, laying a white carpet over the airport. Snowplows had grumbled non-stop and now one was clearing the parking lot behind the trailer. Erik could feel the vibrations from its massive blade shuddering through the thin wall. He checked his watch—4:00 a.m.—then closed his eyes and, wrapping his arms around his torso, drifted into an uneasy sleep. The sound of a key turning in the lock woke him forty-five minutes later.

The attendant brought a blast of cold air in with him. He urged Erik not to get up, saying that he'd wake him after he fuelled the early morning flights. The man returned an hour later and Erik ventured out into the frosty morning to call his boss. Dale's directions were typically curt: the company was flying down a starter on the 8:40 flight. Erik was to offload the parts, get the plane to a hangar, arrange for the repair, and fly the plane back that day.

After he'd unloaded the parts and found a mechanic to fix the plane, Erik settled in at the terminal to wait. Jim Powell, one of Wapiti's veteran pilots, came across him in the early afternoon.

"Isn't this your day off?" he asked. Erik explained what had happened and that he was waiting for the fix on the starter. Jim seized the opportunity.

"I've got a flight to McMurray and I really could use a co-pilot," he said.

Fort McMurray was a booming northern city servicing the Canadian oil sands. Its population of 35,000 had more than quadrupled in the past dozen years, and a year ago Wapiti had started daily flights from Edmonton.

Erik didn't think twice. It beat hanging around the terminal, and the return flight would have him back before the work on the starter was finished.

On the flight to Fort McMurray, Erik and Jim had time to catch up. The two men discussed the situation at Wapiti. Jim had been concerned enough about the airline's safety standards that two days earlier he'd called Transport Canada. He'd informed an aviation safety inspector that Wapiti pilots sometimes had to "bust the minimums" on their approaches into uncontrolled airfields along the company's northern Alberta routes. *Minimums* are the minimum altitudes to which pilots may safely descend to see if visual conditions exist that allow the aircraft to land. When flying on instruments—required at night or in bad weather—minimums are sacred ground for pilots, who are taught never to bust them. Period.

Jim had asked the Transport Canada official whether the pilot or the carrier would be held responsible if a pilot was pressured to bust the minimums and was caught. The inspector told him that it was the carrier's responsibility to ensure its pilots knew the regulations. However, he also cautioned that pilots who broke the rules, either knowingly or unknowingly, wouldn't be completely absolved of blame.

Jim also warned Erik that even though a functioning autopilot was required for single-pilot IFR flights, the autopilots on some Wapiti aircraft couldn't be trusted. To prove his point, Jim engaged the autopilot on his plane and it responded erratically.

Despite these weighty issues and the weather, Erik enjoyed his flight with Jim. The sky was overcast as they descended through snow and heavy fog, and the plane was only a few hundred feet off the ground before the runway appeared. Once on the tarmac, Erik helped unload luggage while Jim went to get a weather update and check on passengers for the flight back to Edmonton. When he returned, Erik knew from the look on his face that something was wrong.

"We're fully booked," Jim said.

"You're bumping me?" *How the hell was he going to get back?*

Jim was apologetic, telling Erik that another Wapiti pilot, Ed Seier, was flying to Edmonton later that afternoon, and Erik could catch a ride with him. Seier was tight with the bosses and the other pilots kept their complaints to themselves when he was around. Erik groaned. He had no doubt that Seier would mention his unauthorized side trip to the Wellses.

Mercifully, by the time Erik flew his own repaired plane back to Grande Prairie that night, Dale and Delbert had both gone home. The next day he was scheduled to begin another six-day run of flying, this time on the p.m. sked. Erik was certain he was about to become the latest member of the "89 Day Club," what Wapiti pilots dubbed the company's practice of terminating pilots before their ninetieth day of employment to avoid having to provide two weeks' notice and holiday pay. He lay in bed sick with worry until exhaustion overtook him and he eventually fell asleep.

A heavy weight of dread filled Erik as he arrived for work on Thursday—whether at the prospect of seeing Dale or flying, he couldn't be sure. A high-pressure system had moved in and settled in a wide band stretching north from Montana through Edmonton and up to Fort Smith, which meant there would be no escaping the weather.

Tonight would be the first time he'd have to rely on his instruments to get into the uncontrolled airports in High Prairie and Fairview. The thought of trying to land in these conditions made Erik nervous. He believed that Dale would want him to take a shot at getting in, no matter the weather, and the best Erik could hope was that Dale would assign a co-pilot on the flight.

That is, if Erik still had a job.

As if the thought summoned the man, Dale entered the hangar. "Kawa will be your co-pilot tonight," he said. "And another thing . . ."

Erik held his breath, but instead of firing him, Dale asked Erik to pick up a set of propellers in Edmonton and bring them back that evening. Relief swept over him. Without waiting for Dale to say more, Erik hurried outside to prep his flight.

Erik was happy to have Andy Kawa with him. After landing in Edmonton at 6:20, the two pilots worked flat out to turn the flight around and get airborne within the allotted half-hour. Erik left Kawa to look after the passengers while he went in search of the props. When he returned Kawa had good news: there were no passengers bound for High Prairie or Fairview. Erik loaded the propellers into the plane's wing lockers, boarded his passengers and prepared to depart.

The cloud ceiling had dropped to below 900 feet by the time the plane took off. The temperature hovered just below freezing, and heavy, sodden snowflakes clung to the windshield before the wipers pushed the slushy mess away. Erik gained altitude and was soon above the cloud and into clear air, where he remained until Peace River Air Traffic Control gave him clearance to begin his descent into the airport. The plane stumbled out of the cloud at 800 feet and when it landed, Erik was ten minutes behind schedule. As he deplaned, he discovered why. The leading edges of the wings were coated with thick, uneven crusts of ice. The sight of it shocked him. He hadn't expected that level of icing to form in less than an hour. Erik climbed back into the cockpit and flipped the switch for the wing de-icer boots, but nothing happened.

Asking Kawa to look after the passengers so he could figure out how to de-ice the wings, Erik hurried to the terminal and minutes later returned with a broom. It wasn't sophisticated, but if there was something he'd learned flying in the Arctic, it was to use the resources one had at hand. Standing in front of the wing, he banged the broom handle gently against its underside. The ice cracked and pieces broke away in sheets, smashing onto the tarmac like windowpanes. Erik heard a voice behind him remark, "Pretty ugly icing up there."

He turned to see a local circuit court judge who, along with his secretary, often flew from Peace River to Grande Prairie. Erik stammered something he hoped might reassure him, but the judge smiled good-humouredly, waving off Erik's words. Northern Albertans were as hearty as the people he'd met in the Arctic, and almost as accustomed to bad weather. But Erik couldn't afford to dismiss the icing. Within minutes of leaving Peace River, he could see a thin uneven bar of it reforming on the leading edge of his left wing. Perspiration blossomed under his moustache as Kawa called for clearance to ascend above the cloud. Flying in icing conditions without reliable de-icing equipment was dangerous, and by the time they began their descent into Grande Prairie, Erik was white knuckled, certain that the plane would stall at any moment. The reported conditions at the airport provided little encouragement: *Ground fog. Weather 500 feet. Visibility one half mile.* Erik was almost on top of the runway lights before he spied them dashing toward him. He pulled back on the yoke and the plane hit with a jolt. The rubber wheels screamed against the icy asphalt before the plane eventually shuddered to a stop.

Erik was stiff with exhaustion. Wearily, he deplaned the passengers and with Kawa's help, unloaded their luggage and put the aircraft to bed for the night. A wisp of something forgotten feathered the edge of his consciousness, but he was too weary to grasp it. He shouldered his flight bag and walked slowly through the midnight quiet to his truck. Tomorrow he would need to do this all over again and the weather promised to be the same if not worse.

Late on the morning of Friday, October 19, 1984, Erik awoke to more snow and overcast skies. Moving sluggishly, he showered then dressed in his uniform of sorts—a white collared shirt, navy dress pants and a dark tie. He padded sluggishly into the tiny kitchen of his basement suite and opened the fridge. As usual, it was empty. On the countertop he spied the tin of his mom's homemade chocolate chip cookies. Earlier that week, Erik's parents, concerned for his well-being, had planned to visit him in Grande Prairie.

"Don't come," he'd told them. "It's crazy here. I'm flying every day and don't know when I'll have time to see you."

His parents had relented, but his mom had sent the tin of cookies. Now he opened it, stuffed one in his mouth and then wrapped up four more for later. He dropped them into his flight bag next to his logbook, pulled on his heavy parka and left the apartment.

Snow continued to tumble steadily, as it had over the past three days. Whorls of flakes skittered across the windshield of his truck as he sped west along 100th Avenue toward the airport. As he exited the thoroughfare and drove north, the Wapiti Aviation hangar rose like the spine of an enormous whale surfacing from an ocean of white. The building was a large Quonset hut with a patchwork of mustard and white squares covering its long curve of roof. Sprawled down the length of it in big block letters was WAPITI.

Erik first checked in with the weather office at the terminal. He'd hoped there would be a change in the forecast, but the SIGMET that had been issued over the past three days was still in effect. A SIGMET, or significant meteorological information, is an advisory that warns pilots of severe or hazardous weather conditions, including severe icing. Erik knew firsthand from last night's flight just how *significant* that icing could be. It had the ability to reduce his plane's aerodynamic efficiency, weigh it down and, in extreme cases—which Erik dared not even think about—cause a crash. He felt a familiar churning in his stomach. While the chances were slim that Wapiti would ground his flight, surely he'd have another set of hands in the cockpit today.

Erik trudged across the snow to preflight his aircraft, the same one he'd captained the previous night. It was a Piper Navajo Chieftain, registration number C-GXUC, one of the planes that Transport Canada had recently grounded citing maintenance issues. Though C-GXUC was back in service, after last night's problem with the wing de-icers Erik wasn't sure he could trust it.

The pilot who'd flown the a.m. sked was wrapping up his shift and gave him a rundown. Erik was already uneasy at the thought of flying into High Prairie and Fairview, and the pilot's report didn't help. The plow hadn't been out that day and there was snow on the runway.

"I barely made it off," he said. Then the pilot dropped another bombshell. He had flown to Edmonton and back that morning with his plane feeling inexplicably overweight. It was only after he returned to Grande Prairie and checked the wing lockers that he discovered the propellers that Erik had forgotten to unload.

That's it, Erik thought. *I'm toast.*

Erik fuelled the plane and taxied to the terminal, feeling like a man heading to the gallows. It was 4:30 p.m. and he knew his passengers would soon be arriving for check-in. He still needed to get a handle on the weather and file his flight plan. The latest aerodrome forecast for the region didn't look good. *Ceiling 1,000 ft broken, 2,000 ft overcast, occasional ceiling 800 ft broken, visibility 4 mi in light snow and fog.*

The conditions were marginal for visual flight and Erik might need to bust the minimums if he had passengers bound for High Prairie on his return.

His thoughts in turmoil, Erik lingered in the weather office. He made a photocopy of the aerodrome forecasts, highlighted the key terminals with a yellow marker, and then filed his flight plan. He checked his watch and, with a start, realized his passengers would be waiting. When Erik arrived at the departure area, Dale was checking them in for him.

"Where have you been?"

Abashedly, Erik held up the forecasts and offered to take over, but Dale waved him away and Erik stood awkwardly by while Dale finished checking in the last of the Edmonton-bound passengers. Finally, his boss asked the question Erik had been dreading.

"You good to go single pilot?"

Erik felt the blood drain from his face.

No, I'm not good to go single pilot, Erik wanted to say. *I'm overwhelmed. And overworked. And exhausted. I need a second set of eyes in the cockpit. I need a plane I can trust. I'd like to overfly High Prairie tonight. I'd like not to be flying, period.*

Numbly, Erik nodded. He turned woodenly and started for the door. Dale called him back, gesturing toward the counter. Erik looked over to see the aircraft journey log lying on top of it. He must have left it behind in the dispatch office. *Where was his head?* Mumbling thanks to Dale for bringing it to the check-in counter, Erik picked up the forgotten documentation and walked outside to his plane.

Dale Wells watched Erik's Piper Navajo taxi down the runway and take off. The Navajo gained altitude heading south and Dale saw it disappear into a low bank of cloud. Then he turned and crossed the snow-swept expanse between the terminal and the Wapiti hangar, his boots slipping on the snow.

It had been a long tough road since he and his dad had started the airline in 1971 after purchasing the assets of Liberty Airways, a Grande Prairie–based air charter and ambulance service with four planes. Dale, twenty-four and a licenced pilot, had convinced his dad that a robust market existed for a local airline, and that they could make a go of it.

Since then his family had worked tirelessly to improve the business, and it was finally beginning to live up to the name he'd chosen. *Wapiti* is a First Nations word describing the North American elk, one of the largest and most majestic mammals to roam the continent. The father-son team soon added a flight school to their charter and air ambulance services. The school generated extra income and Dale loved teaching. His students were doctors, businesspeople, and eager youngsters filled with the same passion for flight that he'd discovered in his youth. Dale relished his hours in the cockpit with his students and enjoyed hearing about their lives.

In 1976 Dale applied for and received approval from Transport Canada to operate a point-to-point commercial passenger service between specific northern Alberta communities, namely Peace River, Grande Prairie, Grande Cache and Edmonton's municipal airport. By 1977, Wapiti had expanded that service to include flights to Whitecourt, Hinton and Calgary.

Dale's professional authority had also grown. Transport Canada approved him to do pilot proficiency checks on their behalf, and soon after he'd begun conducting flight tests for private and multi-engine pilots. A stream of willing pilots knocked on his door, and he hired many of them. Cash flow had recently been good enough for Dale to purchase several new planes.

Finally, Dale was beginning to achieve his dream of building a thriving commuter airline offering passenger flights to the under-serviced northern half of the province. Though demand for flights in and out of these sparsely populated towns was sometimes sporadic, Wapiti was able to stay profitable by operating what was known as a "unit toll air service." This permitted the airline to over-fly certain stops if business was poor and to vary the size of its aircraft depending on the passenger and cargo loads.

Dale's airline had also garnered robust support from the influential community and political leaders in northern Alberta who frequently had to travel to Edmonton—the seat of the provincial government—for business. Among his staunchest supporters were two prominent provincial politicians: Grant Notley and Larry Shaben. Notley, the fiery leader of the Alberta New Democratic Party, chaired a meeting on March 2, 1982, to discuss Wapiti's proposal to begin flights to the smaller communities of Fairview, High Prairie and Slave Lake. By the end of that meeting the eighteen business and government leaders who attended unanimously agreed:

> that support be given to Wapiti Aviation, for the establishment of a regularly scheduled air service, whereby the Carrier could overfly localities in the event that there was no confirmed traffic and whereby the Carrier could use a different size aircraft, dependent upon the amount of confirmed traffic load.

So enthusiastic were Wapiti's supporters about not having to rely solely on Highway 2—a long and often treacherous two-lane artery connecting Edmonton with communities to the north—that they sent unsolicited letters to Canada's Air Transport Commission supporting Wapiti's proposal. One such letter came from Larry Shaben, Alberta's Minister of Telephones and Utilities, who lived in High Prairie and travelled to the capital every week.

Shaben wrote: "I feel that the schedule fee structure and service points as outlined by Wapiti Aviation Ltd. are very appropriate to the needs of Northern Albertans . . . I am in complete support of the entire concept."

Two months later, in May 1982, Wapiti received the go-ahead for scheduled air service between Grande Prairie and Edmonton's municipal airport, and a year after that, to make stops in Fairview, Peace River, High Prairie and Slave Lake. Then, in August 1983, Transport Canada granted Wapiti approval to introduce daily passenger service between Edmonton and the booming oil town of Fort McMurray. When the service started up in September 1983, Wapiti featured one-way midday flights for $57—significantly less than the $70 being charged by its competitors, Pacific Western Airlines and Time Air. Wapiti Aviation had become a competitive force in Alberta's airline industry.

According to Dale, that's when the trouble started. Recently Transport Canada had been singling out Wapiti for closer scrutiny, accusing the carrier of safety violations such as pushing the weather. How else was Dale supposed to get his planes into these rinky-dink airports when they didn't have proper navigation aids? More than a year ago he had applied to get upgraded facilities and a controlled approach for the High Prairie airport, but Transport Canada was still dragging its heels. What was he supposed to do? If he encouraged his pilots to make the stop, Dale would get his knuckles rapped for pushing the weather. If he cancelled flights, he risked losing business.

A few months ago, the situation had gone from bad to worse. Transport Canada had begun sending inspectors to secretly monitor several Wapiti flights as they came into Edmonton. Transport Canada was on the lookout for Wapiti pushing the weather and using one pilot instead of two. On top of that, the RCMP had written Dale a letter alleging violations of regulations according to "a licenced air carrier" or "a reliable confidential source." Dale believed his competitors were behind these complaints and recently he had called Transport Canada and told them, "This nonsense has got to stop."

Instead, the situation had intensified. Three weeks earlier Transport Canada had grounded more than half of the company's fleet, charging that Wapiti hadn't done its 500- and 1000-hour service inspections. If you asked Dale, all of his aircraft were serviceable. Why should he take them out of commission if he didn't have to? The move would cost him money and business and, as far as he was concerned, ultimately play into what his competitors and their friends at Transport Canada wanted: his company's demise.

Dale shuffled through a pile of papers on his desk. He knew influential politicians who'd advocated for Wapiti in the past and he was prepared to call on them if he had to. Dale looked through that night's passenger log and nodded. Larry Shaben, a prominent Alberta Cabinet minister and one of his staunchest supporters, was a passenger on the flight from Edmonton to High Prairie.

PART III

And in the luck of night
In secret places no other spied
I went without my sight
Without a light to guide
Except the heart that lit me from inside

"DARK NIGHT OF THE SOUL"
BY SAINT JOHN OF THE CROSS

THRESHOLD

S econds after Larry cupped his face to the cabin window to try and see the lights of High Prairie, the plane's wings hit the trees. There was a long, ear-splitting *grrrrrrrr*, a monstrous rending of metal. Then, nothing.

When Larry regained consciousness, the first thing he heard was the sound of a man yelling, swearing a blue streak of obscenities at the pilot. A searing sensation tore at his shins and a spike of pain pierced his tailbone. He was disoriented and upside down in total blackness.

Larry's mother had died at forty-nine, the same age he was now, and his father, four years after her. Larry had been in his twenties at the time and the loss of his parents had been devastating. He had since harboured the unspoken fear that he, too, would die young. It seemed this was clearly the moment.

Frantically, he tried to move. Pain gripped his ribcage and he felt a band of material cutting into his thighs. He dimly realized that he was still strapped into his seat, suspended upside down. He fumbled for the buckle with his right hand, and pain lanced through his index finger. He switched hands, and after a moment of grappling, released the clip and tumbled downward. He landed on all fours. His shins burned as if on fire, and he could feel the warm ooze of blood soaking his dress pants. His mouth tasted metallic and when he ran his tongue over his front teeth, he felt a large gap where two were missing. Pain rippled along the left side of his face. Tentatively, he felt his swollen cheek and then, with a sickening sense of loss, his eyes. His glasses were gone. Without them, he was almost blind.

Like a child, he began crawling along the cabin's inverted ceiling, groping desperately for his glasses. Physical injury he could endure, but the thought of being sightless was unbearable. He clawed his way over stinging snow and sharp debris, advancing slowly through the blurry space in front of him. His hands pressed into the nap of something soft and he closed his fingers around it, trying to identify the familiar texture—his ultra-suede coat. He grabbed it and struggled awkwardly to his feet. Larry swept a hand over his left shoulder and felt the smooth fine fabric of his cotton dress shirt where the top of his suit jacket had been ripped away. Shaking, he wrestled unsteadily in the close confines of the cabin to pull on his overcoat. Then, holding out his arms, he advanced toward the flush of cool air in front of him. His eyes darted from side to side through the blackness as if, by some miracle, the ability to see without the thick glasses he had worn since he was a child would return. Instead he detected only dark, shapeless masses; whether seats, wreckage or bodies, he wasn't sure. The moans of the injured surrounded him as he scuffled forward until his outstretched hands connected with the cabin wall. He skimmed them along it until they passed through an opening—a way out. Larry nearly fell through it, and lurching forward, his legs sank like stakes into the deep snow. It filled his rubber overshoes and he felt the icy bite of it against his ankles.

Standing blindly in the inky blackness Larry felt—for the first time in his adult life—utterly helpless.

When Erik saw the trees in front of his cockpit window, he screamed and threw his arms in front of his face. Without the restraining hold of his shoulder strap, his hands were the first part of his body to slam into the instrument panel, followed by his face. His chest was next; it struck the control column hard and a scorching heat ripped through his insides. He felt something smash into the back of his skull.

When he tried to draw a breath, pain knifed through the right side of his chest. Panic swept over him. He lay unmoving, unable to comprehend what had happened. Numbly, he grasped that he was still strapped in his seat and fumbled for his lap belt. When it finally opened, he fell head first onto the ceiling of the cockpit. His shoulder hit hard and his chest exploded in pain. He lay curled in a fetal position, his breath coming in short, shallow gasps. Time stopped. A warm pillow of blood began to pool beneath his head and he tasted the bitter, metallic tang of it in his mouth. One of his eyes was throbbing and filled with blood. But his ears told him everything. The soul-ripping cries of his passengers engulfed him—a suffocating cacophony reverberating in the close confines of the cabin.

Erik coughed and a vise closed around his chest. He could smell the pungent stench of airplane fuel. He could feel it on his clothes. Finally, his brain began to function.

I've got to shut the power down. If there's a spark there will be a fire and the plane will explode.

He raised his head and scanned for the instrument panel. There were no lights above or around him. No instruments. Nothing. The entire nose had been ripped from the plane.

Erik laid his head back down once more and the world around him spun crazily. A choking rush of emotion washed over him. He tried to slow his breathing. A fresh wave of pain skewered the right side of his chest and he felt light-headed. Finally, he willed his shock-ridden senses to settle. Somewhere beyond the hot haze of panic, he felt fresh, cool air. He dragged himself painfully to his feet, peering into the darkness. His fingers, smashed and swelling like sausages, groped tentatively in front of him and one shot through a hole—the broken side window of the cockpit. Erik grabbed the window frame and, with a groan, wriggled through it, collapsing into the deep snow. He lay back, trying to make sense of what had happened.

He tentatively touched the area around his right eye. It was grossly swollen. He tried to ball his hands into fists, but couldn't. They, too, seemed foreign and not his own.

The moans of the passengers trapped inside the plane were excruciating to endure and from somewhere beyond him in the darkness he could hear a passenger yelling: "What a fucking stupid idiot!"

Erik felt tears welling. The passenger was talking about him.

Oh God! What have I done? He wanted to curl into a ball and disappear, but a movement above him drew his attention. Though Erik's right eye was practically swollen shut, through his left he saw an older, well-dressed man stagger from the wreckage. Erik struggled slowly to his feet and the two men stood side by side, stupefied and rooted in place. Snow fell heavy and wet on the shocked men, and the groans of passengers and the nauseating odour of airplane fuel filled the air.

Standing on the margin of a small clearing, Paul Archambault stepped toward the snarl of dense brush. He'd smoked his last rolled cigarette down to a roach and when the heat began to burn his fingers, tossed it into the snow. He swiped at the cut on his forehead, still oozing blood, and tried to clear the fierce humming pressure in his ears. Paul opened his jaw wide and the final wisps of smoke drifted out in a thin, gossamer cloud. His ears cleared. Pitiful, haunting cries of pain floated toward him across the clearing.

Jesus Christ, Paul thought. All he'd wanted to do was to get away from the fuel-drenched wreckage. As he absently rubbed the tender skin of his wrist where the handcuff had chafed it, a horrifying realization struck him. There were a lot of people who weren't coming out of that plane alive and if the cop hadn't taken the handcuffs off before the flight, he could have been one of them.

Paul turned and began wading back along his trail toward the wreckage. Struggling through thigh-high snow, he closed the distance between himself and two figures standing outside the dark hulk of smashed aircraft.

BURIED

Scott Deschamps couldn't move. His head, arms and torso felt like they were encased in cement. He could feel blood running into his eyes, flowing down from a gash in his lip.

I'm upside down.

He tried to wipe the blood from his eyes, but his arms wouldn't respond. Cold seared his bare hands and his fingers curled into what he quickly realized was packed snow. He tried to draw a breath and pain mushroomed through his chest.

I need to stand.

It dimly occurred to him that he had to get his head free or he would suffocate. He tried to reach for some kind of support, but his left shoulder felt dislocated from his body, unhinged and free-floating.

Shaking violently, Scott slowly became conscious of a loud rhythmic roar and realized it was the sound of his own breathing. He stared straight ahead, trying to clear the throbbing that reverberated in his ears, grasping to understand why he couldn't move. Couldn't draw air into his lungs. The world around him was a mixture of muted white and dim shadow. The stench of aircraft fuel and freshly plowed earth assaulted his nostrils.

He knew something very serious had happened. He could taste dirt in his mouth and feel snow compressed inside his nasal passages. It was as if someone had filled a plastic bag, wrapped it around his head and was slowly sucking the air from it. He tried again to reach for support, but his arms were entombed. He sensed one of his hands close to his face, perhaps no more than four inches away. He moved his fingers and felt the icy burn of snow. Then he got it.

I'm buried alive!

Terror gripped him. Trained in avalanche rescue, Scott knew how dire his situation was. Just a month earlier he'd completed an advanced Canadian Ski Patrol course in the Canadian Rockies. What he'd learned was fresh in his mind. If he was to have any hope of survival he needed to try and create an air pocket around his mouth, which might buy him precious time until rescuers found him. *If* they found him. Scott swam his fingers through the dirt until they touched his face. Then he clawed the snow around his open mouth to create a small air cavity. Still, he couldn't get a full breath. He didn't know whether it was because his mouth and nose were obstructed or his chest had been crushed. He could hear himself moaning rhythmically, an eerie wheeze he couldn't control. Somewhere above him others were injured, maybe dying. Maybe dead. He wondered if, like him, they were conscious and facing the horrifying spectre of their own deaths.

"I'm Paul," Paul said as he reached the two men standing outside the plane. Both had battered faces and seemed stunned, in shock or badly injured—or all three.

"Erik," said the younger man. His dark hair was matted with blood and Paul could tell just by looking at him that he was badly hurt.

Beside him was an older, darker-skinned man in a long, fancy coat, who introduced himself as Larry. Though he seemed to stare right at Paul, his eyes had a vacant, unfocused look.

"We need to get those people out," Paul said.

Erik turned to the wreckage, then led them along the plane's exterior toward the tail. He'd taken only a few steps when his legs rammed into a rough metal outcropping. Clumsily, he clambered over it and advanced toward the rear of the aircraft where he began running his hands up and down the fuselage.

Why can't I find the windows? Erik wondered.

His swollen hands bumped into a small, round protrusion where windows should have been. He tried to make sense of what it was. Then he recognized it: the belly light. *Right. The plane is upside down.*

Summoning a mental image of the Piper Navajo, Erik began sweeping his hands down along the curve of the plane's upturned belly until he found an open window and then the cabin door: closed. He knew there was no way to pry the door open from the outside and stretched himself through the window, straining to reach the safety chain. Pain clawed at his chest and his hands fumbled lamely, but he managed to close his fingers around it, removing the pin and then turning the latch. He pulled the door and swung it outward, creating a small shower stall–sized platform suspended several feet above the ground. Fighting his pain, Erik hauled himself onto it and crept inside.

Paul followed while Larry hung back, worried that, unable to see, he'd be more of a liability than an asset.

Inside the rear of the cabin Erik and Paul crowded together.

"Scott," Paul called out.

"Where were you sitting?"

"We were in the last two seats next to the door and he was right beside me. On the aisle."

Erik turned to look at Paul. He could smell tobacco on the man's breath and through his one functioning eye he saw Paul's shaggy mass of long dark hair, thick moustache, and heavy sideburns. With a jolt, he realized that this was the prisoner being escorted by the RCMP officer. Erik also realized that he was the man who'd been shouting obscenities at him after the plane had crashed. Erik's mouth felt suddenly dry and uneasiness tripped down his spine. The prisoner didn't yet know he was the pilot, and Erik wasn't in a hurry to tell him.

Beyond his crippling fear, Scott became aware of scuffling noises directly above him. He heard someone call his name. He inhaled and yelled out, his muffled words filling the tiny hollow of furrowed snow.

"I have to get out of here now. I can't breathe!"

"Are you the RCMP officer?" a voice asked.

"Yes."

He sensed someone trying to dig down to him and then, blessedly, some of the weight that held him down lightened.

Above, Paul pulled two seats that had been raked to the back of the plane and tossed them outside into the snow, followed by a cardboard box, a computer monitor and two briefcases.

"Hold on," he said, "there's metal over you."

"I don't care. Get me out!"

Scott felt himself on the verge of losing control and fought to stay calm. Like a scuba diver with only an emergency pony bottle of reserve air to last him the long distance to the surface, he understood that he was rapidly depleting his scarce oxygen supply.

Get a grip, he told himself. *Get a grip.*

"I need help," Paul called out as he tried to wrench away the metal that hung over Scott like the roof of a crypt.

Erik tried to free the trapped Mountie, but his hands had no feeling. Spasms of pain shot through his chest.

"You're useless," Paul said, shooing him away.

Erik retreated and lowered himself to sit on the open hatch.

Hearing Paul's cry for help, Larry scrambled past Erik to help Paul yank on the large piece of metal, but they couldn't budge it.

Below them, Scott raised his right arm.

"Take my hand," he said.

Paul grasped an arm in front of him, only to realize that it belonged to another passenger who was pinned from the waist down, twisted in a very bad way, and breathing in long, wheezing gasps.

The person's jaw was crushed. It felt to Paul like mush or rubber.

"I need a flashlight," Paul called out.

"I've got a penlight in my bag," Erik answered.

He crawled back inside the cabin and stumbled through it looking for his flight bag. In the mid section, seats had been ripped from their hinges as snow and debris had swept into the cabin. Erik picked his way past the ragged mess, but didn't get far before a tangle of wreckage stopped him. Beyond the impassable jumble, he could hear a man moaning dreadfully, but Erik couldn't reach him. Penlight forgotten, he retreated to the cabin door and emerged into the frigid night air.

Working frantically in the aft part of the cabin, Paul quickly realized there was nothing he could do for the passenger with the crushed jaw. But there was still a chance to save Scott. Tripping over Larry in the confined space, Paul suggested he go outside and try to start a fire. Meanwhile, Paul continued scrabbling in the dark until he found the warm flesh of a hand.

"Is this you?" he asked Scott.

"Yes."

He grabbed tight and tried dragging Scott from under the metal roof, but couldn't move him. The other passenger seemed to be lying on top of Scott and every time Paul tried to lift him, he was lifting the passenger, too.

"Stop," Scott yelled. "You're ripping my arm off."

Paul jumped down from the open hatch and crawled through the smashed window next to it. This time he grabbed Scott by his shoulder. As Paul tugged, Scott tried to shift his position, to create wiggle room by tensing and flexing his muscles. Surely he could free himself. His powerful body had never failed him before. Scott worked out for two hours every day and was in the best shape of his life. Even when he had to wrestle some guy three times his size in a back alley and was being walloped, Scott could always bear down and get a little more strength.

He felt hands clawing away the earth around his shoulder and then his torso, and after a moment he was able to rotate his upper body. He swept his free arm through the air above him, wrapped it around the piece of metal and pulled. But his body still wouldn't release.

Why not?

Scott systematically tried moving his limbs and realized that his left arm was sunk into the ground below him, tethering his body to the earth like a ship's anchor. He twisted his torso back and forth, trying to loosen the dirt around his left shoulder. Searing pain ripped through it. He lay still for a moment, letting the waves of it subside. Strong hands found him once more, and yanked hard. Again, Scott wrapped his free arm around the solid metal slab above him and pulled. His muscles strained and pain washed through him. Finally, the earth's grip released him, and he burst free.

FIRE

"Leave me for a few minutes," Scott told Paul after he'd unearthed him. "I need to catch my breath."

Paul hopped down out of the cabin and went to see about the fire. The reek of airplane fuel was still overpowering, and he wanted to make sure there was enough distance between the fire and the wreckage that they didn't blow the whole thing sky high. He followed the path Larry and Erik had broken through the scrub and deep snow until he reached a small clearing some 20 metres away from the plane. There, Larry had tromped out a circle of snow and lit the cardboard box Paul had tossed from the plane. The fire was almost out by the time he got there.

It seemed to Paul that Larry and Erik had no mind or that they were really dazed. Wasting no time, he loped back to the plane and grabbed the briefcases, several sticks strewn around the crash area, and a garment bag he spied lying near the wreck. When he returned, Paul placed the sticks on the fire and added the papers from inside the briefcases to the flame. Then he handed the empty cases to Erik and Larry, suggesting they use them as seats. As if speaking to halfwits,

Paul reminded them how important it was to keep the fire going and urged them to gather wood.

Erik slowly removed his winter parka and handed it to Paul. He regarded the man who'd left himself in shirtsleeves as if he was crazy, but accepted the jacket.

"I'm happy you're here," Erik said.

Paul put on the parka. Then he took off back down the trail toward the wreckage.

As Paul's outline receded, Larry squinted after him. All he could see was a blur of shapes and shadows. He suppressed a feeling of helplessness and listened intently. He could hear boots crunching through the snow, moving in the direction of the plane. Arms outstretched, he shuffled awkwardly forward, his hands groping blindly in front of him. Snow entered his overshoes each time he pulled one foot then the other from the deep snow, and spears of pain lanced his tailbone and ribs.

Larry had advanced only a few metres when a voice yelled, "Hey, you gonna help out or just stand there?"

Larry could hear Paul swearing under his breath and moved toward him until his lacerated shins rammed into a fallen tree beneath the snow and he stumbled. He extended his arms in front of him to brace his fall, and they jabbed into Paul, who was stepping back over the tree. Paul swore loudly.

"Sorry," Larry said. "I lost my glasses in the crash and I'm blind as a bat without them."

Paul sighed. "Here," he said.

Larry could see an arm extended in front of him and grabbed it. He held on as Paul guided him over the tree and down the path. Together they shuffled toward the plane and then veered left into the torn swath of forest cleared by the crash. Stopping near a small stand of broken trees, Paul placed Larry's hand on the bark and told him to try peeling some off for kindling, and then crunched away into the darkness.

Shards of jagged wood and bark dug into the tender skin beneath Larry's nails and pain throbbed through his broken finger. He was clumsily stuffing brittle swatches into the pockets of his overcoat when Paul returned. Asking Larry to hold out his arms, he dropped a pile of branches into them and, carrying his own armload of wood, led Larry back down the path to the fire.

When they reached it, Paul worked quickly, laying branches over the faltering flame, then asking Larry for the bark to stuff between them. Paul was nursing the fire back to life when Erik staggered back with an armload of wood. He glanced at Larry, and then at Paul.

"Where's your friend?"

"Who?" Paul answered.

"The cop."

Larry's eyes widened and he turned to look at Paul. That's when he realized that the man he'd been following blindly through the wilderness was a criminal.

Inside the smashed fuselage, Scott sat incapacitated. His head throbbed and he felt dazed and disoriented. The world around him moved strangely, slowly, and he wondered if he was dreaming. It would explain why he couldn't get to his feet. Something soft and pliable lay beneath him. He poked at it with his finger and it felt fleshy and forgiving. Somewhere close by a man moaned.

Scott struggled to make sense of his surroundings. Strewn around him were rumpled metal, clothing, luggage, papers and broken Plexiglas. He gradually became aware of the distorted features of an airplane cabin: a seat raked back at an odd angle, an armrest hanging straight down, the oblong opening of an exit hatch. Suddenly, everything became very clear.

He had been escorting a prisoner to face sentencing. The two of them had boarded a small plane in Edmonton that was to fly them to Grande Prairie. *What the hell had happened?*

His mind couldn't connect the dots. He grabbed an outcropping of metal and tried to stand. Not three feet away, the plane's open hatch beckoned. If he could climb through it, he would be outside. Scott dragged himself upright, bracing against the cabin wall. Then his legs gave out and he collapsed onto the soft mound beneath him. His chest exploded in pain, drowning out coherent thought. He was injured, though how badly he couldn't tell. Labouriously, he slid down onto the floor and inched along on all fours until he reached the open hatch. He dragged himself outside and sat on the suspended door, but couldn't find the strength to lower himself to the ground. In the distance, he could see the surreal yellow glow of a campfire. Snowflakes dropped from the sky and the rhythmic moans of a passenger echoed in the darkness.

Moments later a figure seemed to float toward him through the falling snow and a man's outline came into focus. A voice spoke to him and Scott recognized it as belonging to the man who had pulled him from the wreckage: his prisoner.

Paul lifted Scott from the hatchway and half-walked, half-carried him along the trail to the fire. By the time the two arrived, the heat of the flames had melted a pit in the snow about six feet in diameter. Paul removed the parka Erik had given him and handed it to Scott before dragging the garment bag close to the fire's warmth. Then Paul lowered his captor, as if a child, onto it. Larry, in turn, removed his overcoat and laid it over Scott.

No sooner had Paul set Scott down than he returned to the plane and climbed back inside to check on the other passengers. He shuffled slowly through the cabin, letting his eyes adjust to the darkness. In front of him he saw two legs protruding, and on their feet, a pair of large winter boots. Women's boots. Paul reached forward, tugged off the boots and tucked them under his arm. As he advanced through the dim interior he gathered other garments strewn about: a woman's parka, a double-breasted trench coat, underwear, a sweater, a man's pyjama top. He spied a small pocketknife, which he stuffed in the front pocket of his jeans.

Paul moved around touching everyone he could, but they were all dead. The passenger he'd tried to help earlier was among them now, but he heard someone else moaning. Realizing there was no way to get to the passenger from where he stood, Paul slipped back outside and circled around to the front of the plane where he was able to worm through the smashed side window. There, just behind the co-pilot's seat, he found a man semi-conscious and moaning.

Paul pulled on him, but the plane seemed to be wrapped right around him and he wouldn't budge. His right arm was stuffed into the pilot's flight bag. There was no way to free him.

He crawled from the plane once more and scooping up the garments he'd collected, returned to the fire. When he arrived he saw something that lifted his spirits. Larry stood in the soft glow of the flame, smoking. Paul wasted no time bumming a cigarette and when Larry handed over his package, Paul was ecstatic to see that it was almost full. He lit up a cigarette and savoured the sweet burn of smoke as he sucked it deep into his lungs.

"How about I hang on to these for you," he offered and when Larry nodded, Paul felt as if he'd won the lottery. Cigarette dangling from his mouth, he pulled off Scott's running shoes and shoved the winter boots onto his feet. Lifting Larry's topcoat from Scott's body, Paul laid the woman's parka over him and stretched another article of clothing gently over his head before replacing the topcoat. Then Paul handed the trench coat to Larry and the sweater to Erik, saving the pyjama top for himself. Once the men had pulled on their extra layers of clothing, Paul urged them to return to the bush to scavenge more wood for the fire.

Paul knew perhaps better than any of the others that keeping the fire going would be tough. The branches they dug from under the snow were wet and unlikely to burn well. But on a night like tonight a fire meant the difference between surviving and freezing to death. There had been more than a few nights in his past when Paul had been forced to sleep outside in the dead of winter and they'd scared the shit out of him.

Once again, he led Larry through the wilderness, loading his arms with as many branches as the blind, broken-toothed old man could handle before leading him back to the fire. When they arrived, Paul stoked the flames once more and they grew, spreading their warmth to the shocked and shivering survivors. For just a moment they allowed themselves to forget the monumental task that faced them all: staying alive until rescue arrived.

MISSING

n the tiny High Prairie airport terminal building, forty-three-year-old airport manager Luella Wood checked her watch. It was ten minutes before 8 p.m.—the time Wapiti Flight 402 was scheduled to arrive. Standing 5′4″ and 135 pounds, with permed auburn hair and dark blue eyes, Luella had dreamt of being a pilot. Her uncle, a bush pilot, started giving her flying lessons when she was a teen. Sadly, Luella had become nauseous every time her uncle had taken her up. Though she'd been bitterly disappointed with not being able to pursue her dream, the idea of operating an airport had intrigued her enough that years later, she'd taken on the High Prairie airport manager's job.

Inside the squat, single-storey brown terminal building, Alma Shaben sat awaiting the flight. She'd called the airport shortly after seven that evening to check whether the plane would be landing, telling Luella that Larry had phoned just before boarding to warn her that the pilot wasn't sure if they would be able to get in. He'd suggested Alma check with Luella before leaving the house, so if she thought the weather was too bad for a landing, Alma could drive directly to Peace River.

Luella hadn't been sure what to tell her. Over the past few days the weather had truly been a concern and twice that week Wapiti flights hadn't been able to land on account of it. At Luella's 6:00 p.m. weather observation the ceiling had been low, though the horizontal visibility was good. She'd told Alma that if the pilot could get under the clouds he'd probably be okay, but they wouldn't know one way or the other until the plane was overhead and the pilot contacted her by radio. At 7:30 Alma had decided to drive to the airport and wait.

As the flight's scheduled arrival time approached, Luella left the terminal building and walked back to her trailer where the radio was located. She and her friend Edith Guild lived on the far side of the parking lot just a few hundred feet away from the terminal building. The town provided modest accommodation free to the airport manager, but during weeks like this one, it came at a price. More than nineteen centimetres of snow had fallen in the past two days and the wind had swept it into high drifts. Yesterday, Luella and Edith had cleared the sidewalks and had had to do so again this morning. The snow had been thigh-deep in places and so heavy and thick that it kept plugging the snow blower. That afternoon it had warmed up a little and though the plow hadn't been out on the runway, Luella figured it was okay for takeoffs and landings. She'd checked it at 4:30 before a cargo flight was due to arrive. There'd been snow and slushy patches, but it hadn't been icy. She'd walked the runway once more just before Alma arrived, and though a crust had started to form on top of the snow, Luella thought it still looked fine.

She stepped out of the freezing air and into the warmth of the trailer, yelling out: "Edie, anybody call?"

Edith shook her head.

Luella checked the Universal Communications system, or UNICOM, to see if it was loud enough and making its usual humming noise. The UNICOM is a single frequency radio transceiver used at airports with little air traffic and no control tower. Typically, pilots broadcast their location and intentions to Luella over the UNICOM as they were approaching the airport for a landing.

Around 8:05 p.m. Luella started to get an uneasy feeling. She couldn't explain it, but things just didn't seem right.

"They're late, like always," Edie said, but Luella knew that this time something was wrong. She tried to raise the pilot on the UNICOM, but got no answer. Then she began to pace.

At 8:20 Peace River Flight Service called to ask if Luella had heard from Wapiti. She told them she hadn't. Her worry turning to dread, she tried again to contact the flight. No answer. Peace River checked in several more times over the next twenty minutes until, at 8:40, they called to inform Luella that they were initiating a search. They'd notified both the Canadian military's Rescue Coordination Centre in Edmonton and the RCMP, who would be sending a constable from the High Prairie detachment to the airport as soon as possible.

Sixteen minutes later, the pilot of Pacific Western Airlines Flight 594 en route from Yellowknife to Edmonton was 20 kilometres northwest of High Prairie when a distinctive signal shrieked through his headset. When a downed aircraft's emergency locator transmitter, or ELT, distress signal goes off there's no mistaking it. It's a series of shrill, rapid-fire, high-pitched tones that will kick the most placid of pilots into high gear. He immediately radioed Peace River Flight Service to report that he was picking up an ELT signal.

When Peace River called Luella with the news, her heart rose into her throat. She knew that the downed plane was 402. Her first call was to Maurice Pacquette, a local private pilot, owner of a nearby service station and her go-to guy if there were problems at the airport. She told him what had happened and asked him to come to check whether the UNICOM was working and if not, to try using a VHF radio inside one of the private planes parked along the tarmac to contact Flight 402. Though it seemed to Luella like he took forever, Pacquette arrived just minutes later.

At 9:00 p.m. the Rescue Coordination Centre located on Canadian Forces Base Edmonton implemented a major air disaster plan, or MAJAID. The country's highest level of emergency response to an aircraft disaster, it is initiated only if a plane carrying ten or more people is missing. Within fifteen minutes the military had completed a callout for a military search-and-rescue crew and an RCMP constable was knocking on Luella's door. His orders were clear: to ensure a reliable communication link was established between the High Prairie airport and the Canadian military who would soon be launching an air search. The Rescue Coordination Centre also asked Luella to take local weather observations every fifteen minutes and relay them to the military.

She felt her anxiety skyrocket. She was no expert when it came to operating the UNICOM and the military's request for continuous weather observations was in itself a monumental task. Sensing her concern, Pacquette offered to drive into town and get Dave Heggie, a local private pilot with radio experience who could man the UNICOM. No sooner had he left than the phone rang. It was Dale Wells.

Dale had been in his car driving to the Grande Prairie airport when his pager had gone off. He'd pressed his foot on the gas pedal and rapidly closed the distance to the Wapiti hangar. When he opened the door to its cavernous interior, Dale saw his mom and dad inside, their faces pale. Del broke the news.

It can't be, was Dale's first thought when he heard that Peace River Flight Service had called to say that Flight 402 had gone down. Dale immediately got on the phone to the High Prairie airport manager.

"What happened to my plane?"

"We don't know yet," Luella told him, "but the RCMP is here and the military has launched a search."

"I'm getting on a plane," Dale said. "What's the weather like?"

"The clouds are low," she told him, "but if you can get under them, you'll have no trouble landing."

"Okay, I'm on my way."

After the RCMP constable departed, Luella sat slumped beside the radio. A stone's throw away in the terminal building, family and friends were awaiting Flight 402. Reluctantly, Luella left the trailer and walked across the parking lot to the terminal building. There were three people in the main arrivals area: Alma; a younger woman, possibly in her late twenties or early thirties; and a slim First Nations man Luella didn't recognize.

Finally, she found the courage to speak. "The plane has gone down."

Alma's face went white.

No one said a word.

"They've launched a search," Luella added quietly.

Then, with leaden limbs, she headed outside to take another weather observation.

Alma doesn't remember how long she sat in the terminal, only that she was unable or unwilling to move until Luella returned and urged everyone to go home.

"No sense waiting," she'd told them. "We'll call you the minute we hear anything."

Insensible with shock, Alma had gotten into her car and driven home to an empty house. None of her five children still lived in High

Prairie, all having left to attend university or find jobs elsewhere. Three, still at university, lived with their father in his Edmonton apartment where he stayed during the work week. When Alma got home she picked up the telephone and called the number. Seventeen-year-old Joan, the youngest, answered. Struggling to keep her voice from breaking, Alma told her what had happened. One floor separated the residence from that of Larry's close friend and colleague, Hugh Planche, Alberta's Minister of Economic Development and Trade. The minute Joan hung up the phone, she and her brother James ran up the stairs to Planche's apartment and banged loudly on his door. No one answered. Planche, who had been out celebrating the birth of his first grandchild, would not return for another hour. Joan jumped in her car and drove to the University of Alberta where her oldest brother, Larry, was taking a scuba diving course. He remembers being shocked to see his sister at the edge of the pool when he surfaced. Soaking wet and wrapped in a towel, he grabbed his clothes and raced back to the apartment with her. By then James had located Hugh's wife, Sylvia, who worked in the premier's office, and she'd called the premier's chief of staff, Bob Giffin. Giffin, the province's most senior bureaucrat, immediately got on the line to Premier Peter Lougheed at his home in Calgary.

"Stay on top of it," Lougheed told him. "And find out if any other government members from the north are on that plane." Giffin called the homes of several northern MLAs who often flew home on Wapiti for the weekend. He confirmed the whereabouts of all but Grant Notley. When he called the Notley home in Fairview, Grant's fourteen-year-old son answered. Giffin asked to speak to his mom.

"She's on the highway heading home."

Giffin asked his next question very carefully. "Is your dad there?"

"He's staying overnight in Edmonton," the boy said. "He'll be home tomorrow."

Giffin hung up the phone, but wanted to be sure. He placed a quick call to Ray Martin, the only other NDP member of the legislature and a close friend of Notley's. Martin told him that he thought that Grant had stayed over in Edmonton because the Wapiti flight had been fully booked. Satisfied, Giffin updated the premier, and then called John Tenzer, the Alberta government's chief pilot. Giffin's plan was to get Larry's children, Hugh Planche and himself north as fast as possible. Tenzer told Giffin it wouldn't happen that night; with the deteriorating weather conditions, he felt it was far too dangerous to fly. The chief pilot promised Giffin he'd keep him updated through the night, and that the government plane would take off the second it was safe to do so.

Giffin was just putting his head down to catch a moment's rest when the phone rang. His spouse answered it, and a look of concern creased her brow.

"It's Premier Lougheed," she said.

Giffin was instantly awake as he grabbed the phone.

"Grant Notley is on that plane," Lougheed told him.

Giffin started to remind his boss that he'd checked with Ray Martin, when the premier cut him off. It was Martin himself who had called the premier to give him the news.

After hanging up the phone with Giffin, Martin had tried to locate Notley. Unable to do so, he'd called Grant's secretary. She'd told him that her boss had received a last-minute call from Wapiti Aviation saying they had a seat for him.

Despite more than two decades in Canada's north, Sandra Notley was still surprised by how fast and fiercely winter arrived. Raised in Concord, Massachusetts, the vivacious civil rights activist had set out from Edmonton on Friday afternoon to make the 550- kilometre drive north to her home in Fairview. Though her husband, Grant, had planned to accompany her, a meeting had kept him in the city and she'd had to face the five-hour journey alone.

An hour north of the city, she started having car trouble. She'd pulled into a service station in the tiny hamlet of Sangudo where an attendant checked things over. She'd set out once more, and driven another hour when her car broke down. Luckily, she was near Fox Creek, the only town for miles along a barren stretch of Highway 43. She'd managed to get a tow into town, and had then checked into a hotel. Snow had continued to fall heavily through the evening and Sandra, exhausted but relieved to be safe and off the treacherous highway, decided to turn in early. Before she did, she'd called home. No one had answered. Then she'd contacted an NDP aide who'd told her that Grant's meeting had been cancelled and he'd caught a flight out of Edmonton. His plane was believed to have landed at the High Prairie airport, but had been delayed due to engine trouble. Wearily, she'd crawled into bed and fell asleep.

After talking to Luella, Dale Wells had called Peace River Flight Services and the nearby town of Whitecourt to make sure Vogel hadn't diverted. But neither had heard from 402. His heart racing, Wells had quickly fuelled up Wapiti's Cessna 182 and taken to the air. As he flew east toward High Prairie, he still held a thread of hope that his pilot had diverted to another airport and that he and his passengers were unhurt. Dale recalled the terrible look on his dad's face as he'd told him the plane was late. Dale would have liked nothing more than to be able to return to his father with good news.

Though Delbert Wells was the president of Wapiti Aviation and had been its chief of flight operations for eight years, he was scared to death of flying. In 1953, his best friend, a northern doctor, had been killed in a small plane crash while transporting a polio victim from Grande Prairie to Edmonton. When the plane went down in the forest 320 kilometres southeast of Grande Prairie, it had triggered the largest air search in the province's history. Despite these efforts, no one was alive by the time rescuers found the plane. The pilot, the patient and Del's lifelong friend were all dead. Del had not wanted to get on a plane since.

The tragedy also had an impact on Dale, who was seven at the time. Unlike his dad, he'd been drawn to flying, and from the moment he took his first lesson, had known he would be a pilot.

With 12,000 hours of flying experience, most of it in the north, Dale flew the Cessna by feel. He knew the contours of the land as well as those of his own face. He kept the single-engine four-seater just above the cloud, advancing steadily toward the High Prairie airport. Dale trained a close eye on the instruments, but his mind was on his missing pilot. Vogel was no greenhorn. On the check rides that he'd flown with him, Dale had found his handling of the airplane well above average—even excellent. He had appeared sharp on procedures and his accuracy had been very good. He'd logged more hours in the cockpit than almost any pilot Dale had hired and had demonstrated strong airmanship, the ability to think on his feet, and a good awareness of what was going on around him.

Still, in the past few days, Vogel had seemed off his game. Dale thought of the flight documentation Vogel had left behind earlier that day. A pilot forgetting the aircraft journey log was like a priest forgetting his Bible. During passenger check-in Dale had briefly considered taking the flight himself, but the thought had disappeared as quickly as it had come. He was on standby for a medivac and needed to stick around. But the problems with Vogel concerned him. The blown starter. The forgotten props. They were small things—not enough to turf him—though troubling nonetheless.

Dale was beginning to think that the young man was no different from the other prima donna pilots who'd come and gone over the years. They arrived with their big egos and macho attitudes, thinking little operations like Wapiti were beneath them. Dale had invested a lot of time and money giving rookie pilots darn good training and what did he get in return? The bigger airlines snapped up the hotshots and the others were gone the minute something better came along. Erik Vogel had come to him with more hours than most, but Dale knew that he, too, was just building flying time with Wapiti. Dale had also heard that Vogel's dad was a political bigwig out on the coast. As far as Dale was concerned, privileged kids like Vogel had no idea what hard work was or what it took to run a successful airline. They wanted everything handed to them on a platter.

As he neared High Prairie, Dale pushed these unsettling thoughts to the back of his mind and radioed Luella.

"I'm in the vicinity and I'm going to try to locate the ELT signal," he told her.

Luella, who had been dividing her time between operating the radio and taking weather observations, had her hands full. Having Wapiti's chief pilot searching the area was the last thing she needed. Just after 10:00 p.m. she'd taken her third observation, a cumbersome process that involved walking 100 metres beyond the terminal's parking lot where a small beacon sat on a fence post. Luella plugged in the beacon—little more than a lamp with a strong beam—and retraced her steps to the parking lot. Using a handheld ceiling projector, she lined it up to where the light hit the bottom of the clouds and read the measurement on the projector's instrument scale. Then she walked back to the field to unplug the lamp. The whole process took the better part of ten minutes and Luella found that she'd no sooner finished one observation than it was time to start another.

Inside her trailer, the phone had started ringing off the hook. News of the missing plane had swept through the town as fast as a grass fire across parched prairie. Locals were calling to find out what was happening and to offer help.

The scene was the same at the local High Prairie RCMP detachment. Just after 9:30, Sergeant Marvin Hopkins had arrived to find his station in an uproar. Known as "Hoppy" to his friends, he was a fit, 5′10″ bear of a man in his late forties. His light brown hair was styled in the same Brillo pad brush cut he had sported since he was a teen in the fifties, and beneath heavily furrowed brows his blue eyes were keenly alert. He'd been at home with his feet up when one of his members had called.

"Get in here, boss," he'd said. "All hell's breaking loose."

Hoppy soon learned that the Rescue Coordination Centre in Edmonton had launched a MAJAID and that the Canadian Military Command Centre in Trenton, Ontario, was already monitoring SARSAT—the international search-and-rescue satellite system designed to pick up distress signals of emergency locator beacons.

He also discovered that the High Prairie RCMP detachment was being pressed into action. Due to perilous flying conditions, and the presumed proximity of the crash site to the town, the Rescue Coordination Centre had requested the RCMP organize a ground search party to stand by in the event that military planes couldn't get in.

Then came more disturbing news: Minister Larry Shaben, the region's MLA, and others from High Prairie were on the missing plane. For a moment Hoppy was at an uncharacteristic loss. Then he rocketed into action.

He knew several RCMP officers who owned their own snowmobiles, and called to alert them that they and their machines might be needed. Hoppy also called the Peace River detachment, which had a handheld ELT homing device, and asked someone to drive it to High

Prairie as fast as possible. He'd barely hung up the phone when the Rescue Coordination Centre dropped another bombshell: John Tenzer, the Alberta government's chief pilot, had just called to say that government opposition leader, Grant Notley, was also on the plane.

Hoppy lit a cigarette and dragged on it deeply. No matter how it ended, this crash was going to cause a shit storm.

Just up the street, Dave Heggie, a thirty-eight-year-old father of two, was surprised to walk out of the High Prairie movie theatre and find Maurice Pacquette waiting for him. A fellow pilot and volunteer member of Alberta's Civil Air Rescue Emergency Services, or CARES, Pacquette told him what had happened. Heggie dropped his young sons at home and the two men hurried to Heggie's pharmacy to gather and brief a small cadre of local volunteer pilots before they all hightailed it out to the airport.

In his day job Heggie ran the High Prairie hospital pharmacy, but his true passion was flying. Ten years earlier he'd volunteered for CARES to finagle time in the cockpit. Now he was High Prairie's sector commander for the civilian organization designed to backstop the Canadian military's air search-and-rescue system. Heggie well understood the challenge search-and-rescue personnel faced. The small elite military force had the colossal task of covering more than 10 million square kilometres of land, as well as the world's longest coastal waters extending offshore to the Pacific and Atlantic Oceans. Nationally, the Canadian Forces' aeronautical domain extended from the US border to the North Pole, and from approximately 600 nautical miles west of Vancouver Island in the Pacific to 900 nautical miles east of Newfoundland in the Atlantic. When asked what advice he, as a CARES sector commander, would give to other pilots, Heggie's response was chilling: *Don't crash.*

When they all arrived at the airport just after 11:00, Luella was visibly relieved to relinquish her post at the UNICOM. She'd had only Edith to help with the phone and had been running—Luella would later write, "walking wasn't fast enough"—to record weather observations and operate the radio. She told Heggie that Dale Wells, Wapiti's chief pilot, was already in the area, and the military was preparing to dispatch one of its Hercules military transport aircraft from Canadian Forces Base Edmonton.

Southeast of the airport, Dale circled his plane through thick cloud. After he'd radioed Luella, he'd continued southeast along the flight path that Erik Vogel would have been on. Flying toward Swan Hills for several minutes, Dale had picked up a faint distress signal. He'd felt the air being sucked from his lungs. It had to be 402.

He sat numbly at the controls as the signal grew louder and then began to fade again. He banked sharply and turned, his focus fully on locating the downed plane. For the next forty-five minutes he flew a search pattern over the area. During one pass, Dale saw the flare of an oil well torch, but other than that, thick cloud and fog made it impossible to see the ground. The ELT signal was distorted, fading in and out, but he managed to narrow down the crash area to between 30 and 40 kilometres south of High Prairie. It was close to 11:30 when he radioed High Prairie, saying he was going to attempt a landing at the airport. Luella stepped outside to take a look at the cloud ceiling. It had dropped dramatically and was now down to between 50 and 100 feet above the runway. She relayed the information to Dale.

Though supremely experienced at flying in difficult conditions and intimately familiar with the area, even he couldn't argue with tonight's weather. With a heavy heart he banked and, turning the plane toward Grande Prairie, headed home.

CONFESSION

n the snow-draped wilderness 32 kilometres southeast of High Prairie, four men huddled around a feeble campfire. Snow tumbled wetly upon their heads and the burning wood sizzled and crackled, sending wisps of smoke into the air. A wan moon had risen above the trees and though obscured by thick cloud, its faint light stole the night's inky edge.

Erik surveyed the bloodied faces of the surviving passengers, Paul to his left and Larry to his right, both smoking silently. Scott lay on the ground next to him, the topcoat draped over him speckled with snow. Inside the plane, five passengers were dead and another critically injured. Erik was overcome with guilt and remorse.

Tell them. Tell them who you are.

His lips moved soundlessly, but he couldn't bring himself to say it aloud. Blood still dripped from the open gash on his forehead, darkening the snow at his feet. Finally, Erik got it out, his voice thick with emotion. "I'm the pilot," he said.

Scott had not stirred since being set down, but now asked, "How long will it take before they start looking for us?"

Erik glanced reflexively at his wrist, but saw only a deep gash the metal watch strap had sliced into his flesh. The watch itself was gone. He had no idea how long they had been on the ground, but he'd radioed his position just before he'd veered out of controlled airspace. Air traffic control would have been expecting him to contact them and when he didn't, would have sounded the alarm.

Erik explained that the plane's ELT would lead rescuers to them within a few hours. What he didn't appreciate was how difficult the task of pinpointing the crash site would be that night.

Scott checked his watch. They'd been on the ground for two hours and he wondered how long they could last. Like all RCMP officers, Scott was trained in first aid. He'd noticed Erik's laboured, shallow breaths and had taken this as a bad sign—probably a punctured lung and internal bleeding. He'd diagnosed his own condition as a flail chest: a life-threatening injury in which a segment of rib cage breaks in multiple locations, becomes separated from the chest wall and moves in opposition to it.

Larry, too, appeared to be suffering. He had refused to sit down and when he walked, his movements were slow and painfully precise, his arms outstretched to compensate for his blindness. Larry's hands and face were cut and swollen and one of his fingers was bent at an odd angle, clearly broken or dislocated.

Paul, apart from a gash on his temple, seemed fine.

While the others had waded into the bush in search of wood, Scott had come up with a laundry list of things the men would need if they hoped to survive: a radio to contact rescuers, a first aid kit, flares, blankets, a hatchet. Now that he knew Erik was the pilot, Scott asked him about each item in turn.

Somberly, Erik shook his head. The radio and battery had been destroyed in the crash and the plane didn't carry any of the other items.

"No survival gear?" Scott asked, incredulous.

Erik told him there was no legal requirement to carry any of it, and even if there were, it would take up too much space and add weight to Wapiti's often fully loaded planes.

Scott couldn't believe it. He routinely carried as much on his back when hiking or skiing in the backcountry. Without an axe, he knew the men would be hard pressed to gather enough wood to keep the fire going. Already, it was proving a challenge. Every fifteen to twenty minutes, the flame sputtered and the three ambulatory survivors had to leave the warmth of the fire in search of more wood.

"What about a flashlight?" Scott finally asked.

Erik surprised him by saying yes, remembering his penlight. "I have one in my flight bag."

"Where would it be?"

"Right next to my seat," Erik told him.

"I'll go," Paul offered. He knew exactly where the bag was.

"If you find it," Erik told him, "there are four chocolate chip cookies in that bag."

Scott raised his head from the ground and watched Paul leave. Fog shrouded the treetops and a dense stand of forest surrounded them. Scott was no stranger to the wilderness. An only child, he'd spent much of his childhood and teenage years hunting and fishing in the bush around the Vancouver suburb of Delta. By the time he was twelve, he was snaring rabbits and raccoons. At fourteen, he was running his own trapline, selling the skins for profit and even making a few Daniel Boone–style hats from the pelts. Later, he'd moved on to hunting larger game.

He'd always been comfortable in the wild, and he'd never felt helpless in it until now. He squinted into the forest beyond the fire's flickering glow, searching for a shadow of movement or the reflective flash of eyes through the trees. This was bear country. Wolf country.

"My gun," he said, clutching the empty holster on his chest. Frantically, Scott began darting his eyes across the snow around him.

Erik assumed the worst. *He's going to kill me for crashing the plane.*

He staggered back from the fire, his breath coming in rapid, painful gasps. In spite of the cold, hot sweat dampened the back of his neck. The thought of putting more distance between himself and the cop briefly crossed Erik's mind, but his insides burned with pain and his hands hung mangled and grossly swollen at his sides. He knew he wasn't going anywhere.

I deserve this, he thought, closing his eyes.

Scott was frantically trying to recall where he'd left his sidearm. Then he remembered. He'd placed it inside his briefcase and put the briefcase beneath his seat before takeoff. It had to be somewhere inside the plane. He glanced toward the wreck, but Paul was nowhere in sight. Though RCMP regulations required Scott to keep his firearm at his side at all times, there was nothing he could do about it now. He only hoped his prisoner wouldn't find it.

Paul quickly closed the distance to the plane and crawled in through the cockpit window. The trapped passenger was still moaning and Paul could also hear a disturbing repetitive sound above him. *Thud. Thud. Thud.* He realized the passenger was slamming his left arm against the cabin wall. Paul froze. "Don't worry," he whispered to the wounded man, "we're not leaving you. Rescue is coming soon."

As if comforted by Paul's words, the passenger stopped banging. Paul waited a moment and reached for Erik's flight bag, sliding it carefully from around the man's other arm. As quickly as he'd entered, Paul left the plane.

Setting the bag at his feet, he fumbled for Larry's cigarettes. Lighting one, he dragged deeply until the nicotine calmed him. He looked around and spied a black briefcase half-buried in the snow. Paul pulled it out and shook it vigorously, but heard only the sound of shifting paper. Hanging on to the briefcase, he shouldered Erik's flight bag and returned to the fire. When he arrived, he flipped the clasps of the briefcase and opened it. His eyes confirmed what his ears had already told him: it contained only papers. As Paul added them to the fire, Larry wondered briefly if they were his—files that hours before had seemed like the most important documents in the world. Paul snapped the briefcase shut and offered it to Larry as a seat, but Larry shook his head. Then Paul turned his attention to the flight bag. The penlight was not in it, but the cookies from Erik's mother more than made up for that.

"Good thing you removed those handcuffs, huh?" Paul joked to Scott. Though his tone was light, it hadn't escaped him that he probably would have lost his hands—or worse—if he'd still been in cuffs. Nor could the others ignore their good fortune: they were alive while six passengers lay dead or dying inside the plane.

Paul pulled out Larry's pack of cigarettes, offering him one and taking another for himself. Almost too brightly, Paul launched into a string of lewd barroom jokes.

"Did you hear the one about the captain who shipwrecked his boat in the middle of the ocean?"

An uneasy look passed between Larry and Scott and they glanced toward Erik, but Paul was already into his story. Larry laughed politely when Paul was done, but his mind was elsewhere. He could scarcely believe that only hours ago he'd been sitting in the Alberta Legislature during question period. Grant Notley had stood across the floor from him demanding compensation for Steven Truscott, a teenager who had been falsely convicted of murder. Grant's passionate words were etched in Larry's memory: "Does the government consider there is, if not a legal obligation, a moral obligation for restitution?"

He'd agreed with Grant. Larry believed in restitution—in giving people a second chance. *We're often too quick to judge,* he thought. Truscott was innocent, but had spent ten years in prison. Larry had always favoured the underdog and as a member of a visible minority, understood what it was like to be wrongly judged. Perhaps that was why he'd listened so intently to Grant's speech that morning.

Larry felt his throat constrict. Grant had taken the co-pilot's seat—the seat Larry had given up. Now Grant was dead along with others from his close-knit northern constituency.

He looked to his left where Erik sat quietly. Much of his face was dark with blood and his head was bowed. Larry may have been half-blind, but his powers of perception hadn't dimmed.

"I could tell he was hurting physically and emotionally," Larry recalled. Removing his necktie, he handed it to Erik to wrap around his head. Then he asked the young pilot, "What happened?"

Erik didn't know until that moment, but he'd needed someone to ask the question, had needed to talk about the stress he'd been under during the past weeks at Wapiti. So he told the survivors *everything*: the pressure cooker atmosphere at the company, how it pushed its pilots and the weather. Erik admitted that he hadn't wanted to take the flight that night, hadn't believed it was safe. But he didn't feel he'd had a choice. He thought his job was on the line.

"Why hasn't somebody done something?" Larry asked.

"Lots of pilots complained to the government but the company is bulletproof."

"How?"

"The owner has friends in high places."

Larry was taken aback. He was one of those friends. Quietly, he admitted to Erik who he was and that he'd supported the airline. He also told the pilot that another of Wapiti's staunchest supporters, Grant Notley, leader of Alberta's New Democratic Party, was inside the plane.

Erik dropped his head into his hands. A long silence descended on the men and the fire waned, sending a deepening chill into their bones.

"I think it's important to agree on something," Larry said finally, his voice deep with emotion. "If we are asked, we need to say that the others died instantly. They did not suffer."

Paul kicked at the flight bag lying at his feet, stooping to pull out maps and papers, which he tossed on the fire. Then he fished out a hardbound journal and a camera, which he waved in front of Erik.

"You want this?"

Erik didn't answer. He looked past the camera at what Paul held in his other hand: his pilot's logbook. Paul slipped the camera into his pocket and handed the logbook to Erik. Slowly, he opened it and began flipping through the pages. In neat handwriting, on page after page, in column after column, were the hours and minutes—more than 1400 in all—of Erik's hard-earned flying career: daytime hours, nighttime hours, hours on instruments and flying visually when the entire earth seemed to lie at his feet. Alongside them were dates and the names of the captains he'd served and the flights he had flown solo, and as captain, in command of his own aircraft, indeed, his own destiny.

Erik closed his fist tightly around a sheaf of papers and yanked, tearing them from the book. As the others silently looked on, he dropped them into the flames.

SEARCH

At 10:45 p.m., forty-seven-year-old warrant officer Everett Hale had been on standby at the base in Edmonton when he got word that his squadron was to be airborne as soon as possible. Moments earlier, the SARSAT had picked up a signal believed to be from the downed commuter plane. Already dressed and ready to roll, Hale wasted little time getting over to the tarmac to ready the CC-130 Hercules—one of the Canadian military's largest aircraft—for takeoff. Within half an hour, he'd fuelled the plane, started the engines and completed his run-up, and the massive four-engine tanker was rolling down the runway. At 11:10 it was airborne, its flight and search-and-rescue crew heading for the 10-square kilometre area identified by the satellite orbiting far above.

As the plane hurtled north at 350 nautical miles per hour, Hale sat strapped into the flight engineer's seat between and slightly behind the pilot and co-pilot. He stared at the huge central panel of thirty-two neon-green dials lined up like a tray of radioactive petri dishes. His job was to monitor the Herc's systems—hydraulics, fuel, electronics, pressurization and power—and stay alert for any warning indicators. Outside, beyond the expanse of windshield, heavy fog and darkness obscured the night. The weather in the area was extremely poor, ranging from 500-foot ceilings and one-mile visibility to a ceiling of zero feet and one-eighth of a mile visibility. The Rescue Coordination Centre also informed the crew that a Cessna 182 had recently picked up an ELT on a bearing of 110 degrees, 30 to 40 kilometres southeast of High Prairie and had tried to get a visual of the crash site, but hadn't been able to get under the clouds. Hale wasn't surprised. In tonight's conditions there was little margin to fly in and virtually no hope of a visual sighting of the ground.

Beneath an impenetrable mantle of cloud and falling snow, the survivors briefly heard the mosquito-like buzz of a small airplane far above before it disappeared. They looked at one other around the fire. Paul commented on how beautiful they were, busted up and covered in blood.

Larry ran his hands over his face. It was tender with cuts and bruises and the pain in his ribs and tailbone was excruciating. Still, he felt fortunate. A long-ago conversation with a colleague, a Second World War pilot, came back to him. They had flown together in bad weather and when their government plane had landed, Larry's colleague had said: "Any time you can walk away from an airplane, you're lucky."

Larry now understood what he'd meant. Larry hadn't devoted much time to his faith in the past ten years of his hectic political career, but at that moment he silently thanked God and said a prayer for those who had not been so lucky.

He watched Erik hobble away from the fire in search of wood and felt for the young pilot. He wasn't much older than Larry's own children. When he'd been elected as an MLA in 1975, his eldest had been thirteen and his youngest, eight. Larry had thrown himself into his political career and had risen quickly through the ranks of government. But at what cost? During his first term in office he had been an unknown, a backbencher who was only required to be at the Legislature two times a year for six-week stretches when the government was sitting. But in 1979, the premier had appointed Larry to his inner Cabinet where he'd soon established a reputation as a sage of sorts, a wise and thoughtful listener who had the ear and respect of his Cabinet colleagues.

Larry spent not just his days with his colleagues, but his evenings as well. His political life was full of perks—the seduction of power and authority and the unfettered time and independence to fully devote himself to his work. But while he'd been occupied, his five children had grown up, graduated from high school, and left High Prairie for the wider world. Linda, his eldest, was living in the United States, and Carol, his second-born, working as a journalist in Jerusalem. Hard to believe, but the other three were young adults, and though they still shared his apartment in Edmonton, his demanding work schedule allowed him precious little time with them.

And of course there was Alma, alone in the sprawling High Prairie home they had built together. What was life like for her as she waited each weekend for him to return? As she waited for him now?

Larry had desperately wanted to make a good life for his family, but he had also wanted it for himself. His ambition, in part, had been fuelled by regret. His father, Albert, had come to Canada from Lebanon's Bekaa Valley at the age of thirteen. The year was 1919. Because he couldn't speak English, he'd started school in grade one. It took him a year to advance to grade six and he'd been cruelly tormented. But by the time he was an adult, Albert was a successful businessman and owned two general stores in Endiang, a tiny farming community of five hundred people where Larry and his four siblings were born and had lived as children. The stores supported Albert and his family through the Depression, but there were no Muslims in the area and no mosque. So after a group of Muslims came through the town raising money to build Canada's first mosque in Edmonton, Albert decided to uproot his family and, in 1945, moved to the city. He purchased another grocery store, mere blocks from the mosque. The store became a destination for many members of the city's fledgling Muslim community and Larry's father prospered. Later, he established a wholesale toy business that would grow to be one of the largest in Western Canada.

Albert's oldest son, Edward, joined the family business when he finished high school, but Albert had other plans for Larry. He wanted his second son, a bright and capable student, to earn a university degree. The opportunity was rare and came at some sacrifice to the family, but Larry had squandered it. He'd goofed off and, after his first year had flunked out of the University of Alberta. Larry remembered the moment he told his father of this failure as one of the worst of his life. Bitterly disappointed, Albert had died before his son could prove himself.

After his father's death, Larry had floundered for a time, scraping by as a travelling salesman and a department store manager. But as his family grew, he found it increasingly difficult to make ends meet. Alma recalls complaining that a package of four rubber pants she pulled over her babies' cloth diapers cost the same as a pack of cigarettes—a quarter—and there was seldom enough money to afford both. She would silently seethe as she mended ripped rubber pants with Scotch tape while Larry puffed madly on his cigarettes trying to figure out how on God's good earth he was going to feed his family.

In 1967, Larry moved his family from Edmonton to High Prairie. His sole connection to the remote northern community was the Houssians, a Muslim family who ran the local menswear store. He and Alma had paid their friends a visit several years earlier, and during that trip Larry had a chance meeting with the woman who owned the town's general goods business next door. He and Alma had five children under the age of six at the time, and he'd been running a bowling alley in Edmonton. Though they had no money, he secured a promise from the store's owner to call him if she ever decided to sell.

True to her word, the owner eventually called and, seizing the opportunity for a better life, Larry sold their only asset—a lumbering old house overlooking Edmonton's river valley—and moved north to the tiny farming town of 2500 people. But the few thousand dollars left over from the sale of the house wasn't enough to buy the store. Larry's plan had been to secure a bank loan to cover the shortfall, but the managers of the local chartered banks didn't share his vision. None of them would take a chance on an untested outsider with neither collateral nor a track record. In the weeks that followed, Larry's hair began to fall out and he developed a severe case of shingles, but he didn't give up.

Finally the manager of the Alberta Treasury Branch, a small financial institution owned by the provincial government, agreed to loan him the money he needed to buy the business. Over the next decade, the store would not only support and clothe his family, but also allow the son of an immigrant Arab peddler to establish himself as a community leader.

It seemed nothing short of miraculous that Larry was now one of the most powerful politicians in the province. He had a personal staff of four and a government department of hundreds to help him get his job done. But standing cold, blind and battered in the dark wilderness waiting for someone to rescue him, none of it made a difference.

Just before midnight, the crew aboard the Hercules circling several thousand feet above the ground picked up the plane's ELT signal and began working to pinpoint it. That meant first establishing their own position vis-à-vis the nearby navigation beacon at Swan Hills, and then plotting a reverse bearing to the downed plane's signal. To determine the ELT's exact location, the giant aircraft would have to sweep the area, monitoring the signal's strength. The stronger it was, the closer they were to the crash site. The navigator, keeping a close eye on the directional needle, watched for the second it swung 180 degrees indicating they'd flown directly over the ELT, and then plotted the point electronically. The Herc would need to make numerous passes before the navigator could triangulate the ELT's exact location, but it was only a matter of time before they nailed it down. Unfortunately, the signal was weak and distorted, often fading in and out as if obscured by something unseen below.

After overflying the area for an hour, the navigator aboard the Hercules was zeroing in. The pilot radioed the Rescue Coordination Centre to update the searchmaster of the operation on their progress and to request permission to deploy search-and-rescue jumpers once they'd pinpointed the ELT. The searchmaster refused. Poor weather, rugged terrain and heavy snow made it too dangerous. Instead, he made a crew callout for a Chinook—an intimidating twin-engine, tandem rotor helicopter with a wide loading ramp at the rear of the fuselage. Agile and versatile, it was the only aircraft capable of safely getting within reach of the crash site that night.

Some time around midnight, the survivors heard another sound in the distance, this one from a much larger aircraft. The men held their breaths as the plane approached. Though darkness, heavy snow and clouds obscured it and they were bone cold, the sound filled them with hope. As the plane circled far above, Erik assured the others that it was a search-and-rescue aircraft and that it wouldn't be long before they were found.

The promise of imminent rescue compelled Paul to return to the plane and check on the trapped passenger. Maybe, just maybe, he would make it. As he crawled inside the cockpit's portside window, he heard the disturbing rhythm of the injured passenger's exhalations. His breathing had slowed considerably since Paul had last visited and his moans were reduced to barely audible sighs. The hand that had been stuffed in Erik's flight bag hung limply in the air. Paul reached out and took it in his own. He wasn't sure how long he stood there. All he knew was that at some point during that time, the sounds stopped. Paul listened intently for a while longer, but there was nothing. Not a whisper of life.

Witnessing the man's death pinned Paul in place. As he held his hand he sensed something ephemeral, otherworldly, rise and float up into the night. Later he would tell his brother Daniel that he was sure it had been the man's soul leaving his body.

Paul left the plane and wandered aimlessly for a time, chain smoking.

For the previous five days he'd been pacing the floor of a maximum-security cell in Kamloops awaiting pickup by a Grande Prairie sheriff. On Sunday, October 14, Paul had hitched a ride into Kamloops and found a bed at a men's hostel. He'd planned to leave the next morning for Penticton, where he'd heard his younger brother Michael might be living. Around four in the morning a hostel attendant had led two RCMP officers to Paul's bed. They had a warrant for his arrest. The scrappy drifter had laughed in their faces. The charge they'd picked him up on *was* laughable—a misdemeanor, a misunderstanding, even—but the cops hadn't shared the joke. They'd cuffed him and taken him into custody.

At 8:30 on the morning of October 15, Paul had argued his case in front of a judge. He'd offered to plead guilty on the charge of public mischief, hoping to get off, but the judge had refused, ordering him remanded into custody until the Grande Prairie RCMP could fly someone down to bring him in. Paul was pissed. He'd already spent four years of his young life in prison for one thing or another and had only fled Grande Prairie because he couldn't bear the idea of being cooped up in jail again. Now he was in a stinking holding cell waiting for some cop to haul his ass back there.

Jail was exactly as he remembered it: boring as shit. He'd been allowed only an hour of exercise and a little TV each day he'd been there, and he'd already read the only book he could get his hands on. Called *Airport '77*, it was about a plane crash and had filled him with dread. Paul was scared to death of small planes, and the prison keeper had already told him that when the sheriff did show up, that was how the two of them would be travelling back to Grande Prairie.

The only good thing about the day had been the cop who'd arrived to escort him: Scott Deschamps. He'd treated Paul like a human being, and the two had had plenty of time to talk—even share a few laughs. It didn't escape him that he and Scott were practically the same age, yet their lives were completely different.

"What do you think of me compared to what you've read in my record?" Paul had asked at one point.

Scott's response was flippant: "You're one and the same."

Paul didn't know what to make of the comment and had asked more pointedly, "What kind of chance would I have to become a cop?"

Scott had laughed. "Not a good one."

Paul had laughed then too, but deep down the comment stung. As a teenager, he'd taken a naval cadet survival training course and then applied to the military. But they'd turned him down because he had only one kidney. He had lost the other when he was just a child. At the age of five while playing in the front yard, his younger brother Michael had thrown one of his shoes onto the road. As Paul ran to retrieve it, a car had plowed into his small body, throwing him high into the air. The impact had pinballed him onto the roof of an oncoming car and then onto the road. He'd spent a year in the hospital, much of it in a body cast.

As Paul stood alone in the darkness listening to the sound of the search plane approaching then receding, he reflected on the irony of his fucked-up life. Two days earlier—October 17—had been his twenty-seventh birthday. He'd spent it behind bars thinking his life couldn't possibly get any worse.

It was after midnight on Saturday, October 20, when Brian Dunham's phone rang. The military officer on the other end told him that someone with helicopter experience was urgently needed on a search and rescue mission. The request surprised Dunham as he wasn't on standby that night and his squadron flew only Twin Otters, small, fixed wing aircraft. When he arrived at the Rescue Command Centre, he learned that he was to be Team Leader on a Chinook CH-47 helicopter borrowed from the tactical helicopter squadron to respond to a major air disaster.

Standing 5'11" and 180 pounds with close-clipped brown hair, green eyes and a gap-tooth smile, the former navy sonar man and diver was a seasoned Search and Rescue Technician or SAR Tech, and had a job description that read like an adventure novel. SAR Techs are highly trained experts in leading search teams, performing rescue operations, and providing on-site medical care to casualties. They are air, land and sea survival specialists—trained mountaineers, rapellers, scuba divers, spotters, parachuters and advanced trauma medics. Their work requires them to take risks and survive the most strenuous of Canadian weather and terrain conditions.

At 12:51 a.m. the Chinook helicopter carrying Dunham, as well as

Major Peter Dewar, who would oversee search-and-rescue operations from Slave Lake, two doctors, two nurses, six medics and another SAR Tech, lifted off. Within half an hour, the chopper was mushing through heavy cloud and freezing rain, and icing was rapidly becoming a problem.

Subzero precipitation is a hazard for all aircraft, reducing lift and increasing drag and weight. But helicopters are especially susceptible. Spanwise elements of their rotor blades, unlike the leading edges of fixed airplane wings, move through the air at different speeds, and even a small buildup of ice—as little as a quarter inch—can jeopardize the aircraft's ability to stay aloft. The pilot of the Chinook couldn't see ice on the massive twin blades whirling above him, but he could feel the warning signs as the chopper strained to maintain speed and altitude. He was just 42 nautical miles northwest of Edmonton when he radioed the Rescue Coordination Centre to say the Chinook might have to return to Edmonton.

It was 2:00 a.m. and the searchmaster had just received a copy of the passenger list from Wapiti Aviation, confirming that there were high-profile politicians on board. He suggested the pilot try a more westerly approach, but it proved just as perilous. Finally, he advised the pilot to try routing east of Swan Hills and attempt a landing in Slave Lake. Though the conditions were only marginally better, the chopper made it in. Once on the ground, Major Dewar and half the medical team deplaned so that the chopper could return directly to Edmonton with survivors if it could make it into the crash site *and* if anyone was found alive.

After just five minutes on the ground, the Chinook was airborne once more. But with the poor weather and the threat of icing, team leader Brian Dunham knew there were no guarantees they'd be able to reach survivors. He alerted Major Dewar, who called Sergeant Hopkins in High Prairie and told him to get his RCMP ground search party ready to roll.

Hopkins had beaten him to it. His officers were already stationed along the highway east of High Prairie awaiting exact crash site coordinates. But with news of the adverse conditions in the air, they didn't want to wait any longer. Their plan was to head south into the wilderness, advancing in the general direction of the crash area so they could be on hand when the military pinpointed the site. The search party had also commandeered a Bombardier from a local farmer. The truck-sized utility vehicle was equipped with caterpillar tracks that could move easily over the snow, soft muskeg and gnarly underbrush, blazing a trail ahead of the snowmobiles. Carrying two-way radios and a handheld ELT homing device, the RCMP ground search party left the road's hardpacked snow and nosed their snowmobiles into the bush, headlights dipping then rising, light tunnelling deep into the pitch-black forest ahead.

ABORT

ess than a mile into the bush, things began to go wrong for the ground search party. RCMP officers, riding two up on the snow-mobiles, became bogged down in waist-deep snow and the Bombardier was unable to squeeze through the dense trees to lay down a track. When the officers radioed Hoppy, he cursed loudly, lighting one cigarette from the glowing butt of another. There was a lot of heavy equipment on the surrounding farms and in the town, and he put out an urgent request for it. The response came quickly. Cox Contracting, a local business run by two young brothers who knew and respected Larry Shaben, offered every available man and every piece of heavy machinery they owned. That included a wide-pad utility vehicle, a swamp cat and a bulldozer. They would clear a road through the wilderness if that's what it took.

Somewhere high above the soon-to-be-bolstered ground search party, obscured by a thick mattress of cloud, the giant Hercules continued to circle. It had been sweeping the area for several hours to triangulate the position of the downed plane, and had finally pinpointed the ELT. Its crew's orders had been to drop flares to reassure any survivors until rescuers aboard the inbound Chinook helicopter got to them. In the event the SAR Techs could reach the site and hoist the injured aboard, both aircraft were to return immediately to Slave Lake. There, survivors would be transferred to the faster-flying Herc and immediately transported to an Edmonton hospital.

The Hercules had just dropped a series of flares into the thick cloud over the crash site when the Forward Base Commander radioed its crew to advise them that the RCMP ground search party was having a heck of a time making its way in. Still, given the icing conditions the chopper was experiencing, the ground search party might have the best chance to reach the crash site. Major Dewar asked the Herc's crew to divert north toward the RCMP ground party, dropping flares to light the way for almost a dozen men now slogging through the wilderness.

Some 20 kilometres south of the ground search party, four survivors huddling in the deep freeze of night had been listening hopefully to the drone of the aircraft above. It had strengthened steadily and then a series of flares had exploded into the soufflé of dense cloud above them—enormous orange orbs of light ballooning into the darkness.

"We're outta here," Erik yelled.

The men whooped with joy, waving their arms in the air and clapping one another on the back. Feverishly they tossed the remaining wood and scavenged materials onto the fire, sending spires of flame skyward. They surveyed one another's battered faces, the melted pit around the fire, and the torn fuselage of the Piper Navajo in the distance.

"You're wearing a pair of underwear on your head," Paul teased Scott. "I wonder what your buddies at the cop shop would say if they could see you lying there with underwear on your head and a pair of ladies' boots on your feet?"

The cop flashed him an actual grin.

Erik tilted his bloodied face toward the sound of the plane's receding engine, expecting the aircraft to bank and begin a slow arc back. But to his surprise, he saw another flare explode in the distance.

Why would they drop it over there? he wondered.

A moment later a third flare glowed dimly, this one much farther away. Erik's heart sank. "Guys," he said, "we have a problem. They don't know where we are."

"What do you mean?" Paul asked. "They dropped that fucking flare right on our heads."

"I know, but they wouldn't be dropping flares over there if they knew where we are."

Erik couldn't make sense of why the plane that had been circling for hours hadn't pinpointed them. An almost obsessive reader of accident reports, he recalled an article about a lost pilot whose plane had crashed a few years earlier. When rescuers found the pilot, his first question to them had been: *What took you so long?*

The rescuers had told the pilot that there had been no emergency locator transmitter signal from the downed plane. It hadn't been turned on. The horrifying thought occurred to Erik that his plane's ELT might not have been switched back to the "armed" position after one of Wapiti's maintenance inspections.

Erik knew that something serious had happened to his lungs and he could feel the grip of his injury tightening on him. He needed medical attention sooner rather than later, and so did Scott and Larry. Struggling to remain calm, he shared his theory about the ELT with the others. Somehow, they needed to make sure it was working.

Erik plodded back to the aircraft with Paul and Larry trailing. Groping along the outside of the fuselage behind the open hatch, his unfeeling hands managed to find the ELT panel at the tail section of the upturned aircraft. He clawed at its thin metal lip with clumsy fingers, but it was screwed shut. He shook his head, telling the others that without some sort of tool there was little hope of opening it.

Paul reached into the pocket of his jeans and pulled out the pocketknife.

"Here," he said, passing it to Erik.

The pilot's eyebrows rose in surprise. He fumbled to open the screwdriver attachment before Paul snatched the knife back, stepped in front of him and deftly removed the panel. Erik reached inside the dark opening, his hands groping for the ELT unit. He found the six-by-ten-inch box and then located a small toggle switch.

"Is it on?" Paul asked, a note of sarcasm in his voice.

Erik ran his fingers across it, but had no way of knowing which position was on.

"Do you want to use my lighter?"

"No!" The response came out more harshly than Erik had intended, but no way did he want an open flame when the smell of fuel was still so strong. He hesitated, his hand buried within the tail section's interior, uncertain of what to do.

"Just flip it, for Chrissake," Paul urged and Erik felt a prickle of annoyance.

If it was working, Erik would have a 50 percent chance of getting it right when he flipped the switch. But if he chose the wrong position, he risked cutting off their sole lifeline to rescuers.

An idea occurred to Erik that if he toggled the ELT switch every half an hour, he could increase those odds to 100 percent. The problem was he didn't have the strength to continue moving much longer. Scott was immobile and Larry was having increasing difficulty walking. And even if he could walk, he couldn't see. That left Paul. Erik suspected that he'd been stealing from the wreckage and the pocketknife had confirmed it. The last thing the pilot wanted to do was place his life and the lives of his surviving passengers in Paul's hands. But there was no other choice. Erik would have to trust him.

Four thousand feet up and well above the weather, the Hercules flew a direct line from the crash site to the presumed location of the ground search party. As the flares exploded, trailing orange plumes through the night, Hale peered into thick cloud hoping to get a glimpse of something, anything, on the ground. It was no use. The low-sodium flares they used in heavy fog burned hot and fast, flaming out within 1,000 feet to avoid the risk of setting fire to anything— or anyone—below. Hale's attention returned to the green glow of the cockpit instruments. Among them, he saw one of the engines' warning lights flash red. Hale and the pilot exchanged a look of concern. Quickly, they discussed their options and decided to shut down the faltering No. 2 engine to conserve fuel. Then they radioed Slave Lake to advise Major Dewar of the situation. Though the aging Herc was capable of flying on three engines, the major wasn't taking any chances. He told the pilot he was calling out a second Hercules crew to relieve them.

On the ground, the RCMP search party was facing its own formidable challenges. In spite of the added equipment and manpower, progress was excruciatingly slow. Even when they did manage to clear a section of dense bush and advance several hundred metres, trying to chart a course by watching overhead flares burst in a dark, cloudy sky was difficult. After hours of exhausting work, the men were still at least 15 kilometres from the crash site. And for all its might and majesty, the massive Hercules could do nothing but circle blindly, shooting flares like aimless arrows into the night.

Meanwhile, the Chinook had homed in on the ELT and was closing the distance between the Slave Lake airport and the crash site. Dunham hoped that if they could zero in on the signal, the pilot might be able to drop below the cloud so he and fellow SAR Tech Bill Barber could lower to the ground. When the Chinook pilot determined he was on top of the site he took the helicopter into a high hover.

He remained there for almost an hour, alternating between hovering in place for ten to fifteen minutes—as long as he dared without the chopper overheating—then moving into a flight pattern. He repeated this manoeuvre several times while waiting for a break in the weather. It never came.

Instead, something completely unexpected happened. The crew aboard the helicopter suddenly lost the ELT signal. They radioed the Hercules and they, too, had lost the signal. What the hell had happened? It was 3:50 in the morning and the pilot of the helicopter called Slave Lake to advise them of the situation. Not only had the Chinook been unable to get under the clouds, they'd lost the signal and now had only five minutes of flight time remaining before they needed to return to refuel.

Major Dewar's reply was swift: *Go to ground*. The helicopter banked steeply away from the crash area and headed for Slave Lake to wait out the weather.

CRIMINAL

n the deep fold of night, as the pulsing thrum of the helicopter faded first to a distant hum and then to a whisper, a pall of disappointment fell over the men huddled around the sputtering fire. For a long time, no one moved. Erik sat hunched on the briefcase, listening intently for the chopper to circle back; when it didn't, his chest constricted. The silence the chopper left in its wake was a heavy weight on his shoulders. Cold and pain rode his bones like cruel horsemen and his mouth felt drier than he could ever remember. He wanted only to lie down, but feared that if he did he would never rise.

He wasn't sure how much time passed before he could bring himself to look at his passengers. To his right, Larry stood smoking, the end of his cigarette glowing red. His hand shook as he brought the cigarette to his mouth and Erik saw a shudder pass through him. He implored him to sit, but Larry refused.

"I'm fine," he said, but Erik didn't believe it. A thick layer of snow now draped the coat Larry had laid over Scott, who shivered incessantly. Even Paul, who'd kept up a steady stream of chatter, had stopped trying to entertain them, and as much as his jokes had annoyed

Erik, he would have done anything to hear one at the moment. Paul sat mutely puffing on a cigarette as if it was the last one in the world.

"It's too quiet," he said. "I don't like it."

Maybe the rescuers had abandoned them. The thought propelled Erik to his feet. This situation was his fault and injured or not he bore responsibility to somehow help his surviving passengers.

"I'm going to flip the ELT switch," he said. It was all he had to offer.

"Think it's working?" Paul asked.

"If they haven't found us by daylight, we'll take it out and bring it to the fire," Erik said. "If it's not working, we'll try to fix it." He swayed unsteadily and paroxysms of gurgling coughs erupted.

"Why don't you rest," Larry suggested.

"Yeah, pilot," Paul said. "I'll go."

Erik shook his head, raising a hand. Even though he was suffering, he was alive. It was more than he could say for six others inside the plane. He staggered down the path toward the wreckage, bending to scoop a mouthful of snow along the way.

Paul thought about all the pisses he'd taken along the trail on his forays for wood.

"Watch out where the huskies go, and don't you eat that yellow snow," he sang out after Erik, but no one laughed.

When he reached the fuselage, Erik leaned heavily against it and gave in to another coughing fit. He tasted blood in his mouth and braced his hands on his knees, trying to catch his breath.

Stupid! Stupid! Stupid!

He couldn't come to grips with what he'd done. He dimly understood that he'd let the pressure of the situation—the company's expectations; his passengers' need to get home; his intense desire to hold on to his job—override his instincts not to take the flight. But he couldn't for the life of him figure out what had gone wrong *during* the flight. He'd been so fixated on getting into High Prairie that he'd committed the unforgivable sin of descending before passing the airport beacon, dropping to almost 2,800 feet without knowing exactly where he was. Yet he'd been so sure he was close.

Everything was a blur. His traumatized mind couldn't connect his grossly overloaded aircraft, prop ice so thick it was breaking off in pieces that hit the fuselage like hammer blows, and his inability to raise High Prairie on the radio. He couldn't understand how he'd made such a rookie mistake.

Erik shuffled forward, sweeping a hand down the plane's rear flank until he found the open ELT panel. It took a minute for him to locate the toggle switch, and another to manipulate his fingers to flip it. As he stumbled back along the trail to the firepit, the one question he couldn't answer was *Why?*

Erik had lost situational awareness—an understanding of what was going on around him. A shockingly frequent occurrence in aviation mishaps, according to the United States Federal Aviation Authority, loss of situational awareness is responsible for up to 15 percent of fatal crashes. Most of them occur when pilots fly in darkness or bad weather.

On a hot, hazy mid-July night in 1999, John F. Kennedy, Jr. was flying with his wife, Carolyn Bessette-Kennedy, and her sister Lauren when his Piper Saratoga plowed into the Atlantic Ocean off the coast of Martha's Vineyard. The National Transportation Safety Board determined the probable cause as pilot error due to spatial disorientation. A relatively inexperienced pilot, Kennedy was flying without the benefit of peripheral or ambient vision, senses that help pilots judge and maintain proper aircraft attitude. Flying at night in haze, Kennedy literally couldn't tell up from down or left from right.

Richard Leland, director of the Aeromedical Training Institute in Southampton, Pennsylvania, explains that in such circumstances,

The conscious brain can quickly become overwhelmed and important situational awareness cues (i.e., altitude, descent rate, etc.) can be missed. Cockpit tasks are more difficult. Switches are harder to find and placards are harder to read under low cockpit lighting conditions. This puts an increased load on the conscious brain and, in turn, raises the potential for unrecognized spatial disorientation and loss of situational awareness.

Loss of situational awareness isn't limited to the aviation industry. It has been known to occur in a range of high-risk activities from mountain climbing to parachuting to scuba diving. However, the phenomenon has been studied in aviation more than in any other field. When it comes to certain commuter airlines, many pilots encounter a contributing force sometimes called *go fever*—a pressure to fly when they shouldn't. Often young and inexperienced, pilots flying for small bush or commercial carriers find themselves in highly competitive environments that encourage them to push the limits to reach their destinations. Emotion rather than logic becomes a prime decision-making impetus. This pressure to succeed at all costs also contributed to two ill-fated 1996 Everest expeditions memorialized in Jon Krakauer's book *Into Thin Air*. Expedition leaders and climbers encountered the mountaineering equivalent of go fever, propelling them to ignore their designated turn-around time in their push for the summit, catching them high on the mountain as night fell and a storm rolled in.

Whether in aviation, mountain climbing or other high-risk scenarios, several factors can predispose individuals to lose situational awareness. Broadly, these factors are environmental, psychological and physiological. Erik experienced all three. Foul weather reduced his visual information to nil and severe icing had slowed his speed over ground to a degree that put him several miles further back from his destination than he'd estimated. Psychological factors—those imposing an additional processing load on the conscious brain—taxed Erik's ability to determine his exact location using dead reckoning, and impaired his decision-making. He experienced a condition known as task saturation. Flying solo, with an unreliable autopilot, Erik needed to handle more information than his highly stressed brain could process, and missed important cues that would have alerted him to danger. Task saturation explained how Erik allowed himself to descend to such an unsafe altitude, and remain there until he had no time to successfully recover. Physiological factors, most notably fatigue, also impaired his ability to perform. Fatigue is by far the most common physiological factor contributing to aviation mishaps and Erik's cumulative lack of sleep in the days and weeks preceding the crash had impaired his concentration to the point where he was, literally, an accident waiting to happen.

As he trod the now well-worn path back to the fire, Erik could not decipher this deadly chain of events. Reaching the survivors he tottered unsteadily around the perimeter of the clearing, almost tripping over Scott's snow-covered body. Even by the dim glow of the fire, Erik's face looked white and drawn.

"I'm going to pass out," he said.

Paul jumped from his seat and stepped quickly forward just as the pilot began to fall toward the fire. Catching Erik in his arms, he lowered him to the ground where he would remain for the rest of the night.

With Erik's collapse, the task of stoking the fire fell squarely on Paul's shoulders. Over the past few hours he'd lost count of how many trips he'd made into the bush looking for wood. Each time he'd returned more exhausted and disheartened. Every fifteen minutes, the fire burned itself down to its embers and the men were forced to their feet once more.

Never in his life had he felt less like moving. He pulled out Larry's pack of cigarettes, slid it open, and looked inside. Only one cigarette remained. He glanced toward Larry. The older man stood lost in thought on the other side of the fire, his head slightly bowed, the dim glow burnishing his broad forehead. Larry's eyes were closed and around them were dark bruises and cuts from where his glasses had smashed into his face.

"I'm going for wood," Paul said, starting down the path. As he moved away from the fire, Paul pulled the last cigarette from the package and lit it.

"I'll come," Larry offered.

Paul loped on ahead, but when he got to the fallen tree across the path he stopped. Larry would need help climbing over it. As he caught up, Paul pinched the butt of his cigarette between his lips and guided Larry over the tree.

"I'm ready for one of those," Larry said, smelling the smoke.

There was a long pause before Paul answered, "We're out."

Until that point, Larry had managed to maintain his equilibrium, but Paul's confession upset him unreasonably. *The little bugger's a chain-smoker,* he thought, kicking himself for entrusting his cigarettes to Paul.

The men walked in stony silence, advancing down the path that snaked alongside the wreckage and then some five hundred feet beyond it into the crash impact zone. There, the plane had plowed a strip of forest and the going was easier, but where large broken branches had once littered the ground, now there were only twigs. Over the course of the night, the two men had developed a rhythm of sorts, Larry trudging behind Paul, his hand clutching the back of his jean jacket; Paul walking slowly ahead, making small talk by cracking jokes. Now they pushed deeper into the wilderness, stopping often but not speaking. Paul tried without success to unearth heavier limbs beneath the snow and hacked futilely at their branches with the pocketknife. The two men laboured silently for half an hour before Larry spoke.

"Tell me about your family."

The question surprised Paul. It was not what he'd expected. But, reluctantly, he began to talk.

Paul was the eldest of five kids, he told Larry—three brothers and a sister. His parents had divorced when he was ten. A few years later his mom had taken up with a man named Jean-Pierre, a Quebec policeman who was a mean-spirited and abusive drunk. Paul's mom, Gayle, bore the brunt of that abuse. Paul came home one day to find his mother bruised, bloodied and lying unconscious under a chair. Jean-Pierre, pissed as usual, was cleaning his gun. Paul had flown at the man in a rage and severely beaten him. Then he'd moved out. He was fifteen years old.

For a few years Paul bounced between Aylmer, Quebec, and Toronto, Ontario, where his dad lived. Though Paul didn't admit it to Larry, he loved his booze and pot, and when intoxicated, had a habit of taking stuff that didn't belong to him. By age seventeen, that "stuff" included cars. Paul had been staying with his dad in Toronto when one night, after partying into the wee hours of the morning, he had found himself way the hell and gone on the other side of the city. He decided to hotwire a car to drive himself home. The cops picked him up at his dad's place a few days later and packed him off to jail.

That was in 1976 and since then Paul had served four years in Ontario and British Columbia prisons for various break-and-enter and robbery offences. The last time he'd been released from jail, he'd returned home to Aylmer and landed a maintenance job at the

Gatineau Golf Club. On September 12, 1983, while he was working there, a B and E occurred and $10,000 was stolen from the club. Paul, accused of the crime, fled west.

He had plenty of stories he could have told Larry about his time behind bars, but he kept them to himself. If he'd wanted, he could have entertained the men around the fire all night, showing them how he ate in prison, hunched over his dinner plate, elbows outstretched like chicken wings, fork firmly clasped in a fist. Or regaled them with tales of how, when he'd worked as a prison mechanic, he'd turned down the idles on every cop car that came in for repair. If he'd felt like it, Paul could have shown off the eagle tattoo on his right bicep that he'd gotten during one stint in the slammer, or the swirling green serpent an inmate had inked onto his chest during another. But to Paul, the craziest story of them all was the one that had landed him in this fucking mess.

In the early hours of Sunday, August 5, Paul had staggered out of the tavern in Grande Prairie's Park Hotel. Though still summer, the warmth of the nights had begun to wane and the faint promise of autumn's chill was in the air. He'd swayed unsteadily for a minute, then lurched across the wide sidewalk, stepped off the curb, and crossed the road.

The tattered hems of his jeans scraped along the asphalt and a car zoomed by, honking. Loping into Germaine Park, a derelict city lot that was a local hangout for drunks and drug dealers, he'd moved into the shadows to take a piss. Then he'd meandered east along 100th Avenue, past the flashing red neon arrows of Al's News, and the painted brick façade of the Imperial Garden Restaurant. He stopped to light a cigarette and watched as, across the street, Corona Pizza locked its doors for the night. He'd lost track of the hours that had passed since he'd finished his shift washing dishes at the popular local restaurant and lounge, and took off for a few beers with his buddy

Blackie. Now that the bars had closed and the booze was gone, he knew it was time to head home.

Paul shoved his hands deep into his jean pockets and his fingers closed around a set of keys. They belonged to a friend who'd offered his apartment while away working on the oil rigs, and though it was only temporary, Paul loved the feeling of having a secure roof over his head. The apartment was halfway down the next block, less than a minute's walk—one of a half-dozen units tucked away on the second floor of a drab, flat-fronted commercial building in the city centre.

He'd continued east until he arrived at the building, which housed Lee's Sub Shop and Baldwin Pianos on the ground level, and a doctor's office above. Paul stopped in front of a metal-framed glass door. Through the large single pane he could see a steep set of stairs rising up to the dimly lit landing that led to his friend's place. Paul inserted the front door key into the lock and tried, without success, to turn it. He remembered the deadbolt was finicky and jiggled the key in the lock. No luck. He jerked the key roughly, yanking on the door's broad metal handle. At the sound of approaching voices, he stopped and turned to look. A young man and woman swayed down the sidewalk from the direction of the bar. The man's arm was stretched down the small of the woman's back, his hand submerged beneath the fabric of her skin-tight jeans. She was laughing.

Paul's eyes lingered on the couple until they disappeared around the corner, then he turned back to the door and tried again. He rattled the key violently, then felt a flush of anger rise and kicked the door hard with the toe of his shoe. The glass shattered and shards of it flew toward him like translucent arrows before clattering onto the sidewalk. He staggered back and looked around, but there was no one in sight. He yanked the key from the lock, reached through the broken glass, and flipped the deadbolt. Inside, he climbed the steep carpeted staircase, steadying himself on its worn wooden banister. Reaching the landing, he lurched down the short hallway toward his buddy's apartment door, unlocked it, and slipped inside. Without turning on the lights, Paul kicked off his running shoes and groped his way blindly toward the bedroom. Pitching across the threshold, his legs jammed into the bed and he sprawled onto it. He rolled over on his back and stared at the ceiling. The bed seemed to pitch beneath him, and after what could have been minutes or hours, he closed his eyes. Somewhere in the distance a siren wailed. Paul wondered briefly if it was coming for him and tried to raise himself from the mattress. But now that he'd surrendered to the booze and his exhaustion, his limbs felt leaden and wouldn't respond. I'll be fine, he told himself. Then he was asleep.

A few hours later, the cops were at his door. They escorted Paul out of the building where more cops were waiting. When Paul saw them, he flipped out, swinging his arms and trying to run. The cops pinned him to the ground, nearly choking him before hauling him into the station. Paul was locked up inside a windowless concrete room where he slept on the floor. When he awoke, he called out to the attendant.

"What do you want?" the man said.

"I need to get out of here so I can go to work."

Paul worked as a janitor at Corona Pizza and had a shift starting at noon. It was important to him that he get there on time. Theodore Bougiridis, the Greek who owned the restaurant, had taken a chance on him and Paul didn't want to let him down. For some reason, Paul had been straight with Teddy right from the start, telling him about his criminal record. To Paul's surprise, the old guy had offered him a job anyway. Since then, he'd treated Paul with nothing but respect.

Paul couldn't say the same for the prison attendant, who ignored his plea. Furious, he started pounding on the steel door.

"You fucking assholes," he yelled. "I'm a human being just like you."

Paul beat his fists against the door until the tiny hatch in its centre opened and the attendant's face appeared.

"I need you to be quiet," he said.

"I got to be at work."

The attendant regarded him dispassionately and then closed the hatch.

"You want me to steal and rob for a living?" Paul screamed.

"Seems you got no trouble breaking the law," the attendant replied from behind the closed door.

"Go fuck yourself!"

Paul slammed his fist once more into the door. Fuming, he'd paced the room cursing and punching the door. Finally, at about 4:00 p.m., after signing a promise to appear in court later that month on a charge of public mischief, he was released. He'd been taken into custody without his shoes, so he raced back to his friend's apartment to retrieve them and then ran to work. Starving, he'd grabbed something from the kitchen and asked the bartender to pour him a pint to calm his nerves. That's when Teddy saw him.

"You want to come here to drink, but you don't come to work?" he said. "You're fired."

His words were a devastating blow to Paul, who'd liked his job and been proud of the increasing trust Teddy had placed in him. Recently, his boss had let Paul make the night deposit. He loved the people he worked with and the way Teddy and his wife, Donna, treated them more like family than employees. On top of that, Paul had recently fallen for a waitress at the restaurant named Sue Wink.

The next day Paul returned to the police station to provide a statement. He offered to pay for damages if the cops let him off, but by then they had a copy of his criminal record and asked him if he'd be able to help with some thefts that had occurred in recent months.

"Sure," Paul lied, "but I don't know of anyone that's into stolen goods. If I hear anything, I'll let you know."

He left the station wondering how the cops could be stupid enough to think he'd fink on another man. And though Grande Prairie had become the only home Paul had known in his time drifting around the country, he knew he had no choice but to hit the road once more.

ICE

From his icy bed, Scott Deschamps watched Erik collapse. Scott had worried about how long they could hang on and now knew with sinking certainty that time was running out. He couldn't remember the last time he'd prayed, but it seemed like a good time to resume. With the fire's warmth fading, the feeling of vulnerability that had niggled at Scott all night blossomed to full-fledged fear. He looked at Erik lying on the ground and then in the direction of the wreckage where Paul and Larry had long ago faded into the darkness. He closed his eyes and tried to conjure some long-forgotten God.

Please, he pleaded silently, *we're all going to die here if we don't get some heat.*

Moments later, as he lay shivering violently, Scott became aware of a warm yellow glow behind his closed eyelids. He heard the crackle of burning wood and a blessed heat drifted toward him. When he opened his eyes he saw that the remnants of wood had burst into flame.

"Thank you," he whispered.

To his relief, he also saw Paul and Larry approaching down the path. The feeling was short lived. Their hands were all but empty.

The men tossed their meagre findings on the fire and pressed close to the flame, but the heat lasted only a few moments. When it died, it seemed to take the last of their resolve with it.

Hypothermia was making its slow deadly advance on all of them, stealing their warmth by degrees. When it comes to hypothermia, degrees mark the difference between life and death. Once the body's core temperature drops just two degrees below the normal of 37°C, problems begin. Coordination becomes difficult and one's ability to function deteriorates. Everyone but Paul was shivering now, and while it would temporarily help keep them warm, it wouldn't last. Without a fire, the men's core temperatures would continue to fall, their speech would become slurred, and they would grow disorientated. Severe hypothermia would soon set in. Their bodies would experience a complete loss of reflexes followed by coma, ventricular fibrillation and eventually death.

Scott knew what was happening to him. As a ski patroller, he'd studied hypothermia and now recognized its seductive pull; how it lulled its victims from pain and cold to the paradoxical sensation of warmth and comfort that preceded death. For hours he had fought back, willing himself to embrace his pain and the cold—feelings that told him he was alive.

Now as he stared into the extinguished mound of blackened coals, his mind began to turn toward a terrible reality: he was not going to get out of here alive. Thoughts of his wife, Mary, his future, his dreams and ambitions raced swiftly past as if his life was in fast-forward. An image came to him of an old man sitting in a rocking chair on a wide, comfortable porch. He was speaking to a young boy about the things he had not done, the places he had never been, the lessons he had not learned, and the people he would never meet. He counselled the young man as a father would a son, urging him to grasp the opportunities that came his way.

Scott wanted so much more for himself. He realized he wanted to live by the ocean instead of in an isolated northern community. For years he had dreamed of having his own sailboat and exploring the rugged, breathtaking west coast. He wanted to travel the world, to learn another language, to go to university, to run a marathon. Above all, he wanted to have full and loving relationships with his family and friends. Growing up as an only child with few close relatives, Scott realized he had never felt truly connected to anyone. His father, who'd died of emphysema when Scott was eleven, was rumoured to have left a wife and young daughter in Zimbabwe where he'd been stationed during the war. Scott had often wondered about this other family. He had longed to know the truth about it, just as he'd longed for a father's guiding hand to steer him through the confusing years of adolescence and young adulthood. Scott's mother, a working single parent, had had little time for establishing the kind of family life that Scott had longed for.

He regretted upsetting Mary when she'd pushed him on the subject of children. With painful clarity, Scott realized that he *did* want to have a family of his own. Until that moment, he had dismissed the idea of having kids as nothing more than an outdated biological urge. The thought that he would never be a father—never accomplish his dreams—brought a wave of devastating regret that washed over him, pulling him under, submerging him, until he finally accepted the inevitability of his own death.

Defeated by cold, pain and sadness, he opened his eyes. Above him, fog crouched like a heavy beast on the treetops. And then, in the midst of it, there *he* was. Mere feet above where Scott lay, an old man appeared. He had long white hair and a beard. His hands, pale and creased, were folded in his lap and he wore a flowing white gown. The man's face, though heavily lined, was devoid of sorrow or concern. As he stared at him, Scott was filled with profound peace and reassurance, the likes of which he had never experienced. Though not a religious man, Scott knew with utter certainty that he was looking into the face of an otherworldly presence: God, an angel or a benevolent spirit, take your pick. The old man did not speak, but his presence enraptured Scott. Through wide eyes he followed the graceful form as it hovered at the perimeter of the firepit. For the next twenty minutes, the old man kept vigil over the survivors, until, just as suddenly as he had appeared, he was gone.

"Fuck, man, I'm fucking freezing," Paul said.

The others, shaken from their reveries, looked in his direction and saw that the young man—until now seemingly impervious to the cold—was shaking violently. His own deprivations suddenly forgotten, Larry stepped behind him and embraced Paul in a firm bear hug.

Paul's first instinct was to pull away. He thought of his father, a man whose affections he'd longed for, but seldom received. His dad had always felt his oldest son was good for nothing and had told him so on several occasions. Even as a child, he had felt his dad's constant disapproval. As Larry's arms encircled him, it occurred to Paul that few people in his life had given him the degree of affection and unconditional understanding he was receiving in that moment from a near stranger.

After several minutes Paul stopped shivering and Larry let his arms drop.

"What time is it?" Paul asked.

Scott squinted at the face of his watch. "Half-past seven."

"Shit! The ELT."

Scott unfastened the strap of his watch and handed it to Paul, who took it without comment, knowing that the responsibility of toggling the ELT switch was now his alone. He dragged himself down the path toward the plane.

———

At the High Prairie airport, Luella Wood felt sick to her stomach as she left her trailer and made her way across the snowy parking lot to the terminal building. Throughout the night she'd returned every hour or two to check on William Whitehead. The slim, wiry First Nations man sat alone on a couch in the small, darkened lounge area, his back against the armrest, knees tucked into his chest and head bowed. As far as Luella could tell, he hadn't moved a muscle in the ten hours since she'd delivered the news of the downed plane.

Never in her life had she seen such sorrow on a man's face.

The previous evening Whitehead had driven one hundred kilometres south to the airport from the Whitefish First Nations Reserve to pick up his wife, Elaine Noskeye, who was due to arrive on Wapiti Flight 402. Two weeks earlier she'd been rushed by ambulance to the hospital in Edmonton to prematurely deliver the couple's fourteenth child. The infant was in intensive care awaiting surgery, and though Elaine had not been scheduled for release until Monday, she'd missed her family terribly. So the thirty-nine-year-old woman had talked her doctor into letting her go home early to be with her husband and children. That evening marked the first time she had ever flown on an airplane.

Nearby, in High Prairie, a heavy shadow of dread also hung over the tiny, close-knit community. The phone at the RCMP detachment had been ringing off the hook with enquiries and offers of help from local townspeople: farmers, small business owners, concerned citizens and private pilots, all wanting to pitch in any way they could. The local Tags convenience store was delivering free sandwiches and coffee to the airport and police station, and several private pilots were standing by to join the air search as soon as daylight broke around 8:30 a.m.

Hoppy fretted about his officers and the civilian volunteers struggling in the bush. The dense trees, heavy snow and deadfall made the task of clearing a 20-kilometre trail through the wilderness to the crash site next to impossible. Though the men were bone cold and drop-dead tired, they had made progress over the past four hours advancing slowly with the help of the flares that guided them like orange lifelines from above.

In spite of the challenging conditions, however, Hoppy was beginning to think he'd rather be in the wilderness battling the elements than dealing with the shit that had recently started coming his way. He didn't mind the calls of concern from the locals. But word on the crash—including the news that Grant Notley and Larry Shaben were aboard the plane—had leaked to the media and he had news hawks up the hoop. They'd been lighting up all five lines at the detachment and Hoppy had quickly lost patience trying to field their questions. He'd put up a wall, telling staff that he wasn't talking to *anybody* other than search-and-rescue personnel.

In addition to communicating with his officers in the bush, Hoppy had been constantly on the phone with Dave Heggie at the High Prairie airport. Heggie had been keeping him apprised of the military's search-and-rescue efforts and Hoppy knew that the aircraft circling the area weren't having an easy time locating the downed plane. He was deep in discussion with Heggie when across the room he noticed one of his staff gesturing frantically for him to pick up another line. "Sarg . . ." she whispered urgently.

Hopkins held up a finger to silence her so he could hear the latest update on what the military was dealing with. The cloud ceiling at the airport had dropped to less than 50 feet and that ruled out any possibility of an air-rescue attempt until daylight or the weather broke. Now more than ever, Hoppy knew it was vitally important for his ground search crew to get in. He ended his call and looked over at his constable.

"It's the prime minister!" she told him.

Hopkins took the call. Sure enough, it was Canada's head of

government, Brian Mulroney, on the line from Ottawa. He'd met Larry Shaben on at least one occasion and wanted confirmation that he, Notley and the other passengers on board were alive. Hopkins couldn't give it to him.

Aboard the Hercules called in to replace its ailing predecessor, Major Hazen Codner was having a hell of a time. For an hour the second Herc had lumbered blindly through churning fists of grey above the crash site, yet the forty-two-year-old lead navigator had been unable to pick up a signal from the downed plane. Codner, who'd been briefed prior to the Herc's hasty departure from Edmonton at 5:48 that morning, had expected conditions to be a challenge. Crew aboard the previous Hercules had reported that the ELT signal had been in turns intermittently weak and distorted. But Codner hadn't expected it would be non-existent. He was voicing his frustration to the pilot, when the ELT signal inexplicably re-emerged.

Codner immediately got to work plotting a bearing. Though he'd been hurried and half-awake when pressed into action, he was grateful for one piece of good fortune: when he'd grabbed his navigation bag, it happened to contain a topographical map of the area. Now, each time the Hercules passed over the signal and the directional needle swung 180 degrees, Codner manually plotted the position on his map. He'd been at it thirty minutes when the ELT signal disappeared. Codner and the pilot began discussing a possible explanation. Had the battery for the ELT suddenly died? The topo map showed hilly terrain below, which might account for spotty transmission, but not the signal's alternating reappearance and disappearance. The pilot circled the giant Herc once more.

After another half-hour spiralling the area, the ELT signal again reemerged. Codner realized with a jolt that someone below had to be alive and cycling the switch. The crew aboard the Hercules was accustomed to jumping into crash sites and finding only dead bodies. The prospect of survivors on the ground gave them a renewed sense of urgency, and Codner redoubled his efforts to pinpoint the crash location. Staring at the intersecting lines, he was 90 percent certain that the location of the plane was on a high hill west of Slave Lake. He shared his findings with the pilot and suggested he approach the crash site from the northeast, descending low over the wide lake where there were no terrain hazards. Though the cloud deck over Slave Lake was no more than a few hundred feet, dawn was beginning to silver the night and Codner knew that if they could get under the cloud, they might be able to get a visual on the crash site. The five-member crew aboard the Hercules understood the approach was risky. West of the lake, the terrain rose sharply and the pilot would have to ascend steeply to clear the 2,900-foot hill. It was a manoeuvre no by-the-book military pilot would ever attempt, but the crew of Squadron 435 decided to go for it.

Around the guttering fire, the survivors were increasingly desperate for heat. Somewhere far above, beyond the ashen cloud cover, they could hear once again the deep growl of an aircraft circling. Scott, who'd taken part in search-and-rescue operations, knew that when a small plane crashed in an area of dense wilderness like the one they were in, some trees bend and break; others spring back to cover the crash path. Even in daylight, searchers would often see only a faint line of disturbed flora from overhead. The snow, falling heavily, would have rapidly concealed any path that might lead the rescuers to them. He realized that rescuers would *eventually* find the crash site, but would they arrive in time? Vivid in his mind were the images of corpses lying frozen and lifeless in the car wrecks he'd responded to during his time as an RCMP officer in northern Alberta. "Think they see us?" Paul asked.

All night, Paul had been scheming about finding something, anything, he could use to attract the attention of the giant overflying plane. He'd desperately wanted to locate Scott's black briefcase, knowing his gun was inside. Paul figured if he got his hands on it he could fire off a couple of shots and bring the planes circling back. Earlier, he'd even suggested making a roman candle out of one of the fuelladen wings, but Erik, afraid that the fire might spread and gut the fuselage, had stopped him. Now Paul had not only run out of ideas on how to attract attention, but had given up on the campfire as well. To his left, Erik lay silent and unmoving. Paul reached over and grabbed his leg, giving it a shake.

"If we can't see them, they can't see us," Erik mumbled.

Paul felt like screaming at the top of his lungs: *We're alive! We're here!* But he knew it was no use straining.

After a moment Erik spoke again. "My wallet. It's still in the plane."

The others couldn't understand why Erik's wallet should suddenly be so important. They didn't know that, at that moment, he was contemplating his death. Without his ID, the pilot worried that authorities would not be able to identify his body.

Larry stood shivering, as cold as he could ever remember being. He was effectively blind, his ribs and tailbone fractured, his front teeth missing, and his right index finger broken. His hand was buried deep in the pocket of his suit pants. Gently, he closed it around his own wallet, a gold clip that held his ID cards and money. He pulled out the clip and removed the thick fold of bills. Slowly, he let them flutter down toward the smoldering coals. The money ignited into a small flame and Larry watched it flicker for a moment until it died, the corners of the bills curling black before floating away. He surveyed the inert forms of his fellow survivors lying at his feet.

"If you had one wish you could have fulfilled right now," Larry asked, "what would you wish for?"

"I'd like a nice toke of good pot," Paul replied.

Larry laughed. There were countless times during his children's teenaged years when he'd counselled them on the evils of marijuana. He wondered what his kids would say if they could hear the conversation.

"I'd love a cold drink," Erik said. That response surprised Larry until he recalled that the pilot had been complaining of thirst for much of the night, incessantly consuming handfuls of snow to slake it.

"Scott?" Larry asked.

Scott had been thinking of Mary, who'd been beckoning him to follow her into the warmth and comfort of a long tunnel.

"I'd tell my wife I'm sorry," Scott said, "and that we can have a child and make this thing work."

Larry let Scott's words hang in the air a moment before he said, "I'd like a nice warm bath."

The closer they all inched toward death, the simpler their needs had become, Larry thought.

After a moment, Scott spoke again. "I don't think I can hang on much longer."

Paul had been thinking the same thing—that he should just let himself go to sleep, to die where he lay. But admitting the thought made him mad as hell.

"Fuck this!" he said, clambering to his feet. "You're not going to die," he told Scott. "I'm walking out of this and you three are coming with me because we weren't meant to die this way. When this is all over we're going to get together and have a few drinks. C'mon," he urged Larry, "there must be something else we can burn."

The politician wearily followed Paul away from the firepit toward the wreckage. The sky had lightened a shade and for the first time,

Larry could distinguish the blurry lines of the scene around him. As they trudged past the fuselage Larry spotted two dark forms against the snow.

"What's that?" he asked.

Paul told him that it was the airplane seats he'd tossed out of the plane the night before. Scott had assured the men that the seats were inflammable, but they decided to haul one back to the fire and try burning it. When they did, the seat ignited like a torch and huge tongues of white-hot flame immediately shot into the air. Larry yelped as one of them singed his head. "I've burned my hair off."

Paul looked at him quizzically and smiled. As far as he could see, Larry didn't have much hair to burn.

"I'm burning up," Scott yelled out. "It's too hot!"

Paul rushed to his side, drawing Larry's coat up over Scott's head to shield him from the heat. Still Scott protested and Paul began dragging him away from the fire.

"Stop!" he cried out in pain. "Leave me where I am."

Paul let him go. "Scott, do you know that you're a sniveller? You're either too hot or too cold."

Scott ignored the jibe and lay back, waiting for the pain to subside. For fifteen minutes the seat burned brightly, infusing the survivors with welcome warmth. They agreed to save the second seat to make a signal fire, but were soon so cold that Paul shuffled back down the path for the other seat, stopping first at the plane to flip the ELT switch.

Two thousand feet above the men, the Hercules picked up the signal. By the time Paul was wearily hauling the second airplane seat back to the fire, the Hercules was circling back over Lesser Slave Lake's 1,000-square-kilometre expanse, and heading in the direction of Codner's high hill. Strapped in at the rear, Corporal Claude Castonguay, the loadmaster aboard the second Hercules, prepared to open its massive airdrop ramp. As the Herc closed the distance to the distress signal, the pilot slowed the plane's airspeed to 170 knots. Snow and wind buffeted Castonguay as he leaned out, straining to see through the cloud. The pilot eased the yoke forward, steadily descending toward the lake. Finally, at the hair-raisingly low above-ground altitude of just under 200 feet, the Herc broke below the cloud deck, so close to the lake's ebony surface that its crew could see the rugged ridges of wind-whipped water. The plane roared across it with Castonguay hanging suspended above the open ramp. Reaching the southwestern shore of the lake, the pilot began pulling up sharply to clear the approaching hill. The enormous aircraft strained to ascend, vibrating with exertion. Cloud, a thick grey robe above them, began to engulf the Hercules as it crested the hill. The nose of the plane had already disappeared into the murk and the rest was quickly being swallowed when Castonguay yelled out, "Campfire on the ground!"

A cheer erupted among the crew. It was echoed on the ground—at the forward command base in Slave Lake and the Rescue Coordination Centre in Edmonton, in the tiny trailer at the High Prairie airport where Dave Heggie sat monitoring the plane's VHF transmission, and across several land and air radio receivers where others had been anxiously listening.

Within the close confines of Luella's trailer, Heggie sagged with relief. When the Hercules had zeroed in on a high hill west of Lesser Slave Lake, he had feared the worst. If Wapiti's plane had slammed into it nose-first, chances of anyone surviving would have been slim. Heggie was simultaneously astonished and overjoyed to hear news of the campfire. Over the radio, he could hear the crew aboard the Hercules requesting permission for jumpers to paradrop into the site.

The forward base commander refused. Major Dewar knew the visibility was too poor and the terrain too dangerous for jumpers to safely get in.

Heggie picked up the phone to call Hopkins. For the past eight hours, he had delivered nothing but bad news about the military's air search-and-rescue efforts. Now, as he told Hoppy about the campfire, Heggie's voice was filled with optimism.

Hoppy, too, had reason to be optimistic. According to his men on the ground, the search party was within several kilometres of the crash site. The survivors just had to hang on an hour or two more until they could get there.

RESCUE

In the early dawn gloom of Saturday, October 20, 1984, Paul Archambault stood inside the destroyed Piper Navajo airplane. Though he'd been longing for the light of day, he now wished that it was still dark. In daylight, he saw everything in gruesome detail.

Tentatively, he touched the arm of one of the dead passengers. It was cold and clammy and felt like snakeskin. The man's eyes were half-open, his face swollen. An orb of ice the size of a racket ball hung from his mouth.

Paul reached into his pocket and pulled out Erik's camera. He couldn't say why, but somewhere deep in his subconscious, he knew he needed to record this event. He took a couple of pictures of the deceased and was backing out of the plane when something vaguely familiar caught his eye: his duffle bag. He opened it and riffled through his meagre belongings, pulling out the only things he cared about: a couple of photographs of his family and his wallet, which held his life savings: $66.35. He stuffed the wallet and photos into his pockets, threw the duffle bag over his shoulder, and was about to return to the fire when he saw a small, dark object half-hidden under the snow near the rear of the fuselage. Moving closer, he recognized it as Scott's briefcase. Paul yanked the briefcase free and tried to open it, but it was locked. He shook it and could hear the clunk of the heavy gun inside. Clutching the briefcase, Paul made his way back to the firepit, where he distributed articles of his clothing to Erik and Larry.

Scott was only dimly aware of the fact that Paul had been gone for a long time when someone shook him. He opened his eyes to see Paul's face leaning close.

"I found your briefcase."

Scott studied his prisoner uncertainly, and then watched as Paul placed the briefcase at his side. Scott focused briefly on Paul's face, and then his gaze moved past it to the trees beyond. Everything appeared stark in the gentle light. The dense fog that had once obscured even the tops of the bare alder trees had brightened. Paul's voice came to him as if from far away describing the gruesome scene inside the wreckage. Scott couldn't respond, and at that point he didn't care about the dead. He was having enough trouble keeping himself alive.

Somewhere to his right, out of his line of sight, was Erik. Scott had no idea whether he was alive or dead. Scott slid his gaze to his left and saw Larry on the ground curled into a fetal position, his clothing dusted white with snow and his eyes closed.

"Larry!" Scott's voice came out in a cracked whisper. "Larry, wake up!"

Larry groaned and moved a bit. His lids fluttered open and he stared blankly ahead. He'd been thinking of home, his wife, and his children. Unlike his fellow survivors, Larry knew his home was nearby, mere miles away. The frustration of being so close tore at him. As Scott regarded him, he saw the expression on Larry's face change.

"I hear noise in the bush!"

Larry struggled painfully to his feet, his head cocked to one side.

Scott listened too, but could hear nothing save the sound of a plane's engine far above.

"You must be stoned or something," Paul said.

"I'm going to walk out and get help," Larry told the others. He was sure he'd heard the sounds of snowmobiles in the distance.

"We're going to be found here, so we stay together," Paul said.

Larry was adamant. He was tottering away from the firepit when Paul pulled him back, reminding the older man he couldn't see a foot in front of him and even if he could, if he left the crash site and got lost in the bush, no one would ever find him. Erik and Scott added their voices of opposition and Larry eventually relented.

Scott worried that Larry, like him, was so hypothermic that he was losing his ability to think clearly.

"We really need some help, Old Man," Scott whispered aloud. "We're not going to last much longer."

At 8:30 that morning, Canadian Forces Base Edmonton, expecting a break in the weather, dispatched a Twin Otter to try and get under the clouds. Just a minute later, its pilot got word that the Hercules had spotted a campfire on the ground. Hopes were now high that the small plane would be able to get a visual on the crash site. Major Dewar recalled the Chinook helicopter crew and SAR Techs, all of whom had gone to a local hotel to get some sleep.

Just after 9:00 a.m., as Scott was gazing skyward he saw a small patch of blue sky open in the dense fog above him. As he stared at it, a yellow plane suddenly soared across the opening like a bright, beautiful bird. He said a silent thank you to the Old Man for answering his prayers.

The plane disappeared momentarily as it banked and circled back toward the opening. By the time it reappeared, Larry and Paul were on their feet yelling and madly waving articles of Paul's clothing in the air. The plane veered sharply right, radically changing course. This time it arced tightly back toward the opening and as it passed overhead just above the trees, the men saw the plane tipping its wings to wave to them. And as clear as the blue sky above them, they could see the face of the pilot looking down.

In the town of Slave Lake, Brian Dunham and the rest of the Chinook crew had raced back to the airport, arriving just as the second Hercules touched down. Two SAR Techs jumped off to join Dunham's team on the Chinook. They were all aboard preparing for takeoff, when the pilot of the Twin Otter radioed to say he'd sighted the downed plane and four people around a blackened campfire. With the confirmation of survivors, search-and-rescue efforts ramped into high gear. By 9:12 a.m. the Chinook helicopter carrying Dunham, three other SAR Techs and a five-member medical team was aloft and rapidly closing in on the crash site.

On the northwest side of the high hill just below the survivors, a group of cold, exhausted RCMP officers and volunteers were clearing the final kilometre of bush separating them and the crash site, and reported seeing the Chinook roar through the nearby ravine. Over the two-way radio he'd been monitoring for nearly twelve hours, Hoppy could hear one of his men exclaim: "Jesus Christ! That chopper just flew *below* us."

Inside the Chinook, Billy Burton peered intently down into the whitewash of solid cloud. It had been just after midnight when the rookie SAR Tech had dragged his weary body out of bed. Late the previous evening, Burton had returned to base after being away on a two-week training operation in British Columbia. Exhausted, he'd planned to sleep long into the next day. Instead, he'd been awakened by a call saying he was needed on an urgent mission. He'd pulled on the same soiled orange flight suit he had stepped out of only two hours earlier, and headed in to work. When he got there, the 6′3″, 220-pound keener learned that he was to be deployed on a search-and-rescue mission responding to a major air disaster. It was Burton's first big mission and he was excited to get a chance to do the job he'd trained for.

As the Chinook approached the crash site, Burton saw a small clearing appear as if a piece of the sky had suddenly punched a perfect hole through the unbroken cloud deck. Among search-and-rescue personnel, such openings are called *sucker holes* because they can draw an aircraft into an area of seemingly benign weather, only to have bad weather close around them. The pilot of the chopper quickly altered course and flew directly toward the open window of sky. Burton strained forward as the plane neared the hole, and soon he was peering down upon a white landscape slashed black with trees. Among their stark, leafless branches appeared to be a large blue canoe.

Burton's first thought was: *That's strange.* He was trying to figure out why on earth a canoe would be in the middle of the wilderness. Then it hit him: it was *not* a canoe, but the upturned fuselage of a small airplane. His heart thumped crazily in his chest.

Soon the chopper was hovering over the site, its massive twin rotors blowing a whitewash of snow from the surrounding trees. The pilot quickly realized that the dense brush and deadfall would make landing impossible and took up a stationary position a hundred metres away from where the survivors were huddled to avoid catching them in the Chinook's fierce downwash. Team Leader Brian Dunham had already strapped on his harness and grabbed his snowshoes, a portable radio and a penetration kit in preparation to be lowered to the ground. Beside him, the other SAR Techs were following suit, gathering snowshoes and oxygen and medical kits, and preparing the extraction kit for lowering so they'd be ready to face whatever they might find on the ground.

Dunham clipped the winch hook to his harness. He received his safety check, moved toward the open door at the front of the chopper, and took slack from the cable. Peering down, he scanned for hazards on the ground directly below—an area of operational risk known as the *death zone*. Ahead at ten o'clock, he could see the upturned plane, and beneath him, partially obscured by blowing snow, a gnarl of brush. It wasn't much of a lowering site, but it would have to do.

With a Chinook flying as heavily loaded as this one, and hovering at a dangerously low altitude of 75 feet, he needed to be able to cut away quickly from the suspended cable when he hit the ground so he could rapidly put distance between himself and the helicopter. Dunham waited for the flight engineer to give him the thumbs-up and when he did, a crewman began lowering Dunham to the ground. As he neared it, he braced for a shock. The tips of a Chinook's rotors move at supersonic speed, building up a tremendous amount of static electricity and, as the first man to touch down, Dunham knew that he was going to get whacked. What he didn't realize was how severely. As he released from the cable and dropped to the snow a jolt blasted him a foot in the air. He came down hard on his back and for half a minute lay immobile, his limbs buzzing hot and unable to function. By the time he came to his senses and staggered to his feet, another SAR Tech was beside him and a third on the way down. They strapped on their snowshoes and approached the campfire, advancing with difficulty through the heavy brush and snow.

Seventy feet beyond the smashed fuselage, Dunham could clearly see the small campfire. He took in two men standing around the melted pit of snow and two more lying within it, their faces caked with dried blood. A middle-aged olive-skinned man in an ill-fitting trench coat called out to him almost at once.

"Forget about us," he said, indicating himself and the scruffy, younger man beside him. "The guys on the ground need your help."

Dunham was in triage mode and the man's words sent him sailing straight to the most severely injured.

"You don't by any chance have a Thermos of coffee in your pack?" the scruffy man asked.

"Sorry, I don't," Dunham replied.

The SAR Techs assessed the survivors quickly, and then raced across the thigh-deep snow to the aircraft. As Dunham neared the wreckage he shook his head in disbelief that *anyone* had survived. The mass of metal before him was barely recognizable. It had no nose or wings, and the right front quadrant of the plane was completely mangled. Dunham entered the open hatch and sucked in his breath. Four passengers lay dead inside. He retreated, circled around to the forward part of the cabin, and crawled inside where he found two more deceased. The top of one passenger's skull had been sheared away and another person had been impaled. Dunham took a minute to collect himself, then he was on the portable radio reporting his grim findings: 6 Black, 4 Red.

In search-and-rescue terms, *red* refers to survivors requiring immediate treatment and evacuation; *black* refers to the dead. As Dunham was relaying his information, civilian aircraft traffic overhead was becoming an issue. The Twin Otter pilot's initial report sighting survivors on the ground had spread to others monitoring VHF channel 122.8, and soon several media outlets had planes circling the area in hopes of a getting a scoop. Deeming them a hazard to search-and-rescue efforts, the RCMP quickly had the large airspace around the crash site declared a no-fly zone. But as Dunham and his team prepared to hoist survivors aboard the Chinook, one important question remained on the minds of everyone who had heard news of survivors on the ground: who were the lucky ones?

In her High Prairie home, Alma had retreated upstairs with her three youngest children to escape the throng of townspeople in her kitchen and living room, and the media assembling on the street beyond the driveway. She, too, had received word of four survivors at the crash site. It was almost 10:00 a.m. and her sons, Larry and James, and daughter Joan had just arrived from Edmonton. At daybreak, the Alberta government's chief pilot, John Tenzer, had sent word that it was safe to leave for High Prairie and the kids, along with Bob Giffin and Hugh Planche, had boarded the government's nine-seat King Air for the flight. The plane made it only as far as Slave Lake, High Prairie still being too weathered in to land. So Alma's kids borrowed a car from a local automotive dealer and drove the remaining 100 kilometres home.

Giffin and Planche, meanwhile, remained at the Slave Lake airport anxiously awaiting the arrival of the four survivors who were going to be brought there for transfer to the waiting Hercules, which would fly them to Edmonton.

Around the same time the government plane left Edmonton, Sandra Notley was in the motel's coffee shop when she was paged to answer an urgent phone call. One of her husband's aides told her that Grant's plane had crashed near High Prairie the night before. But there was reason to hope. The downed plane had been found and four people spotted alive on the ground.

"I remember thinking to myself that it would be a lot of upset having to go back and forth to the hospital because I was just so sure Grant was one of the survivors," Sandra recalled. "Then I thought maybe they hadn't even been hurt badly enough to need to stay in the hospital." The local RCMP offered to drive Sandra to Fairview. When she arrived, her three children had already heard of their father's death. Sandra's twenty-year-old daughter, Rachel—now an NDP member of the Alberta Legislature—was the one to tell her mother the terrible news.

"I think she suspected because the Mounties had turned off the radio," Rachel said.

In the melee of the rescue scene, Paul stood with a space blanket draped over his shoulders, puffing furiously on a cigarette he'd bummed from one of his rescuers. Above, an enormous helicopter was kicking up one hell of a whiteout, and the deep *whop whop whop* of its two giant rotors rang in his ears. As he watched Erik being hoisted into the air, Paul wondered fleetingly if he'd be on the news and what his folks on the other side of the country would say if they saw their long-absent son on TV. He was fucking freezing and ready to get the hell out of here. As he waited impatiently for the rescuers to splint Scott before hoisting him to the chopper, Paul took out the pocketknife he'd found inside the plane and began to fidget. Seeing this, Scott called him over.

"What are you doing with that knife? Get rid of it."

Paul tossed the knife into the snow and noticed Scott's briefcase. Grabbing it, he handed it to one of the rescuers.

"He can't forget this because his gun and handcuffs are inside."

The rescuer gave Paul a puzzled look before taking the briefcase from him. Then Scott disappeared into a cloud of blowing snow.

Next, the medics bundled Larry into a casualty bag, zipping it up over his head. As he waited for the Chinook to lower the winch cable, Larry called out to Paul. "Can you open this up so I can see what's happening?"

A smile cracked Paul's bloodied face. The old guy hadn't been able to see all night, so why should it matter now? Paul obliged him anyway.

The chopper had momentarily broken from its overhead hover, but moved in once more, its blades thrumming powerfully, generating another fierce downwash. A rescuer yelled to Paul to get down on his hands and knees and cover up. Paul grudgingly complied, but the hoist seemed to take forever and, frozen and fed up, he felt his patience snap. He stood up, threw off his blanket and was walking away from the blizzard of blowing snow when a rescuer hauled him back. The man strapped Paul into a harness and hooked them together onto the winch cable.

At 11:25 a.m., fifteen hours after the crash of Wapiti Aviation Flight 402, Paul Archambault, the final survivor, was lifted into the air. Above him the rotors throbbed with a deafening pulse and below him the crash site disappeared in a white uproar of swirling snow. Paul was cold, sore and hungry, but at that moment he couldn't have cared less.

"It was the greatest feeling in the world," he would later write.

Erik Vogel, as a twenty-one-year-old bush pilot, sits atop a C-185 "taildragger" while flying for Simpson Air in the Canadian north.

Larry Shaben shakes Premier Peter Lougheed's hand during the swearing-in ceremony at the Alberta Legislature in 1975. Larry's personal copy of the Koran sits on the table.

The Shaben family in the backyard of their High Prairie home, 1979. Carol Shaben is in the centre.

A Chinook helicopter hovers above the crash site. To the right is the "blue canoe," the upturned belly of the plane. To its left is the blackened firepit around which survivors spent the night. Right of the firepit are two SAR Techs who, having just finished recovering the bodies of the deceased, prepare to be hoisted aboard the Chinook.

A previously unpublished photo of the downed airplane. The open hatch and broken window through which Paul Archambault escaped are on the right.

Wapiti Aviation's crashed Piper Navajo Chieftain after being turned upright. Erik Vogel was seated in the forward left or pilot's seat, and Larry Shaben in the seat directly behind him. The passengers in the other seats visible did not survive the crash.

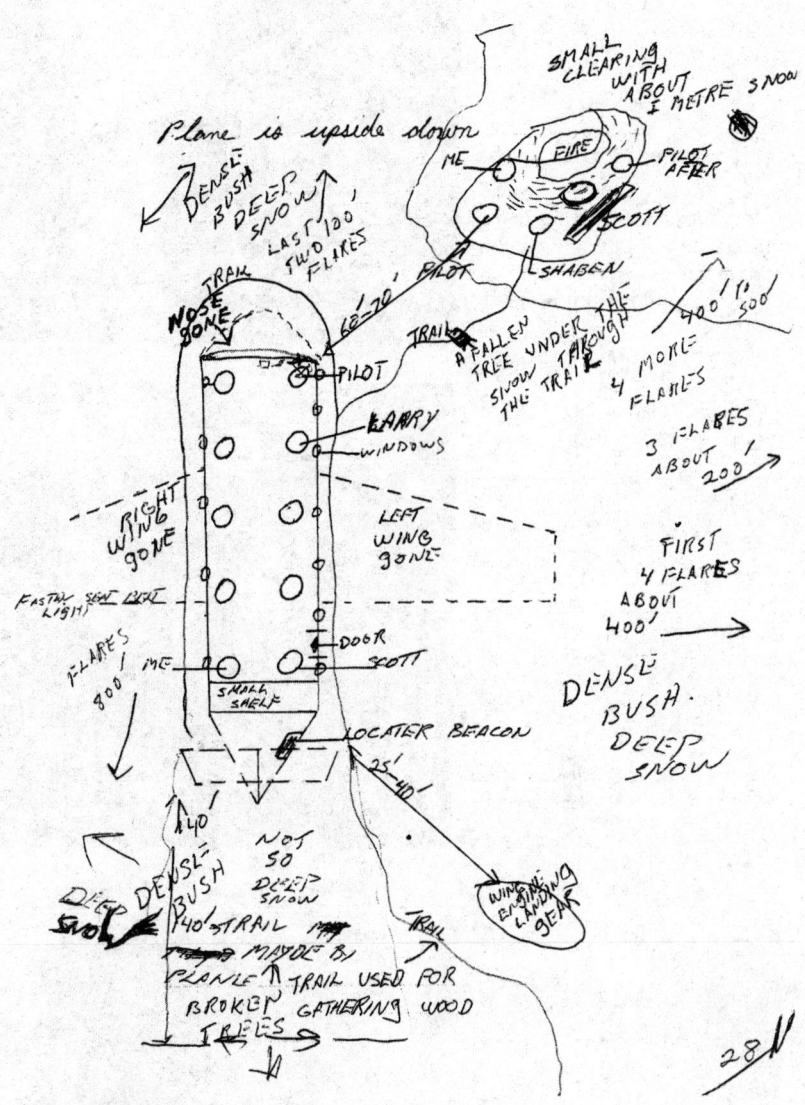

Paul Archambault's hand-drawn map of the crash site from his unpublished manuscript, "They Called Me a Hero," 1985.

Scott Deschamps being transferred to a waiting Hercules in Slave Lake for transport to an Edmonton hospital.

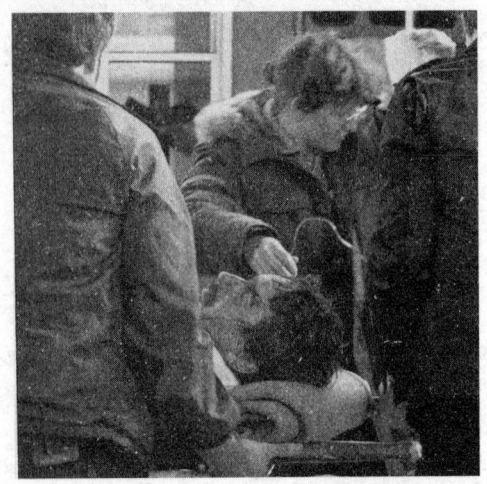

Erik Vogel shortly after his rescue.

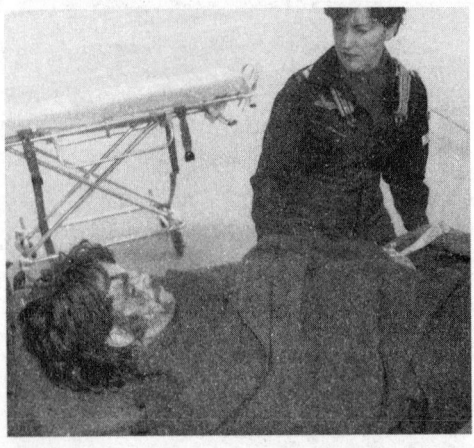

Paul Archambault is taken from the Chinook helicopter on its arrival in Slave Lake.

CBC reporter Byron Christopher interviews Paul Archambault outside the Grande Prairie courthouse following his exoneration on October 22, 1984. Under Paul's arm is a garbage bag containing his life's possessions.

Paul Archambault at the Canadian Aviation Safety Board inquiry into the crash at Grande Prairie's Golden Inn on February 26, 1985. Fellow survivors recall him clutching his unfinished manuscript entitled "They Called Me a Hero."

Larry Shaben and Paul Archambault enjoy a cigarette together during a break in the crash inquiry proceedings.

Paul Archambault (standing) poses for the cameras next to Erik Vogel during the 1985 Canadian Aviation Safety Board crash inquiry.

The survivors together at the Canadian Aviation Safety Board inquiry for the first time since the crash. Left to right: Erik Vogel, Scott Deschamps, Paul Archambault, Larry Shaben.

Scott Deschamps looks on as Paul Archambault receives his lifesaving award in Grande Prairie on March 1, 1985.

Paul Archambault and Sue Wink in Grande Prairie during happier times, 1985.

Erik Vogel (left) and Scott Deschamps at the start of their five-day hike of the West Coast Trail, 1985.

Scott Deschamps and his half-sister, Joanne Deal, in front of Scott's home during her only visit to Canada, 1998.

Erik Vogel at the fire hall in his early days as a firefighter. Back row, left to right: Tom Chapman, Kris Andersen, Erik Vogel (centre), Norm King, John Titley. Seated, left to right: Captain Bob Zetterstrom, Lieutenant Brian Davis.

Erik Vogel (right) and fellow West Coast Air pilot Brent Mclean on the float of a de Havilland DHC-6 Twin Otter during Erik's final days as a commercial pilot.

The author at her home with the survivors on their twenty-year reunion in October 2004. Left to right: Erik Vogel, Larry Shaben, Carol Shaben, Scott Deschamps.

PART IV

As you go the way of life you will see a great chasm.
Jump.
It is not as wide as you think.

NATIVE AMERICAN PROVERB

HERO

For Brian Dunham, the Wapiti search-and-rescue mission and its unlikely assortment of survivors was one of the strangest and most memorable in his twenty-five-year career as a SAR Tech. After Dunham hoisted the four survivors aboard the Chinook, Dr. Kenneth Betts, the military medical officer, tended to their injuries. The doctor had quickly assessed the two men who had been hauled up on stretchers—Erik and Scott. What Betts found wasn't good. The pilot had a potentially life-threatening collapsed lung and a head injury, in addition to having lost a lot of blood. Scott had blunt chest trauma and hypothermia, and was in extreme pain. Larry had broken ribs and a probable compression fracture of his spine, while Paul appeared only scraped up. Betts radioed Slave Lake, requesting immediate transport of the four survivors to Edmonton for further assessment and medical treatment. Word came back quickly that the Hercules was refuelled and standing by to fly the men south.

Hearing this, Larry insisted that he not be sent to Edmonton, so the medical team on the chopper decided that he and Paul, having more minor injuries, would be admitted to hospital in Slave Lake. Paul, who had been reclining in the back of the Chinook, sat up. "I have to be with Scott," he said. "Wherever he goes, I go."

"Why?" Dr. Betts asked.

"I'm a prisoner in his custody," Paul replied.

Betts regarded Paul skeptically and then turned to Scott, who nodded. Then he added, "He saved my life."

Just before eleven in the morning, the Chinook descended from the clouds over Slave Lake like a noisy, inelegant bird. By the time it touched down, a small army of local paramedics and medical personnel was waiting to meet it. So was Bob Giffin. The premier's right-hand man watched intently as medics unloaded two men on stretchers from the aircraft. Both were hooked to intravenous lines, their bloodied faces half-hooded by blankets. Giffin didn't recognize either of them, or the lad on the third stretcher that followed. He moved anxiously toward the helicopter's open ramp and peered inside. There was his old friend, his face battered, hobbled by pain and limping badly but refusing to be offloaded on a stretcher. Larry wanted to step down from the plane under his own steam.

"Larry!" Giffin shouted.

"Bob," Larry replied, "call Alma right away and tell her I'm okay."

Giffin raced to the terminal building. When he reached the Shaben home in High Prairie and asked to speak to Alma, a woman whose voice he didn't recognize asked him to wait. Giffin could hear sombre background conversation. He waited a long time before the woman returned.

"Alma doesn't want to come to the phone." (She later admitted that she'd feared the worst and couldn't bear to take the call.)

"Tell her Larry's okay."

"He's okay!" he could hear the woman shout and then the room exploded in cheers.

Alma didn't cry when she heard the news. She drew her three grown children into a tight embrace. Then the four of them grabbed their coats and, along with close family friends, drove to Slave Lake.

"I walked into the hospital and there he was," Alma recalled. "He had a black eye and scratches all over his face. The media was everywhere, but I didn't see anybody but him."

Larry wrapped his arms around his wife and held on as if he would never let her go.

"The tears came then," Alma said.

But there was no good news for the family and friends of most of the passengers. Several had made their way to the Slave Lake airport in anticipation of the Chinook's arrival. Reporter Byron Christopher was on the scene that day, having jumped a plane from Edmonton as soon as the news of survivors broke. Christopher was standing beside a pay phone in the terminal when two teenage girls burst through a nearby side door.

"Do you have any information on the plane crash?" the older one asked him, her voice desperate.

"Four survived."

"My mother, Pat Blaskovits, was on that plane. Did she make it?"

"I don't know," Christopher told her, though he did. He'd seen the four survivors being taken from the plane and knew that they were all men. But he didn't want to be the one to break the news to the girls, so he directed them to an office at the end of the hallway reserved for the families.

"The girls ran down the hall, knocked on the door and walked in," he recalled. "The door closed. I could hear voices and crying. The girls were in there for only minutes when the door flung open and they ran past me, opened the exit door and ran toward a vehicle in the parking lot. The older girl had her hand to her face. She was sobbing uncontrollably. It was awful to see that. The memory of the two girls running by me crying is locked in my mind as though it happened yesterday."

That scene would repeat itself for several other families, but for none more publicly than the family of Grant Notley.

At the High Prairie RCMP detachment, Marv Hopkins' long night was unfolding into an interminably long day. After fourteen hours supporting and coordinating the ground search crew, his team had broken through the bush to the site shortly after the Chinook left with the survivors. Bone-weary and frozen stiff, they now faced the gruesome task of helping to remove six bodies. Brian Dunham and another SAR Tech had stayed behind to recover the bodies of the deceased and prepare them for transport to High Prairie when the helicopter returned.

Major Dewar had called from Slave Lake to give Hopkins the names of the reds and the blacks and tell him that the latter would be taken to High Prairie for medical examination. Among the dead were two townspeople and four others from neighbouring communities. As if dealing with the devastating impact that the crash would have on the small town wasn't enough, Hopkins had to fend off the crush of media that had descended on his detachment. He'd refused to talk to them while the search was underway, but now that the plane had been found reporters hounded him incessantly for any scrap of information. Phone lines were lighting up, all five ringing steadily, but Hoppy was determined not to release any information until the deceased's next of kin were notified.

Then he got a call from NDP MLA Ray Martin, frantic for news of Notley. The two men were much more than political colleagues; they were best friends, each man having stood up for the other at his wedding. As far as Martin was concerned, that made them family. Hoppy explained that he wasn't at liberty to give out the information, but Martin insisted. In the background, Hoppy could hear the hushed din of voices—party faithful and political colleagues, he would later learn, who had gathered at the Alberta Legislature to await the news.

"As deputy leader of the party, I need to know," he remembers Martin saying. "Political arrangements will have to be made."

Hoppy hesitated.

"Was he killed or wasn't he?" Martin pressed.

"For your information only," Hoppy said, his voice halting, "he passed away."

"Grant's gone," he heard Martin cry out, and a chorus of grief erupted around him.

The news spread with the force of a hurricane. Soon radio and television stations were awash with reports that Alberta's iconic, long-time government opposition leader had been killed. The story of the crash tore across the nation and then spread to the international wire services where it was picked up by newspapers from the *New York Times* to the *Jerusalem Post*.

That's how I learned of it.

The summer I turned twenty-two, I left Canada for an educational tour through Jordan, Israel and the Occupied Palestinian Territories. At the end of five weeks—on the morning the group of fourteen Arab American university students with whom I'd been travelling left for New York—I stood on the front step of the Jerusalem YMCA and waved goodbye. The previous day, I'd spontaneously landed a job at a local news agency. I had no idea where I was going to live or how I would get by on the US $200 a month salary I'd been promised, but naïve and idealistic, I didn't care.

I lost some of that blitheness during the next three months as I experienced military occupation first hand, but the fragility of life didn't truly hit home until the morning I picked up the *Jerusalem Post* and read a tiny news item about a Canadian commuter plane crash near my hometown 10,000 kilometres away. Seeing my dad's name at the end of the article was beyond surreal. I read the story a second time, suppressing a bubble of hysteria rising in my chest. The words were there in black and white: my father was one of four men who'd survived a plane crash in which six others died.

Two months would pass before I could get time off from my job to go home for Christmas. That delay was excruciating. I called my family every Sunday, always asking to speak to my dad—to reassure myself that, yes, he was alive. On the phone, he was always calm and comforting, as if life was as it had always been.

Except it wasn't. Had I been able to follow the headlines that dominated the local and national newspapers after the crash, I would have known that it had forever changed many lives. Though Grant Notley's death commanded most of the media's attention in the early days, another story began to emerge from the whisperings of those close to search-and-rescuers' efforts: how an accused criminal aboard the plane had allegedly saved the life of his RCMP escort and the two other survivors.

Immediately following the crash the man at the centre of the story was under guard in Edmonton's Royal Alexandra Hospital. Paul had been cleaned up, X-rayed, given a change of clothes, fed, and admitted for observation. He'd even been permitted to stop in at Scott's room to return his watch before being taken to a private room on the third floor of the hospital. A warden from the Edmonton Remand Centre came to see Paul, and after questioning him, left him in the company of a guard. The two men were alone in the room when the guard pulled out a pair of shackles.

"Is that really necessary?" Paul asked.

"It's the policy."

Paul was furious.

"How fucking stupid," he would later write. "I crash in a plane. I help others stay alive until rescue arrives. Point blank, I went through a very traumatic experience and I had to be chained to my bed like an animal."

That same afternoon, as my dad was being bundled into an ambulance to be transferred from the hospital in Slave Lake to the one in High Prairie, the media had swarmed. One of the reporters congratulated him on surviving his ordeal, suggesting he had been heroic.

"No," he corrected him. "Archambault is the hero. He saved Deschamps' life."

That evening the chief of police paid Paul a personal visit and offered his congratulations on a job well done. Later, on a trip downstairs with his guard for a smoke, Paul was sought out and thanked by Scott's wife, Mary, who had just flown in from the west coast.

On Sunday, October 21, Paul awoke stiff, sore and still shackled to his bed. The only good thing he remembered about that morning was the shot of Demerol he'd managed to persuade the doctor to give him. It softened the edges of his pain and made him feel better than any pot he'd ever smoked. After another examination, the doctor assessed him to be fit for discharge. Paul argued fiercely for another shot of Demerol but the doctor, after a long shrewd stare, shook his head. Soon after, a police guard escorted Paul to the Edmonton Remand Centre. When he arrived, he was immediately searched and stripped of his meagre possessions, including Erik's camera, which he'd stuffed in his pocket. The authorities booked him, handed him prison clothing, and put him in isolation.

Paul was crestfallen. He hated prison and here he was, locked up yet again. He began to think about how short life was and that he needed to *do* something with himself. That night he asked for and was granted a paper and pencil. With it, he began to write the story of the accident. He'd filled five pages when, for some inexplicable reason, he tore them up and flushed them down the toilet.

Back at the Royal Alexandra Hospital, Erik was facing his own ordeal. He was in serious condition when paramedics had wheeled him into the emergency room. Doctors and nurses had fluttered around his bed like ghosts, their faces drawn and serious. Words floated in the air as he drifted in and out of awareness: *internal bleeding, surgery* and *next of kin.* Erik had no idea whether he would survive his injuries or if he wanted to. If he survived, how could he live with the mental anguish over what he'd caused?

Outside his room, journalists hovered like beggars waiting for a handout. Erik was semiconscious and alone when a nurse leaned over his bedside to speak softly to him.

"There's a guy in the waiting area and he wants to see you," Erik remembers her telling him.

Erik looked at her quizzically. His parents had not yet arrived from the west coast and he had no family to speak of in Edmonton.

"He won't go away," the nurse told him, adding that the man had said he was a friend.

Erik could only nod his head weakly before closing his eyes. When he opened them, a familiar face slowly came into focus. It was Duncan Bell.

Duncan took Erik's hand and held it so long that Erik felt uncomfortable.

"I know what happened," Duncan told him. "I figured that if anybody needed someone who understands what they're going through right now, it's you."

Erik was overwhelmed, though at first Duncan's presence seemed a bitter irony for the young pilot who had felt little sympathy for Duncan's mistake two years earlier.

Duncan stayed with Erik the rest of the day and most of the night. At one point, as he surveyed Erik's battered body, he joked, "You're going to have the same scars that I do."

Duncan's understanding became an immeasurable comfort, and his unconditional acceptance helped strengthen Erik for the terrible onslaught that would follow.

On Monday, October 22, Paul awoke in lock-up. Completely isolated, he had no idea that the crash was dominating national headlines. *Notley Dead*, proclaimed one newspaper. *Party Leader and Five Others Killed in Plane Crash*, read another. *Town Devastated*, stated a third. The official account of the dead:

GRANT NOTLEY, 45, a thirteen-year elected representative of the Alberta government, husband of Sandra Notley and father of three

CHRISTOPHER VINCE, 30, a personnel administrator with the Alberta government's department of Social Services and Community Health, who had recently moved to the north from Calgary with his young wife, Frances

ELAINE NOSKEYE, 39, of the Atikameg Reserve, wife of William Whitehead and a First Nations mother of fourteen

GORDON PEEVER, 33, director of finance for the Alberta Vocational College near High Prairie, husband to Virginia and a father of six

PATRICIA BLASKOVITS, 51, assistant director of nursing in Fairview, married to Norman and a mother of eight

TERRANCE SWANSON, 28, a recent PhD graduate in plant pathology, who'd just landed his first job with the Department of Agriculture and left behind his two young daughters and pregnant wife, Sally.

Paul knew nothing of the names or identities of the dead, but the images of the battered faces of his fellow survivors were seared into his memory. He was haunted by guilt over the trapped passenger he could not save. And he was angry. That morning Paul demanded to see the warden. A few hours later the deputy warden paid him a visit.

"Why can't I be with the other guys?" Paul asked. "I'm not a rapist or a rat, so why the isolation?"

The deputy warden had nodded thoughtfully and a short time later Paul was transferred to a regular prison cell. He wouldn't stay long. After eating lunch, a police officer arrived to escort him to the airport. He told Paul they would be flying north to Grande Prairie that afternoon and that Paul would finally face the charges that had put him on a plane in the first place. As he walked out of the remand centre, he looked up at a TV screen to see Larry's face on the news. Paul wasn't allowed to stop and watch, so he had no idea that his life was about to drastically change.

Larry Shaben wore a bathrobe and a weary grin. His two front teeth were missing and his face was bruised and swollen as he spoke to reporters in his High Prairie hospital room. After being rescued, Dad had insisted on being transferred to his hometown hospital. On Sunday morning, he finally agreed to meet with the media. What he had to say would add weight to rumours already swirling about the heroic efforts of a prisoner aboard the plane.

"I think most of the credit goes to that young man, Paul Archambault," Dad told reporters. "He saved the mountie's life by getting him out of the plane. Paul Archambault did an outstanding job."

Paul's story would soon capture the imagination of a nation. Reporters chased the police car he was travelling in on the way to the Edmonton airport and besieged him when he arrived there. Dressed in the ill-fitting clothes the hospital had given him after his arrival, Paul shrank as reporters peppered him with questions from all directions.

"Did Grant Notley die on impact or after?" one asked.

"I don't know," Paul answered. "I didn't know anyone other than Scott, my escort."

"Tell us what happened," another demanded. "Would you call yourself a hero?"

"I just did what I thought had to be done," he said. "The thing that bothered me was listening to a man moan until death. I really feel bad that I couldn't get that one person out who was still alive. He lasted hours," Paul added, his pact with Larry and the other survivors forgotten.

As Paul was flying north to face the judge, the Alberta Government was convening in the Legislature. The session lasted only thirty-six minutes and the premier put forward only one motion: that this House stand adjourned until next Friday at 10 a.m. in honour of their deceased colleague. Members from across party lines, some choking back tears as they spoke, paid tribute to Grant Notley and to the three other deceased who were public servants and members of government staff: Mrs. Swanson, Mr. Vince, and Mr. Peever, and to the families of Mrs. Noskeye and Mrs. Blaskovitz. Then the House stood for a moment of silence.

After Paul's plane landed in Grande Prairie, a small cavalcade of media tailed the police car that drove him from the airport to the courthouse. Several reporters had been on the plane with Paul, intent on covering the hero's trial. Paul felt a jumble of fear and nostalgia as he looked out at the city he'd fled. Snow crusted the roads and fields, and the big prairie sky shone bright blue and diamond hard. He stared at the familiar streets, the distant downtown buildings nearby the bars he'd gotten drunk at more times than he could remember, and the river valley where he'd bedded down on warm summer nights. Soon the car approached the centre of the city where the local RCMP detachment, courthouse and other government buildings were clustered. When the car reached the courthouse, it descended a ramp that led underneath the drab, cement building to a service entrance. Ice crackled under the tires as Paul was transported from the brittle brightness of day into dark shadow.

He was led into the courtroom before the judge arrived, and took a seat beside his escort. The room was small but stately, decorated in shades of beige and rust. A wide centre aisle cut through it, leading to the judge's imposing bench. Behind it hung a massive provincial coat of arms on a checkered wall of raised and inset brick. At the front of the room were two counsel tables and a modest seating area where Paul waited nervously. The judge entered and Paul was called forward to the prisoner's box.

Justice Kenneth Staples was in his early forties, with dark brown hair and a gentle, reserved manner. The case before him was highly unusual. The accused had saved the life of his RCMP escort after a plane crash, and had gathered wood and maintained a fire during the night to keep the survivors alive.

Judge Staples listened intently, first to the crown prosecutor who presented details of the case and then to the accused who answered his questions in a soft-spoken voice.

"I was taken with his conduct," Staples would say later. "He wasn't a show-off. He was quiet and respectful."

The judge sat thoughtfully for a moment after the Crown and the accused had had their say, and then asked Paul to step out of the prisoner's box and stand on the floor in front of the bench.

"You are to be highly commended for your conduct," Staples said, then dismissed the mischief charge. He ruled that the time Paul had already spent in custody since his October 15 arrest would serve as his sentence on the charge of failing to appear. The judge then excused him from the courtroom.

Paul Archambault was a free man.

He couldn't believe it. A huge grin split his face as a court worker led him downstairs to collect his personal effects. A woman behind the long front counter handed him a green garbage bag. Inside, he was relieved to find his blue jeans, shirt and jean jacket, which he promptly changed into in a nearby washroom. They smelled something fierce of fire.

His pleasure was short lived. Riffling through his pockets, Paul discovered that his wallet was gone. The Edmonton Remand Centre hadn't returned it when he'd left that morning. He wished to hell he'd hidden it somewhere they wouldn't have found it. Still, as Paul left the provincial courthouse and walked into the bright afternoon sunshine, there was a spring in his step. Outside, a clutch of reporters surrounded him. With cameras rolling and microphones thrust in front of him, Paul found himself once again the centre of rapt attention.

"What are you going to do now?" a reporter asked.

It was a question Paul hadn't had much time to think about. He'd expected to be locked up for awhile. He didn't want to reveal too many details about his life, but he did tell reporters he didn't even have the coins to wash his smoke-smelling clothes. He would have liked to say that he was heading back east to see his mom in Aylmer, but being flat broke, that was out of the question. Plus, there was an outstanding warrant for his arrest in Quebec stemming from the B and E and theft at the golf course he'd worked at the year before.

Though he had no permanent address, Paul kept a post office box in a town just across the Alberta–British Columbia border. Thinking fast, he told reporters that if anyone wanted to find him, he could be reached care of general delivery in Dawson Creek.

"How will you get there?" a reporter asked.

"I'll be travelling the way I like best: thumbing," Paul told them. "That way my feet are on the ground and I like the view."

Paul hung around Grande Prairie for a few days, but his new status as a hero made him uncomfortable.

"It was pretty scary being called that," Paul recalled. "It was hard to walk down the street because everybody would stare at me and it kind of blew me away. Like, one minute they couldn't give a shit who I was and then the next minute I'm something great."

In an interview the day after his exoneration, Paul was blunt with reporters. "I'm going to tell it to you straight. I'm tired of everyone calling me a hero. I didn't do anything different than a whole lot of other people would have done in that situation."

But most people didn't see it that way. Teddy Bougiridis, the owner of Corona Pizza who'd fired him two months earlier, was one of them.

"So you're a hero now, eh?" he said with a happy grin when Paul showed up at his old haunt. Coming from his former boss, Paul didn't mind. It had cut him deeply when Teddy had let him go, and it felt good to redeem himself in Teddy's eyes.

Paul also appreciated the way complete strangers stepped in to help. Shortly after his exoneration, Grande Prairie's *Daily Herald Tribune* established a fund to help him get back on his feet. Within a few days, it had collected $300 from local citizens. But their generous donations weren't enough to keep him in Grande Prairie.

"I wanted some time to get my thoughts together," Paul recalled. Several days later he quietly left the city.

"I'm keeping my plans to myself," was all he would say. "I want to lead my own life. I don't want to get hounded."

One thing Paul did after he left town was visit his uncle, Denis Archambault, a criminal defence lawyer in Prince George, British Columbia. Denis was not only sympathetic to individuals who ended up on the wrong side of the law, but also understood and appreciated his nephew in a way few others did. In his legal work Denis had crossed paths with an innovative psychiatrist by the name of Bennet Wong, a consultant with the government's justice department who helped rehabilitate troubled youth. Wong and his partner, Jock McKeen, had recently opened The Haven Institute, a residential personal development retreat on an island on Canada's west coast. They were reputed to be doing groundbreaking group therapy with people struggling to find their way in the world. Denis suggested Paul enroll in a one-month seminar at The Haven, and offered to foot the bill. Paul agreed.

In the meantime, the story of Paul's heroism continued to prompt financial donations from people across the province, all wanting to help him get back on his feet. This, too, made Paul uncomfortable. He told one reporter that he hoped Albertans who wanted to contribute to a fund for him "won't go crazy." All he needed, he said, was money to keep him going for a month on the island.

"I've got to find out a little more about myself and fix myself up mentally," he said.

Days later, as the cold whip of winter lashed the rest of the country, Paul was aboard a British Columbia ferry heading across the Strait of Georgia en route to Gabriola Island.

INQUEST

Erik Vogel lay in a no man's land between life and death in Edmonton's Royal Alexandra Hospital. Reports of the crash filtered through his semi-conscious brain like dark, slow-moving shadows.

When his parents arrived at his bedside, the first words he remembers his father saying were, "What the hell were you thinking?"

A jetliner pilot who had never experienced the pressure cooker atmosphere common to small commercial carriers, Erik's father couldn't comprehend how his son could have made such a colossal error in judgment. Erik shrivelled at the shame he had brought upon his dad, who had a high profile in aviation circles as well as BC's Lower Mainland municipal politics.

The weight of the grief and pain he had caused his passengers and their families, and the notoriety he'd inflicted on his own, drained Erik. His condition worsened. His fiancée flew in to be at his bedside, and an old school friend, expecting the worst, called to say goodbye.

It seemed to Erik that his future had been shattered beyond redemption. As he drifted in and out of consciousness, he tried to recall the desire for flying that had propelled him toward his terrible fate. Not so very long ago, he had been absolutely certain that it was his destiny to fly. Now, he was equally certain his flying career was over.

As Erik was losing his will to live, events were conspiring to bring him back from the brink. The first arose from a fortunate turn of fate that briefly put Erik and Scott in the same hospital room. Hours after he'd returned from the emergency department, several RCMP officers paid a visit to Erik's bedside to obtain a statement. Weak and guilt-ridden, he'd been prepared to take all the blame and tell them everything that had happened. Scott, lying in the bed next to him, told Erik to keep his mouth shut.

"You don't have to talk to anyone until you get yourself a lawyer," Erik remembers Scott telling him. "They're going to use any statement you make to press criminal charges."

Scott's intervention gave Erik pause. The charges he felt certain the authorities would lay on him might not be a foregone conclusion.

Then he received a phone call from Sandra Notley, who'd heard that the young pilot was in critical condition. Her forgiveness had filled him with gratitude.

The final event was an interaction with investigators from the Canadian Aviation Safety Board, or CASB, who visited Erik sometime during his early days in the hospital. Created by an act of Parliament, the CASB had been operational less than a month. The fledgling safety board owed its existence to Justice Charles Dubin, a prominent Ontario Court of Appeal judge appointed in 1979 as a one-man commission of inquiry on aviation safety in Canada after a series of plane crashes. During his inquiry, Dubin discovered that the Aviation Safety Bureau had destroyed evidence, and he concluded that the agency, deeply rooted within Transport Canada's massive bureaucracy, could not objectively investigate aviation safety when it was also responsible for setting regulations, and for licensing pilots and air carriers. Dubin recommended that the Aviation Safety Bureau be abolished and that an independent tribunal be created to investigate aviation accidents and conduct public inquiries.

The high-profile crash of Wapiti 402 was just what investigators from the newly minted CASB needed to cement their role as an effective and powerful watchdog. And their ace in the hole was Erik Vogel. More often than not in plane crashes involving multiple fatalities, the pilots don't survive. As a result, authorities often conveniently cite pilot error as the cause—a practice referred to in the aviation industry as *blaming the dead guy*. This time, however, the CASB had a pilot who could tell his side of the story.

By Monday, October 22, they had launched an investigation into the crash and a national team of investigators had converged on Erik's hospital bed. What they told Erik during that first meeting made an impact: Transport Canada had known for a year and a half before the crash that Wapiti Aviation had repeatedly violated safety standards. In fact, in August 1984, Dai Griffiths, a Transport Canada inspector, had written a lengthy memo to government authorities about the airline's safety transgressions, based on interviews with three pilots, two of whom had recently been dismissed by Wapiti. The pilots told officials that Wapiti indirectly pressured them to fly in poor weather conditions and that they felt they'd be fired if they didn't complete certain flights. The memo stated: "There is total disregard for regulations, rights of others and safety of passengers. If they persist in this matter of operation for a much longer period we are virtually certain to be faced with a fatality."

With Erik's help, CASB investigators were confident they could not only shut down Wapiti, but also fix Canada's broken aviation safety system.

Erik Vogel had a reason to live.

———

Even with a cause to champion, the weeks and months following the crash were crushingly difficult for Erik. As he found out more details about the passengers he had killed, and news of the crash continued to dominate headlines, his stomach tightened into a fist of guilt and remorse that would not unclench.

After ten days in the hospital, Erik returned to White Rock. By mid-November, the CASB had finished its field investigation of the crash site and written a letter to the highest levels of government requesting special surveillance of Wapiti Aviation. The CASB also announced it would hold a public inquiry, and in January 1986 it subpoenaed its key witness, Erik Vogel. Over the following weeks, CASB investigators inundated him with files and exhausted him with interviews as they began building their case.

A day did not pass when he didn't think about the crash, but the CASB's insistence that the fault lay with Wapiti and with Canada's inadequate aviation safety system gave Erik hope of resurrecting his flying career. That hope was short lived.

"No one wanted anything to do with me," Erik recalled of the bleak months that followed his high-profile accident. He applied for dozens of flying positions both locally and on the other side of the country, the continent, the globe. He sent résumés to carriers as varied as Georgian Bay Airways in eastern Canada, United Airlines in the United States, and obscure operations in the Maldives. Rejection letters arrived one after the other. His only lifeline was the belief that he wasn't solely to blame for what had happened that October night.

In Grande Prairie, Dale Wells was facing his own kind of hell. The night of the crash, it was he who made the difficult phone call to Erik's parents to tell them their son's plane had gone down. Since then he'd barely had a moment to breathe. On Monday, October 22,

1984, Transport Canada inspectors had descended on Wapiti Aviation, sequestering its records and subjecting Dale and his dad to four straight days of interrogation, despite the fact they were still reeling from the devastating impact of the crash. Aviation officials had also released a damning media statement: "The most recent base inspection of Wapiti Aviation was a maintenance inspection conducted October 1, 1984. At that time it was discovered that the Company failed to meet a regular maintenance check on part of its fleet."

If Dale hadn't been so angry, he might have laughed out loud. As far as he was concerned, his planes were all serviceable and the only deficiency inspectors had found during their recent airworthiness maintenance audit was that Wapiti had not conducted the "special" 500- and 1000-hour inspections for some of its fleet. What aviation officials failed to mention was that Wapiti had kept up with all of its required 100-hour inspections, that the company had immediately completed the additional inspections, and that the planes in question had been back in the air within twenty-four hours.

Shortly after the crash Dale had told one of his pilots that he was "surprised Vogel had flown into the ground as he was considered conscientious and a careful pilot." But he hadn't spoken to Erik since the crash and hadn't seen him the day Erik returned to Grande Prairie to get his truck from the yard outside the Wapiti hangar.

As the weeks progressed, Dale felt as if his detractors would settle for nothing less than Wapiti's total destruction. Aviation inspectors surveyed its operations like sharp-eyed raptors, monitoring maintenance activities, scrutinizing Edmonton departures and constantly hassling pilots to produce valid licences, medicals and PPC cards. By early November, one of the victim's families had launched a lawsuit against Wapiti alleging "wanton or reckless operations."

On December 10, three inspectors arrived at Wapiti to conduct a full audit. The results of that days-long ordeal were outlined in a double-registered, special delivery letter, which arrived on Christmas Eve, 1984. In it, Transport Canada notified Dale that they were suspending elements of Wapiti's operating certificate for safety reasons, including the company's right to fly single-pilot IFR, and flights into several northern airports. Dale would also lose his status as chief engineer. But an even more personally devastating result of that year-end audit concerned Dale's father, the man who had literally sold the farm to support his son's dream of building a thriving northern airline. In Transport Canada's estimation, Delbert Wells, Wapiti's president for the preceding fourteen years, "lacked sufficient knowledge of the intricacies of the present operations to permit him to competently discharge his duties as operations manager."

On February 26, 1985, the CASB convened a public inquiry into the crash at Grande Prairie's Golden Inn, a cheerless ten-storey building just a few minutes' drive east along the highway from the airport. Erik was filled with dread as he conferred with James Duke, the lawyer his father had hired to represent him at the proceedings, which took place inside the hotel's large, dome-ceilinged conference room.

Outside that conference room, the three surviving passengers were experiencing entirely different emotions. Larry, Paul and Scott hadn't seen one another since shortly after their rescue, and the joy of their reunion was unbridled. They shook hands and clapped one another on the back. Larry embraced Paul warmly. Paul felt a flush of affection for the two well-dressed men who stood beside him—one his former captor, the other a politician who had vouched for his character. In Paul's hand was a binder containing the initial pages of a handwritten manuscript he'd begun to write during his month at The Haven. The exercise had been a revelation, and had given him the courage to begin changing his life.

One of the vows Paul made while at the retreat was to keep in closer touch with his family. He'd contacted his parents after the crash, and when he got off the island, they'd paid for his visit east. Paul had first flown to Montreal, where his father was living. From there he'd hopped a bus to Ottawa, just 15 kilometres across the provincial border from his hometown of Aylmer, Quebec.

A slim, attractive woman in her mid-fifties, Gayle Archambault sat on the bench of an Ottawa bus station anxiously awaiting her son's arrival. Her short auburn hair was freshly set and she'd carefully applied a half moon of shadow above her blue eyes. She wore a voluminous fur coat and clutched a large black purse primly in her lap. Gayle appeared self-conscious beneath the glare of TV cameras, her bright red lips pursed in a thin line. The media had tracked down Gayle in Aylmer shortly after the plane crash and she'd enthusiastically told reporters when her son would be arriving home. There is no way of knowing whether she felt honoured or annoyed by the media's attention that day, but what is clear is that the minute she saw Paul's bus pull into the bay, she forgot about the cameras. She slid to the edge of her seat in anticipation and when she saw her son descending the stairs of the bus, her eyes lit up and an enormous smile creased her face.

Unaware that reporters and TV cameramen had gathered to witness his homecoming, Paul stepped down unselfconsciously onto the pavement. He was clean-shaven, sporting his typical uniform of blue jeans and a jean jacket, and had a new black duffle bag slung over his shoulder. A camera flash flared. Paul's face briefly registered surprise, and his eyes darted uneasily toward the cameras trained on him and then into the small waiting crowd. When he saw his mother, he ran forward and embraced her. Paul held on for a long time.

The story of his return hit the local news that night. The next day the Aylmer police came knocking on his mother's door. They arrested

Paul on an outstanding warrant dating from September 12, 1983, for allegedly breaking into the pro shop at the Gatineau Golf Club and cleaning $10,000 out of the cash box. The charge was far more serious than the one Paul had recently faced in Grande Prairie, but the judge was equally sympathetic. Though Paul pleaded guilty, the judge sentenced him to just a year's probation without surveillance.

For the first time in many years, Paul felt truly free. He told reporters in an interview after his court appearance. "I feel it could turn my life around. I want to put the past behind me, starting today."

Though his mother desperately wanted her eldest child to settle in Aylmer, he knew his stay would be temporary. It was not just the subpoena to be in Grande Prairie for the crash inquiry that drew him back west, but his feelings for a woman he hadn't been able to get out of his mind.

Inside Conference Room A, seventy people sat shoulder to shoulder in rows of straight-backed, metal-framed chairs. The clamour of voices filled the air and television cameras and media crews dotted the room's perimeter. On the far wall was a bank of large windows across which brown curtains were drawn. Pinned to the centre of them was a large Canadian flag. On a raised platform in front of the flag, three men in dark suits sat like judges behind a long draped table; senior members of the Canadian Aviation Safety Board who had flown in from Ottawa. On the floor facing them, at another long table, sat representatives of the federal departments of Transport and Justice, accident investigators and their legal counsel, Dale Wells with his legal team, and finally, Erik Vogel and his lawyer. It was the first time Erik had seen his former boss since the accident and Erik's stomach was turning cartwheels.

Bernard Deschenes, the inquiry chairman, opened the proceedings, telling the audience that the inquiry was to be a fact-finding mission solely aimed at identifying the safety deficiencies that had led to the accident and making recommendations that might help prevent future reoccurrences. "We will not point an accusing finger at anybody," he said.

After tabling the exhibits and providing a clinical synopsis of the crash, Norm Hull, chairman of the CASB's technical panel, called Erik to the stand. Though he'd gone over details of his testimony half a dozen times with Hull and other members of the panel, Erik's mind felt thick and doughy with stress. He made it through the testimony about his flying experience and the events preceding the flight without difficulty, but Erik faltered when it came to the area of questioning Hull called Accident Flight Segment 3: The Actions and Events from Initiation of Descent to Impact. Sweat trickled from his armpits as he recounted the details of his descent, and his eyes darted to Dale Wells who sat stone-faced at the front of the hearing room, flanked by three lawyers. The men conferred often, and Erik watched them scribbling notes as he spoke. Even to his own ears, his explanation sounded feeble. In truth, Erik's approach into High Prairie that night *was* illegal. If Hull had asked him to justify why he had done it, he would have been hard pressed to give him an answer.

At one point during his agonizing testimony, Erik glanced up into the audience and saw Larry, his brown eyes warm and sympathetic behind large, thick glasses. Larry had never judged Erik and it was clear he was not judging him now. Erik pressed on and at 11:15 a.m., Deschenes called for a five-minute break in the proceedings.

As Erik slouched limply at the witness table, Paul appeared at his side. After a brief hello, Paul leaned in toward Erik as if he meant to speak, his hands on the back of a nearby chair. Erik lifted his eyes questioningly and as he did so, saw a photographer training an enormous camera lens on them. Erik shot Paul a withering look, then stared grimly ahead as a camera flash flared white. To his annoyance, the photograph, staged by the media who'd asked Paul to stand next to him, would be picked up by the wire services and appear in papers across the country the next day.

After a fifteen-minute recess, Erik returned to the stand where Dr. Bryce Hansen, the CASB's expert on the impact of human factors in aviation, took over. Dr. Hansen's line of questioning shone a spotlight on the tense operational atmosphere at Wapiti, drawing out information on the uneasy relations between Erik and company management, Erik's significant weight loss after joining the airline, and finally his chronic state of fatigue. When investigators had interviewed Erik after the crash, they'd quickly determined that stress and fatigue had likely played a critical role in the accident. Though Erik didn't have the benefit of his pilot's logbook to refer to, he'd recounted his punishing schedule in the days preceding the crash, including the unscheduled medivac flight and blown starter, which had forced him to spend a grim night in the refuelling trailer at the Edmonton Municipal airport on October 17. The investigators had questioned him repeatedly on his pre-crash schedule, taking careful notes, which they later transcribed into a preliminary report. Erik had an outline of that report in front of him and frequently referred to it during his testimony.

"Did you have an opportunity to sleep?" Dr. Hansen asked.

"No."

"What time did you finally manage to get away from Edmonton the next day?"

"I believe it was about 10 p.m."

"And what time did you arrive at your residence?"

"It would be after midnight," Erik answered.

"And what time did you retire for the night?"

"I had made a phone call home. I have a fiancée in Vancouver, and I retired after that. Twelve-thirty, one."

"Then your time on duty would have totalled fifteen- or fifteen-and-a-half hours, is that correct?"

"That sounds correct," Erik confirmed.

"And that was following two-and-a-half-hours' sleep?"

"Yes."

"How were you feeling by the time you went to bed that night?" Dr. Hansen asked.

"I was tired," Erik said, adding that he'd let his co-pilot fly the leg back from Edmonton so he could rest.

Dr. Hansen nodded. "But to reiterate, you did not have an opportunity during the day or during the flight to sleep?"

Erik said that he had not. He also detailed his three uncomfortable exchanges with company management.

"Would you describe how these incidents affected your state of mind at the time," Dr. Hansen asked.

"Besides being uptight, it weighed heavily. You keep wondering if you are going to keep working tomorrow."

By that point, the sympathy of the audience was with the young pilot. Quiet murmurs of dismay began to ripple around the room and reporters scribbled furiously. Dr. Hanson picked up steam as he neared the finish line.

"And calculating duty time for the three days previous, the sleep over that same period of time was nine hours . . . are those totals correct?"

"That sounds correct," Erik answered.

"As a final question," Dr. Hansen concluded, "in any of your training as a professional pilot have you been required to receive any instruction in aeromedical subjects, things like disorientation, hypoglycemia, fatigue, illness . . . ?"

"No, sir."

"All right. Thank you," Dr. Hansen said with a note of satisfied finality. "I have no further questions."

With that, the inquiry chairman adjourned the first day's proceedings. It was 5:30, and Erik had been on the stand for six hours. He felt completely wrung out, but as his lawyer, CASB investigators, his father, and many former Wapiti pilots who attended the inquiry to support Erik gathered around, he felt a glimmer of redemption. When the crowd cleared, Erik saw two women patiently waiting to speak to him: Sally Swanson and Virginia Peever, the widows of two of the men who had died on Flight 402.

They thanked him for telling the truth.

The next morning, Erik walked a little straighter as he entered Conference Room A. His nerves felt less jagged and he found a moment to talk to his fellow survivors. Reporters asked the four men to stand together for a picture and in that one Erik smiled broadly.

At 9:05, he took the stand for the second day. This time, he fielded questions from John Bassie, the chief counsel representing Wapiti Aviation. Not more than a minute had passed before Bassie asked Erik where his pilot's logbook was.

"I burned it in the fire," Erik told him.

"I see," Bassie replied, and then asked Erik about what the notes were that he had with him on the witness stand the day before.

Erik frowned. "An outline from one of the reports."

Bassie regarded him steadily. "And I take it from that, you have problems recalling?"

Uneasiness rippled through Erik. After circling around seemingly peripheral issues about Wapiti's flight checklist and flight dispatch system, Bassie began his assault.

"Mr. Vogel, yesterday you mentioned a medivac flight which you said was October 17, 1984. Is that correct?"

"Yes, sir . . ."

"And are you sure about your date being October 17, 1984?"

"Yes, I believe I am."

Bassie turned and plucked a paper from the tabletop behind him. "Have you seen this before?"

In his hand was a Wapiti charter invoice. Bassie placed it on the stand under Erik's nose and Erik nodded.

"And you recognize your signature where it says pilot's signature?"

"Yes."

"And that document is dated October 16, 1984?"

"That is correct."

"So your medivac flight was October 16, 1984. Is that correct?"

"That one, yes."

"That's the flight you were talking about yesterday, is that correct?"

"I believe it was," Erik said.

"Mr. Vogel, now that we know that the medivac flight was on the 16th and not the 17th, could you tell us what you did on the 17th?"

Erik flushed, his memory completely blank. "I'm afraid I can't. I was under the impression . . . in the hospital when we were going over this, that that was the date . . ."

"If I told you you went to Fort McMurray at 14:05 with Mr. Powell. Do you recall that?"

Erik began to sweat. "I recall that, yes."

"It was not an authorized flight by the company, was it?"

Erik swallowed. His lawyer, Jim Duke, quickly asked the Chairman, "Sir, is this relevant to safety? Where are we going with this line of questioning?"

"I didn't hear the question," the Chairman answered. "Mr. Bassie . . . ?"

"Was it authorized?" Bassie asked again.

"The flight itself was a scheduled, authorized flight, sir," Erik replied.

"But you were not authorized to go?"

Erik felt the air leave his lungs. "No."

"That starter problem, then, was on the 16th, was it not?"

"It was the day of the medivac, yes."

"Would it be fair to say that on the 17th of October, 1984, you did not work at all?"

Erik was flustered now. "Was I not . . . there are not records of my flying?" he stammered.

"I'll show you the company records," Bassie offered, almost congenially. "I've marked the area in question with the photostat copies of them, Mr. Vogel, to assist you."

Erik studied the journey log in front of him. There it was: the medivac to Edmonton had *not* been on Wednesday the 17th, but Tuesday the 16th. He'd slept in the refuelling trailer on Tuesday night and on Wednesday, as a favour to Jim Powell, Erik had flown to Fort McMurray as his co-pilot while awaiting the starter repair. That left Wednesday and Thursday nights during which Erik had presumably gotten plenty of sleep.

Later, after agonizing long and hard about the events of that week, Erik would put the pieces together—how he'd arrived home after the starter fiasco, late on Wednesday, October 17, his one day off that week, and resumed flying the next day, Thursday, October 18. Thursday had been the day he'd picked up the props in Edmonton, banged ice from the wings with a broom handle, and first battled the fierce weather system that would bring down his plane on October 19. But in that moment at the inquiry, Erik was mute, his brain numb.

At the table behind him, members of the CASB investigative team were in shock. They hadn't thought to question Erik's recollection of events, to cross-check them against the company records. Phyllis Smith, the CASB's lawyer, was the first to speak.

"Mr. Chairman . . . I did want to express a concern . . . Mr. Bassie and Wapiti have had the group reports for some five weeks and none of this information has been brought to the attention of the technical panel . . . And one of the things that was discussed in some detail at the pre-hearing conference is that an ambush of the type we were expected to avoid, has appeared at this hearing."

Bassie, well seasoned in the thrust and parry of the courtroom, didn't miss a beat.

"That's a problem that will always be faced by an inquiry of this type, Mr. Chairman," he interjected. "Whoever conducted the investigation had access to all these books. There was nothing held back . . . There is no ambush here. It is just a situation where something was not done."

"Or missed," suggested the chairman.

"Or missed," Bassie concurred.

"Yes," the chairman agreed, looking at Bassie. "I think we'll give you the benefit of the doubt."

Bassie pressed his advantage. "And the other problem we faced here is that we did not know what Mr. Vogel would say. We knew he lost a whole day, we knew that this idea that he worked so hard those two or three days . . . was not correct. We thought that Mr. Vogel would look at it and realize that he was wrong and say so. But he didn't."

"Mr. Chairman . . ." the CASB's legal council tried again.

"End of argument," the chairman cut her off. "File the documents."

The rest of Erik's testimony unfolded like slow torture. The spirit of "respect and cooperation" the chairman had insisted on during the inquiry did not seem to Erik to be part of Mr. Bassie's repertoire. He found himself constantly on the defensive, his credibility questioned and undermined at every turn. After another hour of cross-examination, it was the inquiry chairman who finally asked the question Erik had been dreading: "Have you come to an explanation as to why you were still in the Swan Hills when you descended to the altitude of 2,800 feet?"

"I made an error in navigation," Erik admitted. "I believed I was farther ahead than I was."

When he stepped down from the stand, he felt as if he'd been gutted in front of the entire audience.

His testimony spawned a host of sensational news stories detailing how Erik had recanted his original version of events. Erik's contradictory account on the second day of the inquiry not only called into question his credibility and skills as a pilot, but completely undermined the CASB's attempt to show that human factors—particularly fatigue—were a major cause of the crash. As for the CASB's hopes of making the crash of Wapiti Flight 402 a precedent-setting case that would improve aviation safety—they had been dashed.

By the time Dale Wells took the stand later that day, the CASB's team of investigators had elected to avoid the now-uncertain territory of pilot fatigue and focus instead on Wapiti's safety standards. Harry Boyko, the CASB's head of operations, questioned Dale on everything from his airline's recent maintenance audits to allegations that management refused to assign co-pilots when the weather was below single pilot minimums.

"Can you tell me . . . has the operations manager ever rejected a request by a pilot for a co-pilot?" Boyko asked, picking up on Erik's testimony of the previous day during which he'd recounted his uncomfortable exchange with Delbert Wells over wanting a second pilot for the October 16 medivac.

"Not to my knowledge under normal circumstances," Dale replied.

"Have you ever refused that request?"

"Not when it was required by the weather."

Boyko persevered, trying another tack. "How many times in situations where a pilot has requested a second pilot have they been refused that second pilot?"

"I can't think of any instances."

"So you are saying that you have never really refused a co-pilot in the past twelve months?"

"Not to my knowledge."

Boyko later questioned Dale on Erik's assertion that, in order to satisfy his boss, he felt he needed to descend as low as 800 feet to get in to High Prairie before bailing on a landing attempt.

Dale's response was unequivocal: "I have never advised him to go to take a look at 800 feet. We were concerned about, you know, a safe operation and keeping a good reputation and developing our traffic with our passengers. And I had never at any time told any pilot to go take a look and go down to 800 feet."

It was John Bassie, Dale's chief counsel, who revisited the issue of Erik's fatigue. Bassie carefully led Dale through an accounting of Erik's scheduled flying hours in the days leading up to and including the crash, beginning with the emergency medivac on October 16, which had resulted in Erik spending the night in the refuelling depot trailer.

"If there was any reason that Mr. Vogel did not receive adequate sleep on the evening of October 16, 1984, do you have any explanation for it?"

"There was no reason for it as far as operation of the air service is concerned," Dale replied.

"Now, after he returned to Grande Prairie on October 17, was he assigned duties for October 18?"

"He was assigned to fly the evening flight departing Grande Prairie."

"Do I take it from that that he was assigned no morning duties?"

"He had no morning duties assigned."

"Okay. If there was any lack of sleep on the part of Mr. Vogel on the evening of October 17, can you give any explanation from the company's point of view as to why that may have happened?"

"I could see no reason whatsoever for any lack of sleep," Dale said.

"Okay. And did Mr. Vogel conduct the flights on the afternoon of October 18?"

"Yes, that's correct."

"And how many hours of flying time is that?" Bassie asked.

"Three hours of flight time."

"When was he next scheduled to work for your company?"

"Well, his next schedule was the same for the Friday as he flew on the Thursday, which is the five o'clock departure from Grande Prairie to Edmonton with a return through High Prairie and Peace River–Fairview."

"Again, I take it he was not assigned any duties on the morning of October 19?"

"That's correct."

"And if he did not get a full night's sleep on the evening of October 18, is there anything from the point of view of your company that you can give as a reason for that?"

"Nothing in the operation at all that should have kept him from getting a proper rest," Dale said.

"So is it correct, Mr. Wells," Bassie concluded, "Mr. Vogel did not have any flying duties with your company for the morning of October 17, the morning of October 18, the morning of October 19, 1984?"

"That's correct."

"And is it also correct that for October 17, 18 and 19, he flew only in the afternoon?"

"For assigned duties, that's correct."

"On any of those days, October 16, 17, 18 or 19, did Mr. Vogel complain to you about being tired or fatigued?"

"No, sir."

"Mr. Wells, is there any doubt that Mr. Vogel was the pilot-in-command . . . at the time of the fatal crash?"

"There is no doubt whatsoever."

"He was the pilot-in-command at the time that aircraft took off?"

"Yes."

"And as a pilot-in-command, is it not correct that he could have declined to depart if he so desired?"

Dale's answer was unwavering: "Yes, that's correct."

During the inquiry, more than twenty witnesses would take the stand, including Larry, Paul and Scott. Mechanics, passengers and pilots—most former Wapiti employees—lined up behind Erik to admit that they, too, had experienced safety deficiencies. In the end, the inquest left many unanswered questions. For Erik, however, it had been a nightmare that was almost as bad as the crash itself.

The four-day hearing ended on March 1, 1985. After his closing remarks, Chairman Deschenes announced that the RCMP and the St. John Ambulance Association of Canada wished to make a special presentation. Local RCMP Inspector Donald Webster stepped to the front of the room, a large framed certificate in hand, and called Scott Deschamps, sharply dressed in his navy RCMP uniform, to stand beside Paul. Scott beamed as Inspector Webster asked Paul to step forward. Then, in front of a flurry of flashes, the inspector presented him with a life-saving certificate.

Paul smiled shyly as he accepted the award. "I'm very touched," he said. "I only did what I had to do."

Receiving the award filled Paul with a kind of wonder. Never in his life had he been recognized for an accomplishment. When reporters finally finished questioning him, he slipped quietly out of the hearing room and stood alone beneath one of the hotel's large second-floor windows. Paul held up the certificate, proudly examining it beneath the sunshine streaming brightly down.

"What are you going to do with it?" asked a reporter. It was Byron Christopher, who had been at the Slave Lake airport the day of the rescue and witnessed the two girls who'd just learned of their mother's death. He'd met Paul two days later at the Grande Prairie courthouse.

"I'm going to mail it to my father," Paul said. "Maybe now he'll be proud of me."

Though Paul hadn't completely turned his life around, he felt like he was well on his way. When he'd returned to Grande Prairie a few weeks earlier, he'd sought out Sue Wink, the waitress at Corona Pizza with whom he'd been smitten. To his delight, instead of rebuffing his advances as she had when they'd worked together months before, she seemed to have had a change of heart. She looked at him differently, told him he'd grown up a lot. She even offered him a place to stay and their romance quickly blossomed. Paul recognized the stirrings of a happiness he hadn't experienced for many years.

As Paul's life was looking up, Erik's was headed in the opposite direction. He desperately wanted to put the crash and the public humiliation of the inquiry behind him. He might as well have wished for the moon. In June 1985, Transport Canada suspended his pilot's licence. Families of the deceased filed a spate of lawsuits naming him, Wapiti Aviation and Transport Canada. The province of Alberta launched a fatality inquiry into the deaths of six passengers, which was scheduled to open on June 17 at the Grande Prairie courthouse, and subpoenaed

Erik to appear. Mercifully for Erik, the inquiry was postponed due to a scheduling problem, sparing him the ordeal of testifying again so soon. It was rescheduled for late October, and hung over Erik like a threatening shadow.

Downhearted, broke and unemployed, he needed desperately to put the crash behind him. Soon he would do just that, disappearing into the west coast wilderness with a man whose life he had almost ended.

AFTERLIFE

On Scott Deschamps' release from hospital, he'd spent a month on medical leave in White Rock trying to take stock. Soon after that he told a reporter, "All of a sudden I was reborn a healthy twenty-eight-year-old with my whole life ahead of me. That experience definitely changed my outlook in the sense that I now have a greater appreciation of life."

Yet Scott didn't know how to make sense of it all. In December, after the RCMP had denied his request for a transfer to the west coast, he'd returned to duty in Grande Prairie. The reality of being back at his job chafed at him. He'd initially coped by immersing himself in preparation for his inquiry testimony. He'd resurrected the laundry list of safety equipment he'd asked Erik about the night of the crash, which the plane hadn't carried: flares, a first aid kit, an axe—anything that would have eased the physical ordeal he and the others had endured. But he kept coming back to the questions he couldn't answer: What had he experienced on that snowy hillside as he lay dying? What caused the apparition of the Old Man? Why had he been visible only to him?

Scott was certain he wasn't going to find the answers policing the streets of Grande Prairie. The day after his testimony at the CASB inquiry, he announced his decision to quit the RCMP.

"During the crash I spent fourteen hours lying in the snow unable to move," he told reporters outside Conference Room A. "That environment facilitated a time of reflection which prompted my decision. I've always wanted to go to university ever since I can remember and I've never done it. I was always working. Now I realize that life is so fragile. People talk about the right to life. I don't talk about the right to life; I talk about the privilege it is to live because any one of us can be killed at any time. It is so easy and it happens so quick. So if you haven't done the things that you've always wanted to do, it's time to do them."

Several months after he made that statement, Scott found himself sitting in an office at a deserted Canada–US border crossing examining the passports of people with immigration issues. He'd landed the job as an immigration officer a week after returning to White Rock. During the two-month training period that had followed, he'd enrolled in a distance education program for a Bachelor of General Studies at Alberta's Athabasca University. But still, none of these changes were enough to dispel his sense of urgency that life was passing him by.

Scott momentarily closed his eyes, shutting out the glare of fluorescent lights from the ceiling above him. Outside, sparse streams of car headlights flared into night. It was past midnight and he felt restless. Constrained. He watched a set of headlights grow brighter until a car pulled up to the window of a nearby booth and the officer inside briefly checked the driver's passport before waving him on. As the car's red tail lights receded down the dark stretch of highway, Scott wondered: *What am I doing wasting my time here?*

The truth was that he'd never had a deliberate plan for his life. After high school, he'd knocked on the door of a local youth detention center and they'd hired him on the spot. At the time, Scott had been proud of the fact that, at eighteen, he'd been the youngest corrections officer they'd ever hired. Because of his wilderness experience, he was soon asked to take young offenders into the bush to teach them essential life skills. Five years later, when Scott applied to the RCMP, the choice was more a matter of natural progression than passion. It suddenly occurred to him that his decision to become an immigration officer had been a mistake.

Scott didn't want to waste any more time sitting around doing insignificant things. He needed answers. He needed understanding that would make life feel purposeful again. Scott immediately began typing up a notice of resignation, which he laid on his boss's desk at the end of his shift that night.

Without the distraction of a job, Scott's once well-ordered world began to unravel. The worst casualty was his marriage. He and Mary had been so young when they got together, their decision so impulsive. While the first few years of their marriage had been fine, it had been hard to maintain their relationship after Mary had left Grande Prairie for her job on the coast. Scott had hoped that quitting the RCMP and moving back to White Rock would solve things. But he'd been naïve. His experience the night of the crash had changed him profoundly and it seemed to him there was no going back—to his RCMP career, his unexamined life, or his relationship. A short time after leaving his immigration job, Scott ended his marriage.

Though more than six months had passed since the accident, its reverberations continued to rock him. Those close to him were puzzled, expecting the young man who had always been grounded, reasonable and methodical to just get over it. But it wasn't that simple. Questions—big questions—weighed on him. What was the vision he'd witnessed? Was it a miracle? A sign from the Creator? He had touched the face of death before the Old Man pulled him back from the brink. How *could* he get over it?

———

According to the American psychiatrist and author Robert Jay Lifton, the sense of being personally adrift is not uncommon among survivors of atrocious events. Having a near-death experience, survivors can close down and remain numb and incapacitated, or they can confront what has happened, opening out to a greater appreciation of life sharpened by the experience of survival. Though Scott didn't fully understand it, he was being propelled toward the latter. Before he could begin a quest for greater wisdom, spirituality and understanding, however, he first had to deal with the decidedly earthly reality of being unemployed, single and homeless. Scott could think of only one person who could fully understand his state of mind. So in the spring of 1985, Scott Deschamps moved in with Erik Vogel.

Moving day was grey and drizzly as Scott and Erik hauled Scott's meagre belongings into Erik's 800-square-foot bungalow, which he'd purchased during the two years he spent driving a bus before joining Wapiti. The house, located on Habgood Street just blocks from White Rock's waterfront, was tiny, but fortunately for Erik, Scott had abandoned many of his material possessions along with his former life. However, he had hung on to one substantial piece of furniture, a massive, homemade butcher-block table. The two men strained under the weight of it as they dragged the solid slab of wood on legs into the cramped kitchen of Erik's home.

As the spring of 1985 rolled into a hot, dry restless summer, Scott and Erik found themselves hiking Canada's rugged West Coast Trail. The 75-kilometre stretch of wilderness along the southwest coast of Vancouver Island—part of a treacherous coastline known to mariners as the Graveyard of the Pacific—is one of North America's most gruelling treks. Ragged submerged rocks and giant, rolling breakers extend almost 30 kilometres offshore and, when combined with frequent and fierce storms, have been the demise of hundreds of large ships and tankers. Some say there is a wrecked ship for every mile of coast along the Graveyard of the Pacific.

A stiff wind whipped large waves onto the southern stretch of that remote coastline as Scott and Erik trudged along its rocky shore. A strong and seasoned hiker, Scott had allotted just five days to traverse the entire West Coast Trail, a journey that typically took seven. It was late on the fourth day as the two men picked their way across a slippery sandstone rock shelf, their bodies straining under the weight of 27-pound backpacks. Offshore, one of a dozen shipwrecks they'd seen lay like a rusting corpse in the waning light.

During the first three days, Scott and Erik had covered more than half the distance between Port Renfrew and the trail's northern terminus in the tiny fishing village of Bamfield. Along the arduous trail, they'd encountered dozens of perilous coastal surge channels, hauled themselves high over running water in rudimentary cable cars, slogged through boggy, old-growth rainforest, crossed steep canyons on rickety foot bridges, and climbed up and down sheer green ravines on countless rough-hewn, wooden ladders. They'd encountered slugs the size of bananas and hoisted their food into trees each night to avoid attracting bears or cougars. But they had also witnessed spectacular vistas. The black dorsal fins of orcas cut the waves off the Pacific coast and eagles circled above, their white heads clearly visible against the blue sky. Sea lions lumbered clumsily on rocky offshore shelves, and tide pools teemed with life. The wild log-strewn beaches humbled them and the mossy glow of sunlight filtering through the forest's giant, ancient foliage seemed otherworldly.

For Scott, returning to the wilderness was like a homecoming. As a youngster, he had spent a lot of time in the bush with his dad, an avid outdoorsman. One of the few legacies Joseph Deschamps had left his son was a love of the outdoors. The two had spent many hours hunting and fishing together in the wilds surrounding their Delta home, and after his dad died, Scott had found a rare sense of connection and belonging in these untamed places that he had experienced nowhere else.

It had been Scott's idea to hike the West Coast Trail. He'd persuaded Erik that the two of them, carrying only light packs, could easily complete the trek. Erik had relented only after Scott promised him they wouldn't starve. Contrary to his promise, Scott had packed just a small shoebox-sized supply of food, and had jogged long stretches of the route, forcing Erik to keep up a punishing pace. Now, as they hiked a misty stretch of beach, their feet stuttering along the shell-strewn sand, Scott suddenly realized his priorities were very clear. He would search for an understanding of the miracle that had occurred the night of the crash, and he would complete the bucket list that he'd begun as he lay dying on that snowy hillside. He thought about what had seemed vitally important to him that night—getting a university degree, travelling, sailing the west coast, learning another language, running a marathon and just spending time outdoors doing things like this that made him feel vital and alive. As he strode on, the bucket list unfurled, solidified, one goal after the next, until it included all the things Scott wanted out of life.

Though weary, Scott felt lightness return to his step when he and Erik finally rounded a long point of land and saw their campsite ahead. The sweeping curve of beach was strewn with enormous logs, and wisps of campfire smoke spiralled into the air. Offshore, the sun was melting like a fuzzy orange lozenge into the Pacific Ocean mist, and the gentle cascade of Tsusiat Falls whispered in the distance. Exhausted but happy, the two men reached the surprisingly busy campsite and dropped their packs on the sand. Other hikers had already claimed the higher ground, and after enjoying a wash in the falls' cool water, Erik and Scott pitched their tent close to the shore.

That night, as several hikers gathered together around a vigorous campfire, Scott shared his story of survival. The faces of those around the fire glowed with incredulity as he recounted the plane crash and long night in the wilderness. Beside him, Erik slumped grimly, but Scott didn't seem to notice. Pointing to Erik, he concluded his tale with more good humour than he'd felt in many months: "This is the pilot who flew the plane."

Gasps of disbelief erupted and several hikers challenged Scott's claim. Sitting awkwardly in the shadows, Erik didn't rush to back him up.

That night, Scott slept soundly. It was Erik who awoke yelling when the rising tide began surging into their tent. He quickly collapsed the poles and grabbed Scott to wake him, narrowly avoiding Scott's fist, which had come hurtling out of his sleeping bag toward Erik's face. Though taken aback, Erik would later chuckle about Scott's reaction, when he reminded him about the warning Scott had issued several weeks earlier as the two men discussed sharing a tent: "Never touch me when I'm sleeping or I'll take a swing at you."

It wouldn't be the last time Scott surprised Erik. After he moved out late that summer, Scott showed up at Erik's door one day with a six-pack of beer and a seven-page typewritten legal document. It was a statement of claim Scott had filed in the Alberta courts for damages resulting from the plane crash. Named were Wapiti Aviation, Delbert and Dale Wells, and Erik Vogel. Scott insisted it wasn't personal, and Erik said he understood.

For a short, intense week in the British Columbia wilderness, Erik had been able to put his troubles behind him. But back in White Rock they returned with a vengeance. Late one August afternoon, Erik stood over the large butcher-block table in his kitchen, opening one rejection letter after another. Unable to work as a pilot after his licence had been suspended, he'd applied for dozens of different jobs, to no avail. Finally, his neighbour had put in a good word for him for a temporary position mowing lawns with the BC Housing Management Commission. Erik at last reached for a beige envelope bearing the commission's name and opened it. The brief letter inside read:

Dear Erik,

We are pleased to confirm our verbal offer of the short-term Groundskeeper position in our Burrard Region effective September 3, 1985. The rate of pay for a Groundskeeper II is $12.03 per hour and your services will be required until approximately October 11, 1985.

It was a far cry from flying, but at least it would help pay the rent. Sometime before he began his job as a groundskeeper, there came a knock on his door. Erik opened it to see an official-looking man standing on his front step.

"Erik Hunter Vogel?" the man asked.

Erik was loath to acknowledge his identity. When he finally nodded, the stranger handed him a subpoena to appear at the rescheduled Alberta government fatality inquiry. Erik felt sick. During the first inquiry, he'd cooperated openly with authorities, made himself available and tried to do what was right. As a result, he'd been publicly humiliated and had lost his pilot's licence. He had no job prospects other than five weeks mowing lawns, and no money. He'd also put his dad through the humiliation of having to stand behind a son who had committed a high-profile error that had cost the lives of six people, not to mention the financial burden of paying a pile of expensive legal bills. Erik studied the subpoena for a moment. The date for his appearance was October 30, 1985. It would mean flying back to Grande Prairie. That city held nothing for him but bad memories. Clutching the subpoena in his fist, Erik walked into his kitchen, opened the cabinet under the sink, and tossed the document into the trash.

If Grande Prairie held only grief for Erik, it seemed to offer nothing but promise for Paul Archambault. After the CASB inquiry, he'd been rehired at his old job and settled there.

Whistling happily near the end of his seven-to-three shift, he dragged a damp mop over the worn linoleum kitchen floor of Corona Pizza. Paul had opened the restaurant early that morning as he'd been doing for going on six months. It was almost quitting time as he emptied the grey water from his bucket into a large industrial sink in the restaurant kitchen and rinsed out his mop. He tied off a couple of large green garbage bags, hoisted them over his shoulder and headed down the back stairs to the alley. Outside, the air was hot and still. Paul tossed the bags into the metal bin and pushed his thick hair back from his brow with a sweep of his bare forearm. He wore his hair slightly shorter than he had before the crash and one of the girls at work had given him a gentle perm, which suited him. He was lightly tanned, and though he'd filled out during the months of good living, he still looked fit in a black crewneck T-shirt emblazoned in yellow: "Corona Mafia."

The shirt elicited a lot of chuckles from customers and staff, but as far as Paul was concerned the words carried a shred of truth. After the inquiry, Teddy Bougiridis had hired Paul back as janitor. Teddy was a big-hearted bull of a man, an immigrant who ran his business like a benevolent godfather. The number of full- and part-time staff at his booming restaurant and sports lounge was upwards of sixty. Many had been with Teddy and Donna for more than a decade. Paul counted himself lucky to be among them again.

Since he'd been back, Teddy had given him increasing responsibility. In addition to keeping the place clean, his boss often loaned Paul his car and asked him to pick up liquor orders or drive staff to and from work. On occasion, he even let him cook. Paul had put a cap on his own drinking and was the guy Teddy and Donna called on to get patrons home safely if they'd had too much booze. The Bougiridises ran a tight ship, but they were happy to offer work to anyone willing to follow their rules, and this time around Paul made sure he was at the top of their list.

Teddy's daughter, Elpeda Palmer, was twenty the first time her dad hired Paul. When her dad told her about Paul's criminal record, she'd disagreed with the decision. But as far as Teddy was concerned, everyone deserved a chance to prove himself. After all, he had come to Canada from Greece with nothing but a hundred dollars in his pocket. Elpeda's concerns were still there when her dad rehired Paul after the crash, but before long she warmed to him.

"He looked like Grizzly Adams," she said, adding that Paul was smart and capable.

Soon she came to view him like an older brother and appreciated his kindness to her, her sisters, and other members of her family. Elpeda eventually trusted him enough to allow him to play with her two-year-old daughter at the restaurant while she worked.

Paul, for his part, was willing to do anything Teddy and Donna asked of him, and they reciprocated by giving him extra work to supplement his income. The storage shed Paul built in their backyard from scrap lumber is still standing more than a quarter century later.

"Paul was close to everyone and he was very loyal," Donna Bougiridis recalled. She and others who'd known him before the crash noticed a change in him. He was less selfish, more caring. He had vowed to end his troubles with the law and, so far, had kept his word. And because he'd saved one of theirs, local RCMP officers treated him well whenever they saw him, which was often. Corona Pizza was not only a popular eatery for the locals; its downstairs lounge was a frequent after-hours watering hole for many cops.

Paul warmed to the eclectic mix of people in Grande Prairie, people who found a sense of community among the resourceful, unpretentious individuals who populated Canada's isolated, northern prairie. Few in the north judged a man on his past or who his family was. Because of Paul's heroic actions and his presence at one of Grande Prairie's most popular restaurants, he had gained acceptance among a wide circle of people. Affable, humble and a natural storyteller, he got on well with almost everyone he knew.

Paul recalled that time in his life: "I'm striving to be better for myself—mentally, physically, morally—and I'm not doing too bad."

The biggest reason for Paul's happiness, however, was the woman with whom he had fallen in love. At thirty-six, Sue Wink was nine years his senior and a divorced mother of two. When she left her husband, she'd moved to the east side of the city where she rented half a duplex owned by Teddy and Donna. For Paul, it had become home.

Working and living together, he and Sue were inseparable in the months following his return to Grande Prairie, often acting like teenagers experiencing their first puppy love. During that time, Paul's status had grown from local hero to national celebrity. The event that catapulted him to widespread recognition was his appearance in May 1985 on *Front Page Challenge*, a popular current events show considered an institution on Canadian television. It featured a panel of prominent journalists who had to guess a news story by questioning a guest hidden from view. Many high-profile personalities including Indira Gandhi, Malcolm X, Boris Karloff and Ed Sullivan had appeared on the show.

Producers at the Canadian Broadcasting Corporation offered to pay for Paul's rental car, hotel room and travel expenses to Prince Albert, Saskatchewan, where an episode of the show was being taped in front of a live audience. He rented a brand new Mustang and invited Sue along on the eight-hour road trip. The two felt like honeymooners that week and Sue recalled only one disagreement. It happened along a deserted stretch of prairie highway, when Paul began slowing down for a scruffy-looking hitchhiker who appeared drunk. She'd pleaded with Paul to keep driving, but he wouldn't listen.

"Sue," she recalled him saying, "that's how I get around."

When the TV show began, Paul appeared on a raised platform behind the panel and a moderator. Dressed in blue jeans, a sky blue t-shirt and jean jacket, Paul stood under the glare of lights to thunderous applause from hundreds of spectators who packed a large auditorium. Sweat beaded his brow as the panelists began asking questions in an effort to unearth his identity. He was so nervous he initially got several of his answers wrong, forcing the moderator to gently correct him. It may have been Paul's uncertainty that finally tipped off the third panelist to question him, Canadian author and journalist Pierre Berton.

"Is this a happy story?" Berton asked.

"No."

"Is there any death involved?"

"Yes."

"More than one death?"

"Yes."

"More than ten?"

"No."

"Is this the plane crash that killed Grant Notley?"

"Yes," Paul replied.

Again the audience erupted with applause and the panelists turned in unison to regard their unusual guest.

During the commercial break that followed, Paul was escorted to a chair on stage where the panelists continued to question him, this time about his actions that night.

Betty Kennedy's voice was a mixture of awe and motherly pride as she asked Paul about his survival skills: "How did you know all those things?"

"I probably heard a lot of things in my past that didn't mean anything," he said, "but they were buried in my subconscious mind. When I needed to use them I just dug deep and grabbed."

"So you're a survivor?"

Paul smiled. "You better believe it."

"Did a lot of good things come your way out of this? Did it change the course of your life?"

"It's changed me in the sense that I've got so much attention from the news media, and people I don't know approach me and say good things and it just kind of blows me away."

"Did they never do that to you before?" Kennedy asked sympathetically, clearly taken with the humble young man in front of her. "Were there not many people who said good things to you before?"

"Sure," Paul said, a mischievous grin softening his expression. "But I didn't know so many people before."

Kennedy laughed heartily, and a chuckle of approval rippled through the audience before guest panelist Laurier LaPierre picked up the thread of conversation.

"How much has it changed your values and your soul?"

"My values?" Paul seemed momentarily at a loss. "My values probably remain the same, I just appreciate things more. Doing what I did," he said quietly, "I did that because I was the least hurt. I was capable. I was in the right frame of mind. And that was an experience all in itself."

After several more minutes of questions, Pierre Berton asked a final one: "Do you consider yourself a brave man?"

Paul dropped his gaze as he thought for a moment.

"I don't know," he finally said.

When Paul and Sue returned to Grande Prairie, life fell again into an easy rhythm. To his relief, the media scrutiny subsided and though he found himself bristling a little when people greeted him with: "Hey, Hero," he tried to take his new status in stride. Of course, there were perks. At the local disco he and Sue often frequented, women he didn't know would ask him to dance, and while he was committed to Sue, he didn't mind the attention.

Sometime that summer Sue transferred from her waitressing job upstairs to work as a bartender in the downstairs lounge. Paul knew the move made sense, allowing them to take turns looking after Sue's kids, but he didn't like it. The lounge was open until 2:00 a.m. and drew mostly men. Though the tips were good, he hated the thought of Sue fraternizing with the customers who frequented the bar, especially late in the shift when they were more likely to be drunk and disorderly. Still, he tried to make the best of it.

Mid-afternoon one July summer day, as soon as he finished up his janitorial duties, Paul yelled goodbye to his boss and fellow employees and headed for the door. His and Sue's house was a 3-kilometre walk away, but if he hurried, Paul could usually squeeze in an hour or two with her before she left for her shift. The northern sun was high in the sky, and warmth radiated from the sidewalk. Flies buzzed lazily inside storefront windows, and kids wheeled by on banana bikes, their Creamsicles melting quickly in the heat. Paul picked up his pace, moving through the afternoon lull of the city, a jaunty spring to his step, his chin tilted slightly skyward. When he passed people on the street now, he would look them in the eye, often nodding or saying hello.

He continued a kilometre southeast long the railway tracks, his running shoes crunching on the dry, pebble-strewn bed between the rails until he reached the road leading to their house. As he neared it, Paul turned up a back alley. Dandelions winked bright yellow along wooden fences and ahead he could see his yard. Paul loved approaching the house this way. Earlier that summer he'd pulled the weeds from the overgrown backyard, plowed the unruly quack grass and planted a huge garden. Entering the yard, he proudly surveyed the neat strips of green in front of him. Bushy arrows of carrots and radishes lined the near side of the garden bed, giving way to staked rows of peas and runner beans. Paul snapped a tender bean from its stalk and popped it into his mouth. He, Sue and the kids had recently begun eating from the garden and loved it. Paul had also built an outdoor barbeque out of brick and cooked many meals there.

As he bounded happily up the steps, Paul could hear Sue's laugh coming from the kitchen. On either side of the steps, still-green tomatoes hung on the vine, plumping in the heat radiating from the back wall of the house. He pulled open the screen door to see her on the phone, her auburn hair a lovely contrast to the pale skin of her face, her cheeks flushed pink beneath the rims of huge round glasses. Catching sight of him, Sue quickly ended her call.

"Who were you talking to?" Paul asked. Something about the look on her face sent a knife of jealousy stabbing through him. Sue sometimes chatted with Scott Thorne, one of the local RCMP officers who often came by Corona Pizza after his shift. He was handsome, with a full head of dark hair and a thick moustache, both of which looked to Paul as if they'd been combed for hours. Unlike the other RCMP officers, with whom Paul got along fine, he didn't like Thorne. Nor did Paul appreciate Thorne's loud mouth or the way Paul thought he talked down to women. Most of all, however,

Paul didn't like the way he and Sue flirted whenever they were together. Paul felt a hot rage rising.

"He's just a good friend," Sue insisted, but Paul had trouble believing her.

He slammed his palm hard against the door frame, turned, and stumbled back toward his garden. This time he stomped through the beds without regard for the tender shoots.

The unusually dry summer of 1985 gave way to fall. On the west coast, one morning after another dawned cloudless and clear, but Erik could not appreciate the good weather. His weeks unfolded in soul-destroying succession as he mowed lawns in the "projects" of Vancouver's impoverished downtown east side. He ground out the days incessantly ruminating over the details of that fateful night. As he told a reporter at the time, "I spent the whole year trying to forget about it, but I can't go a day without thinking about it."

His job ended and the anniversary of the crash came and went. Flying jobs remained non-existent. Though Erik's pilot's licence was no longer suspended, the high-profile nature of his crash firmly closed doors before he could even get a foot in. Erik had become a pariah in the aviation industry. He submitted applications to local firefighting units in the Lower Mainland and waited, trying desperately to bury the past.

It caught up with him on October 30, 1985. Though Erik had ignored the subpoena to appear at the rescheduled provincial fatality inquiry into Wapiti Flight 402, the courts hadn't. The inquiry opened that day in Grande Prairie, with Judge Carl Rolf presiding. When he discovered that his key witness hadn't bothered to show up, the judge immediately ruled Erik Vogel to be in contempt of court and issued a warrant for his arrest.

Unbeknownst to Erik, the warrant was only effective in Alberta, or he may well have ended up in jail. Still, he refused to attend the inquiry and found himself constantly looking over his shoulder, shuddering every time there was an unexpected knock at his door.

Friends urged Erik to testify.

"You're making us look bad," one of his former flying buddies told him.

In early November, Erik got a phone call from the Burnaby Fire Department asking him to come in for an interview. Dressed smartly in a suit and tie, Erik had impressed his interviewers. It wasn't often that they got an experienced pilot looking for work as a firefighter. When one asked Erik if he could start training immediately, Erik sat up, his face earnest and alight with hope.

"Absolutely," Erik replied.

The interviewer in the chair across from him leaned forward and fixed him with a level stare. "Before we offer you a position," he said, "do you have any issues with the law?"

Erik's mouth went dry and he felt his stomach lurch. He'd vowed not to participate in another inquiry, especially one led by people who had nothing to do with aviation, but now the matter of an outstanding warrant could cost him the chance for a new career.

"Nothing I can't clear up," he said.

Erik returned to Grande Prairie in December 1985 to testify at the fatality inquiry. This time, however, his mission wasn't to change the course of aviation safety, but to change his own life.

"I should not have been out that night," Erik admitted in a media interview at the time. "The flight shouldn't have left. I cut a corner, which I shouldn't have done. I'm not proud of it. I know what I did was stupid. I was exhausted. I was tired. I was in a hurry. I just did it."

Erik unflinchingly accepted responsibility for his actions. When he finished his testimony and boarded a plane to fly out of Grande Prairie, he still carried a heavy burden of guilt, but for the first time since the crash, Erik felt like he might finally have a chance to begin again.

FATE

Though my father seemed to have put the crash behind him by the time I returned to Canada in late 1985, I knew it weighed on his mind. On more than one occasion he pondered his last-minute decision to give up his usual co-pilot's seat after boarding Flight 402. What had prompted it? Why had he lived when others—colleagues, neighbours and constituents—had died? Was there divine intervention at play? These questions undoubtedly plagued him when he returned to the sombre atmosphere in the government chambers of the Alberta Legislature where Grant Notley's high-backed leather chair sat empty. Colleagues don't recall Dad talking much about the crash, but said he seemed unsettled for some time after it.

In spite of his highly visible public life, my dad was in many ways an intensely private man, seldom sharing his innermost feelings with anyone. He spoke little of the passengers who had died, but I know the question *Why not me?* surfaced every weekend back in High Prairie when he passed by the Peever home or saw Gordon's widow, Virginia, or one of their children. He called Sandra Notley and Virginia Peever after the crash, but did not share details of those conversations. Still, I had to wonder. Did the inexplicable reality of having survived strip the weight from his words of condolence, stretching them thin?

After his release from hospital, Dad also travelled north to the First Nations reserve of Atikameg to visit Elaine Noskeye's husband and fourteen children. A devoted family man, Dad must have noticed that her absence filled every corner of their modest home, the uncertainty of a future without a wife and mother reflecting itself darkly in fifteen pairs of eyes.

The crash certainly cast a shadow on the periphery of his days and nights. For months afterward, my mom said, he awoke to nightmares and was haunted by the deaths of the other passengers—those he knew and those he didn't. Randy Wright, his executive assistant, recalled a day the following spring when authorities delivered a box to his office at the Legislature. In it were possessions that had been retrieved from the crash site after the snow melted.

"Mr. Shaben asked me to look at it," Randy told me. "He couldn't bring himself to examine the contents of that box."

Nor did my dad seem eager to examine any debris the crash may have left within him. He hurled himself back into his political life. That included flying on Wapiti Aviation to and from High Prairie most weekends. Within a month of the accident the airline had been besieged with negative media, and locals had begun to call it *What-a-pity*. Dad knew Wapiti badly needed a public vote of confidence. He admitted being terrified to fly again, but he also understood how critical the airline's passenger service was to people in the isolated communities of northern Alberta. He and Grant had fought hard for that service and Dad wasn't going to turn his back on it. He confided to Randy that there was another, more private reason. "I had to prove to myself that I hadn't lost my nerve." So, as was his way, stoically and with little fanfare, Dad got back on a plane.

He demonstrated the same unwavering approach to political service. Regardless of any turmoil or uncertainties he experienced, outwardly he appeared patient, purposeful and exquisitely rational. He was devoted to his constituents and worked hard, especially for the disadvantaged, Métis and First Nations communities in his riding, improving infrastructure and ensuring they had drinking water, new roads and schools, and improved television transmission. Minister of Housing at the time, he revamped a faltering government program that provided homes for needy rural Albertans, including off-reserve Métis and Treaty families. The program had been beset with problems such as vandalism and property damage. Dad supported a monumental change to the program: offering families the opportunity to own their own homes if they faithfully paid their rent without interruption for eight years. Almost immediately, rent payments arrived on time, vandalism ceased, and upkeep dramatically improved. He also supported initiatives offering construction skills and training to eligible housing recipients, and engaging them in building their own homes. As an added benefit, the residents' newly acquired skills resulted in improved employment opportunities.

"It was about restoring peoples' pride and sense of responsibility," he told me.

Sometime in the summer of 1985, Dad had a surprise visit from Paul Archambault. Paul had been in Edmonton to see his brother Michael and decided to pop in to the Alberta Legislature. I imagine Paul standing awestruck—as I had been when I first visited my dad there—in front of the turn-of-the-century stone building's soaring bell-shaped dome and stately columned wings. Inside the main doors, the Legislature is even more impressive, with an intimidating rotunda made almost entirely of gleaming white marble. The floor shines like ice as sober-faced men and women in dark suits rush across it, the click of their heels echoing in the expansive space.

In the middle of the rotunda is an enormous circular fountain, and the sound of cascading water is everywhere. Paul's mouth must have hung open as he craned to look at the ornate balconies perched atop massive marble pillars that rise more than a hundred feet toward a pale blue ceiling high above. Until that moment it's likely that he hadn't thought of Dad as anything other than a fellow survivor. Now Paul probably wondered uncertainly if it was right to just drop in on him.

"Call me," Dad had said, and Paul had done so on several occasions. Their talks had been easy and filled with banter. When they'd met again in person at the inquiry, Dad had given him his business card and invited Paul to visit him anytime he was in Edmonton.

Paul made his way up to the fourth floor's wide mezzanine overlooking the lobby, circling it until he found the wing of offices he was looking for. The door marked 403, large and made of solid dark wood, hid a suite of offices assigned to the Minister of Housing and his staff. Paul pushed it open and entered a spacious outer chamber with several desks and a small seating area. An attractive dark-haired woman looked up at him.

"Yes?" she asked, a note of wariness in her voice.

"I'm here to see Larry," Paul said.

Her eyebrows shot up. In his office and at the Legislature, everyone except his elected colleagues called him *Mister* Shaben or *Minister* Shaben or *The Honourable* Larry Shaben.

"Is he expecting you?"

"Sure."

Upon hearing Paul's response, two other women sitting at nearby desks looked up. As Paul began shifting his weight nervously from one foot to another, a lanky redhead about his own age, neatly dressed in a suit and tie, emerged from an office door. Randy Wright. The receptionist cast him a quick, questioning look.

"He told me to drop in any time," Paul said.

"What's your name, please?" the woman asked.

"Paul Archambault."

Now all eyes were overtly on him in surprise and recognition, but Paul was probably too uncomfortable to notice.

"Please take a seat, Mr. Archambault," the receptionist said kindly. "I'll let Mr. Shaben know you're here."

Paul dropped stiffly into a chair, absently fiddling with the loose watchstrap around his wrist, as he was in the habit of doing when uncomfortable or distracted. Then a door at the end of the chamber opened and my father emerged. Randy recalls how his face lit up when he saw Paul. Dad came over to him and wrapped an arm around his shoulder. He asked the receptionist to hold his calls before guiding Paul into his private office and closing the door. Not many people had that kind of one-on-one access.

Dad remembered that first visit as an especially happy one. Paul clutched his now-finished manuscript. Dad was surprised at the size of it, half-an-inch thick, dozens of handwritten pages in neat block letters. On the title page were the words: *They Called Me a Hero.*

"You should let me read it," Dad said, full of curiosity.

"No." Paul looked sheepish. "I'm still working on it."

Talk had then turned to happy news. Despite their sometimes tumultuous relationship, Paul and Sue had gotten engaged.

Dad was overjoyed. He'd met Sue briefly during the CASB inquiry the previous spring, and saw immediately that Paul was smitten with her. Paul's stunning reversal of fortune heartened him. So many of my father's days were shadowed by difficulty. The recent collapse of the oil and gas industry, on which Alberta relied, had brought crushing hardships to the people he'd been elected to serve. Just after he'd been appointed to the Cabinet in 1982, the bottom had fallen out of the housing market as interest rates soared to more than twenty per-cent. People who had flocked to the province to service the booming oil industry found themselves unable to pay mortgages they'd secured with five-percent down payments. Many simply left. Houses were abandoned and scores of commercial properties lay empty.

As head of the Alberta Housing and Mortgage Corporation, Dad was besieged with requests from developers pleading for financial relief, pestering him to either postpone their loan payments or grant them permission to forgo them altogether. Two local banks had folded, and Dad seemed constantly on the defensive.

He had told his staff never to lead people down the garden path. One of the first questions he or his executive assistants would ask when people came to them for help was: "What do you think I can do to solve this problem?"

Lately, however, it seemed there was little he or anyone else could do to make a positive difference in people's lives. Perhaps that was the reason Paul was especially welcome.

"You're invited to the wedding," Paul told him during that first visit.

Dad promised Paul that no matter when or where it was, he and Mom would be there.

Alberta's tough economic times weren't the only thing troubling my father. Big changes were afoot in his government. That June, Premier Peter Lougheed, the man who'd inspired Dad to pursue a political career, announced he would not be seeking re-election, stepping down after eighteen years in public office. Principled and passion-ate, Lougheed began his political rise to power in 1965, winning the leadership of Alberta's small "c" Conservative Party. By 1967 he'd managed to wrestle six seats from the Social Credit Party, which had enjoyed an uninterrupted majority for thirty-six years. Wielding a law degree from the University of Alberta and an MBA from Harvard, Lougheed swept into office in 1971, capturing forty-nine of seventy-five seats.

Dad had joined the Conservatives in the early 1970s, attracted by the party's youth, energy and inclusiveness—qualities embodied by its new leader. "He was wise," Dad said of his political mentor. "He recognized that the face of Alberta was changing through immigration and through the multicultural nature of our province, and that in order to be an effective government, he needed to include people."

When my father was elected as a Member of the Legislative Assembly in 1975, he was one of sixty-nine Conservatives forming Alberta's new government. Incredibly, the premier chose him to respond to the speech from the throne, the address given by the lieutenant governor to open the legislative session and set the agenda for the new government. "It was a recognition of his potential," Lougheed said when asked why he'd singled out a newcomer for the honour.

Dad clearly remembered that day. He brought his Koran from the top shelf of a bookcase at home for the swearing-in ceremony. Few noticed when the Bible was quietly exchanged for the Muslim holy book just before my dad stepped forward to take the oath of public office. For the son of uneducated Lebanese immigrants, it was a life-changing moment.

Alberta found its voice under Lougheed's leadership. The charismatic new premier fought for stronger provincial input into national decision making and for the province to control its natural resources, particularly oil. He took on Canada's centrist government, led by Prime Minister Pierre Elliott Trudeau, over the National Energy

Program, a controversial initiative that increased revenues to the federal government from Alberta's resource-rich oil and gas industry. To many western Canadians, the program was akin to colonial exploitation, giving politicians 3,000 kilometres to the east control over Alberta's energy resources. Lougheed retaliated by putting new oil developments on hold and ordering cutbacks in production. The eventual result of the political hardball was a revenue-sharing agreement that many believe marked the beginning of western Canada's emergence as a true partner in Canadian confederation.

My father also found his voice in government, and after one term as a rookie backbencher, was appointed to Cabinet. Lougheed would later reflect: "Larry had an ability to grasp complex issues. He had a sense of both rural and urban Alberta, and added to that, a talent for communicating to a broad cross-section of the public. You put those together and you get an exceptional minister."

But power didn't come without compromise. Quietly proud of his ethnic and religious heritage, my dad walked a fine line when it came to his public persona. Though his position had made him the highest-profile Muslim politician in Canada's history, he was circumspect about his faith and Arab identity, both of which had been misunderstood and maligned in North America. Feeling that he had to work twice as hard to gain credibility and respect, my father downplayed his ethnicity and religion. When Middle East politics ignited in the early 1980s following Israel's invasion of Lebanon, the pressure on him from Arab and Muslim communities to use his political influence had been high. Even I had urged him to speak out. Dad refused, telling me he could accomplish more through thoughtful and discreet conversations with his colleagues. I didn't understand. Instead I judged him as either afraid or unwilling to jeopardize his position by wading into the contentious realm of Muslim and Middle Eastern politics.

Looking back, I now realize that my dad wasn't in politics for power and position, but because he wanted to make a difference. Like Lougheed, he wanted to help create a country where there was room for everyone regardless of ethnicity or religion, and under Lougheed's leadership, Dad believed his government could make it happen. But with the premier stepping down, my father became less certain about what the political future would hold. Still, he felt he owed a debt to his country, and perhaps to God, for the inexplicable gift of his continued existence. So as 1985 drew to a close, he decided to run for another term in office and began the arduous task of campaigning for his fourth election, slated for the following spring.

It was past midnight on a bitter winter evening when Paul looked in on Sue's children to make sure they were still fast asleep. In the past year he had grown attached to them. Though things between Sue and him had been rocky at times, he'd been overjoyed when she'd agreed to marry him and couldn't imagine his life without her. Tiptoeing out of the bedroom, Paul grabbed the keys to the old Mustang he'd recently bought and headed for the door. The air was biting and the snow seemed luminescent under a bright moon. The door of his car creaked as Paul opened it and lowered himself into the bucket seat, stiff with cold. The engine groaned several times before finally starting and Paul sat for a few minutes waiting for the car to warm up. He cranked the fan and a blast of frigid air made him shiver. Eventually, two domes of cleared glass began to appear on the frosted windshield. Paul had had a few beers, but his mind felt clear and sharp with purpose.

Over the past few months rumours had begun to surface among the staff at Corona Pizza that Sue and Scott Thorne were having an affair. Though no one spoke about it openly when Paul was around, he knew the rumours the same as anyone else. Jealousy consumed him as he recalled a recent argument during which he'd confronted Sue about how she openly flirted with Thorne and a few of the other regulars.

"I got to make tips," she'd told him.

Recently, Paul had taken to dropping in at night, but that hadn't gone over well. The last time he'd showed up unannounced at the lounge, he'd found Sue chatting with a customer and had lost his temper. After that incident, she told Paul to stay away from the lounge when she was working.

Tonight, Paul had tried to keep his mind on other things, but it had kept swinging back to Sue and Thorne the way a compass needle points north. He drove west down the deserted city streets and pulled up to the curb near the restaurant. His heart was pounding as he approached the front door and pulled it open. Inside the small foyer, a set of stairs led down to the lounge. Paul could hear music playing loudly and the raucous jangle of voices. He shoved his hands deeply into the pockets of his jeans and started down, his eyes trained toward the long bar at the back of the room.

Scott Thorne's back was the first thing that came into view. Sue was laughing at something Thorne was saying, her face inches from his. Paul felt his heart constrict. Sue glanced up then to see Paul standing there, a look of anguish on his face. She laid a hand on Thorne's arm to silence him and whispered something in his ear.

If the man standing so close to Sue hadn't been a cop, Paul would have beaten the shit out of him. But if there was one thing Paul hated more than another guy messing with his lady, it was jail time. If Paul so much as touched Thorne, the cop would make sure Paul was locked up. So he turned on his heel and bounded back up the stairs, angry, hurt and betrayed. All the time Paul had been with Sue, he'd secretly feared he wasn't good enough, that she had her sights set on greener pastures.

By the time he reached his car, he could hardly breathe and tears stung the back of his eyes. He raced across the city, fish-tailing around icy corners as he hurtled toward home. Once inside he grabbed his duffle bag and started throwing clothes into it. He wasn't thinking, only reacting the way he had always done when life turned against him: by hitting the road.

Paul shot out of town, speeding west on the dark, snow-slick highway. He drove fast. Recklessly. He was headed for the only sanctuary he knew: his uncle's home in Prince George. Paul never made it. Somewhere along a lonely stretch of asphalt past Dawson Creek, his car smashed into a bridge abutment and careened off the highway.

The next day Sue got a phone call from the Dawson Creek Hospital with the news that Paul was in serious condition. She booked the night off work, arranged care for her kids, and hopped in her station wagon. When she walked into Paul's hospital room two hours later, her jaw dropped. He looked like a broken puppet. Above his bed was a thick grey metal frame with a series of ropes and pulleys leading to a brace that held Paul's leg suspended in mid-air. Stainless steel rods protruded from his bloodied skin, passing through clamps attached to the frame. Sue felt sick as she stared at the hardware piercing his battered flesh. One of his arms was immobilized in an L-shaped plaster cast with only his fingers visible, and his face was swollen and bruised.

The doctors told Sue that it would be at least a month before Paul could leave the hospital. Though numbed by painkillers, he was still lucid enough to kick up a fuss.

"He wanted to come home," Sue remembers, "but the hospital didn't want to release him."

Paul persisted and eventually the doctors agreed to transfer him to Grande Prairie. Still, Paul didn't make it easy.

"He refused to go in an ambulance," Sue said. "He wanted to come back with me."

In the end, given the choice between staying in Dawson Creek or being transferred by ambulance to Grande Prairie, Paul finally gave in to an ambulance ride.

While relieved to be back in a city with people he knew, Paul's troubles were just beginning. In the days and weeks that followed, he hounded the doctors for medication to ease his pain. They gave him Demerol, but unlike the Edmonton hospital after the plane crash where doctors had quickly cut him off, the Grande Prairie medical staff was more obliging. With each shot Paul found himself feeling blissfully happy, his suffering and his troubles far away.

He'd been in the hospital three weeks when Sue began to notice that he was asking for painkillers all the time.

"What are they giving you?"

When he told her it was Demerol, she got mad. She'd seen how Paul had struggled to get a handle on his addictions before the plane crash and it was awful to see him revert to his old ways.

A week later, when the doctors finally sent Paul home, he left with a prescription for strong painkillers. Still unable to work, he lay around the house. On occasion, he'd hobble into the restaurant to say hello. Elpeda remembers Paul showing up one afternoon in a cast blackened with dirt. He'd wrapped it in a plastic bag, and when he removed it, his foot was filthy, his toenails overgrown and in need of trimming.

Each night when Sue returned from work, she found Paul high on pills, which were disappearing from the bottle at an alarming rate. She hid the bottle and started to hand them out instead of letting Paul take them himself.

But one day she came home to find that Paul had discovered the stash and taken the whole thing. Another night it was Paul who arrived home late. Convinced that Thorne was inside the house, Paul smashed his fist through a window. Sue rushed outside to find him badly cut, his hand bleeding profusely.

By the spring, Paul was able to return to his job at Corona Pizza, but his addictions had also returned, and they were powerful. In addition to drinking and taking pills, he'd started snorting cocaine.

In the months he'd been off work, the slump in the oil and gas industry had begun taking a toll on Corona Pizza and the Bougiridises' other commercial interests. Teddy, who had long supported his family in Greece, found himself unable to provide the financial assistance they had come to rely on. As a result, his relationship with his family deteriorated and Teddy's health began declining in tandem with his fortunes.

Paul thought the world of Teddy and Donna. The couple had not only hired him when he was down on his luck; they had trusted him and looked out for him like parents keeping an accident-prone son away from the knife drawer. Now, with their energies diverted, and Sue's affections seemingly elsewhere, Paul found himself sliding toward a dangerous precipice.

The incident that pushed him over the edge happened during the summer of 1986. Sue had been growing increasingly uneasy with Paul's drug use, and the two frequently fought bitterly, sometimes even violently. Though she drank, Sue didn't use drugs and didn't want them around her kids. In the past she had always trusted Paul, but now she began to worry about going to work in the evenings.

As Sue made her way home from the restaurant one night, her mind was already racing ahead to the state she'd find Paul in when she arrived. The house was quiet as she let herself in. She called his name softly, but he didn't answer. She let her eyes adjust to the dim light, and then tiptoed down the hallway to check on her kids. Both were fast asleep. Breathing a sigh of relief, she returned to the living room. With a start she noticed Paul sitting on the couch, his head flopped back against the cushion, eyes closed. On the coffee table in front of him were a syringe, a spoon and other heroin paraphernalia.

"That's it," Sue said, "you've got to go."

Though he protested, she was resolute. Sometime shortly after, Paul left the only home he'd known in a dozen years. He remained in Grande Prairie for a time, limping into the restaurant in the mornings to open up and do the cleaning. Elpeda thought he might have been living at the York or Park hotel, both popular drinking establishments nearby with rooms above their sprawling main-floor taverns. Paul called Sue and begged her to take him back. She acquiesced, but then had to ask him to leave again.

Sometime that fall or early winter, as Corona Pizza was slipping toward the end of its days—the restaurant would close the following summer—Sue and the Bougiridis family lost track of Paul. What he did or where he drifted over the next two years is unclear. What is certain, however, is that Sue Wink left Grande Prairie for the province of New Brunswick, nearly 4,000 kilometres away, where Scott Thorne had been transferred.

One of the last times Sue recalls seeing Paul isn't a memory she's proud of. It was sometime in the weeks following their breakup. She was working at the bar in the sports lounge. The music was blaring, the room full of regulars, when Paul showed up. He stood uncertainly at the bottom of the stairs for a moment and looked at her. Sue lifted the arm of the record player behind the bar, stopping the music. In the abrupt quiet, conversations died and several customers turned their heads to look at Paul. In a city the size of Grande Prairie there were few secrets, and Paul and Sue's breakup wasn't one of them. As customers shifted uncomfortably, Sue grabbed another record from the shelf and slapped it on the turntable. Then she lowered the needle until it settled into a groove on the well-worn vinyl. The rich, leathery voice of Tina Turner filled the room. The song she was singing: "We Don't Need Another Hero." Across the lounge, Paul looked stricken.

"I took it off before it finished," Sue recalled twenty-seven years later, her voice full of regret.

By the fall of 1986, my father's political star was soaring. In May of that year, he'd won his fourth consecutive election and the new premier, Don Getty, had appointed him Minister of Economic Development and Trade, one of the most senior and coveted portfolios in government. My dad's new position was a nod to his increasing influence. So, too, was the premier's request that he chair two of the government's most powerful committees: Treasury Board, and Priorities and Planning.

As his increasing responsibilities consumed him, the crash receded to the shadows. Soon, however, two incidents would bring Larry's unsettled emotions rushing back. The first was an unexpected visit from Paul sometime that fall or early winter. Larry and Paul hadn't spoken since before Paul's car accident, and Dad recalled being stunned by his appearance, too lightly dressed for the weather and much the worse for wear compared to their last encounter. Paul's hand was a mess of welts and scars, and he walked with a pronounced limp. Now twenty-nine, he'd recently arrived in Edmonton where he was temporarily staying with his brother Michael.

Dad was sad to hear the news about Paul and Sue. Though Paul tried to downplay the significance of their breakup, Dad suspected that it had hurt him deeply. "He was a guy who was in need," my father told me. "He needed somebody to appreciate his worth as a human being."

In his fierce desire to make something of his life, Paul was not unlike my father. But in terms of the cards fate had dealt them, the two men were worlds apart. Dad asked Paul if there was something in particular he needed, anything my father could do to help. Paul shook his head. At the end of their meeting, Dad reached into his wallet and pulled out fifty dollars, which he pressed into Paul's battered hand.

"He took it," Dad remembered, "but that's never what he came for."

The second incident happened just a few months later on a wintry night in early December. Dad and Mom were driving north from Edmonton to High Prairie. On April 17 of that year, after months of continued surveillance and investigation, the federal government had shut down Wapiti Aviation. The airline had immediately launched a lawsuit against Transport Canada for damages, challenging the legality of the decision in court. Though a federal judge had restored Wapiti's operating certificate a month later, the closure had taken a toll on the carrier's regular passenger traffic, and service to smaller communities like High Prairie had been curtailed. As a result, Dad had been forced to revert to making the four-hour drive home from Edmonton every Friday night and then back again every Sunday afternoon.

That night, he'd been happy to have his wife's company. As was always the case after a week's gruelling schedule, he was exhausted, so he'd asked Mom to take the wheel. They were on an isolated stretch of highway east of High Prairie when Dad spotted a distress signal.

"We saw a car's lights go off and on a couple of times and from the angle of the lights, it was in the ditch," he said.

Mom wanted to keep driving.

"Alma, stop!" she remembers Dad saying. "Stop the car. They need help."

As she pulled to the side of the road, Dad was surprised to see that the two stranded motorists were young men. Dad offered to take the wheel from my mom and they opened their doors to exchange seats.

"I talked to the guy for a few minutes," Dad remembered, "and turned to open the back door to let him in."

Meanwhile, Mom sat uneasily in the driver's seat watching the other man circle around to her side of the car.

Suddenly, a fist smashed into the left side of my dad's face. The force of the blow knocked him to the pavement, shattering his glasses and sending them flying into the snow. His head exploded in pain as he felt a boot connect with his cheekbone. On the other side of the car, Mom screamed as the second man grabbed her hair and tried to pull her from the car. Her hands gripped the steering wheel in fear and then she, too, felt a fist slamming into her head. Dad somehow managed to crawl to his feet and lunge across the front seat of the car. His attacker was trying to drag him back out, but Dad was able to grab the arms of Mom's assailant, who was now yanking her from the car by her hair. Through the haze of terror that overwhelmed her, she felt her assailant's hands release her and heard Dad yell: "Run, Alma! Run!"

Without thinking, she did just that. She ducked under the arms of the man Dad held and dashed onto the road. She began running down the centerline of the dark, snowy highway, hysterically waving her arms at oncoming traffic.

"No one was stopping," Mom recalled. She shudders at the memory of hearing her assailant's even, reasoned voice behind her as the first motorist slowed for her.

"Don't pay any attention to her. She's drunk."

As the motorist sped up again, Mom looked over her shoulder at the young man, and beyond him, to her car. Inside she could see the dark silhouette of his accomplice hammering a fist repeatedly downward, but no sign of her husband. A cold certainty came over her that if she didn't get a grip on herself, Larry would not survive. Taking a long, choking breath, she managed to calm herself, stepping once more toward oncoming traffic.

This time when a car slowed and its driver rolled down his window, my mom spoke to him with as much clarity as her heaving voice could manage.

"I'm Alma Shaben," she told him, enunciating her last name, which was well known in the region.

More cars had now begun to slow along the highway. Though vast, the north was still a small community, and she hoped someone in one of the vehicles would recognize the name of their elected government representative.

"My husband, Larry Shaben, is in the car," she said, louder this time. "Someone's killing him."

"That's Larry's wife!" she heard a man yell from an open truck window and relief flooded through her. It was short lived. As soon as the truck's door opened, Mom's assailant took off. With horror, she watched him reach the driver's side of their car and jump behind the wheel. He floored the accelerator and the car shot off down the highway, Dad still inside.

My father was in deep trouble. Not only had his attacker kicked him repeatedly, he'd pushed his head and shoulders between the seats, pinning his arms so Dad couldn't fight back. The young man had then tried to light Dad's hair on fire and had bitten his hand with such force that a large gash lay open across his knuckles. Dad had fought blindly, using every ounce of his strength to throw off the young man. Fear gripped him as he felt the car begin to move.

"I knew that if they drove down the highway with me, that would be it," he told me. "I'd be dead."

With his upper body immobilized, Dad raised his feet and jammed them into the steering wheel, bringing his heels down hard. He heard the driver swear as the car began swerving, and then felt a series of jarring jolts as it left the highway and careened into the snow-filled ditch. That's when my father remembers the men *really* getting angry. Both piled on top of him and were beating him senseless when a group of truck drivers pulled them off.

As my father recuperated in the hospital over the following days, he thought long and hard about his life, and how God had spared him for the second time in twenty-six months. It was that sense of unfathomable providence that would eventually set him on an entirely new path.

ATONEMENT

Hi Erik,

Just a short note to let you know that I am still behind you in every way. I am doing just fine and so are dad and all the kids. How is everything with you? I hope things are looking good for your future. Things will soon slow down and then you can get on with your life. This you well deserve.

I hope you and your girlfriend are doing okay. Lord only knows you two and all your family are very special people and you all deserve a better life than what you have been dealt. I wanted to let you know I still care about what happens to you. Whatever you do, don't give up hope. I still want to fly as one of your crew when you become a captain.

Don't you blame yourself for anything because everything happens for a reason. Just you keep that in mind. Well, I have to go. The plane will be in in about twenty-five minutes. You tell your dad for me that he has a very valuable son that he should be proud of.

Take care and remember we are all hoping for you and will never stop hoping. Caring for you as a brother, and wishing you all the best,

Carla Blaskovits

Erik put the letter back into its envelope and placed it inside an old flight bag that he had been filling with newspaper clippings and legal documents since the crash. Carla's letter meant the world to him. She had been so young on the day she and her sister had rushed into the Slave Lake airport to discover that their mother, Patricia, had been killed in the crash. Carla had since found work with an airline and Erik couldn't help but wonder if her mother's death had something to do with that decision. He had first met Carla during the CASB inquiry and she had stayed in touch. Erik was humbled by her capacity for forgiveness, particularly when Erik couldn't forgive himself.

The question he still couldn't answer, years later, was *why* he had descended below a safe altitude before the needle of his ADF swung, indicating he was over the airport. Not a day went by that he didn't think about it, and his continuing legal battles didn't make things any easier. In 1989 Erik was subpoenaed to appear as a witness in a lawsuit against Transport Canada filed by Sally Swanson and Virginia Peever, who were suing the federal government for negligence. The widows' claim, in part, alleged that for five years prior to the accident, the Canadian government had known Wapiti was repeatedly violating safety regulations, yet had failed to act. Erik had also been named in a defamation lawsuit by Wapiti Aviation against the CBC for a documentary on the crash in which Erik, along with several other former Wapiti pilots, had participated.

These legal claims dogged him as he tried to settle into his new career as a firefighter. He would later become single-minded when it came to safety, and to saving lives, but on one occasion during his early firefighting days, his determination not to be the one to let anything bad happen on his watch may have clouded his judgment.

The incident happened during a house fire. When firefighters arrived at the scene, the homeowner was unaccounted for and thick, black smoke billowed out of the building. Adrenaline was pumping through Erik as he entered the front door. Unbeknownst to the crew, a fire was raging in the basement and a flashover—the most dangerous time of a fire when heated combustible gasses inside a structure suddenly ignite—was imminent. The firefighter behind Erik recognized the danger and bailed out, but Erik— though he'd been taught that his own safety was paramount—was so focused on saving possible victims that he crawled deeper into the house. Outside, the fire truck's air horn sounded once, then a second time—a signal to get out—but Erik didn't hear it above the roar of the fire. He could feel the heat of flames below his hands and knees and through his turnout gear, and was at risk of being caught in the flashover, when another firefighter grabbed him from behind and pulled him out.

Erik also needed to find a way to climb from the financial hole his actions and legal battles had created. He started a second job driving a truck, working his way up from dump trucks and hospital laundry trucks to eighteen-wheelers.

The other debt he felt he owed was to Carla and the other victims of his crash to make sure accidents like his didn't happen again. In the years following the crash, Erik had obsessively followed news of similar small plane crashes. By late 1986, both the CASB and the Provincial Fatality Inquiry had released their findings. In addition to identifying potential safety lapses by Wapiti management, the reports each cited human factors as significant contributors to the crash. Erik began studying accident reports in which factors such as pilot fatigue and anxiety had played a role. Gradually, the answer to the question that had plagued him—*why?*—became clear. Pilots on smaller carriers were often overworked, exhausted, pressured, and just plain scared. Bodies were piling up as a result and no one was doing anything to prevent it.

Erik started speaking out. He offered to talk to pilots at flight schools, warning them of potential hazards. In his two years of training at a top aviation college, his instructors had never once told him what the real world of flying was like—how in the absence of a reliable safety net, pilots were the last line of defense. And even now, no one wanted to listen. One flight school owner whom Erik approached complained that he would be bad for business. With cruel irony, student pilots he tried to talk to dismissed Erik's advice, saying it would never happen to them.

Erik understood. When he'd learned of Duncan Bell's crash, he'd responded the same way. Still, he didn't give up. Determined to make an example of himself, he published letters in aviation safety newsletters. One, titled "It Won't Happen to Me," detailed the effects of pilot fatigue that he now realized had led to his fatal decision making on the night of the Wapiti crash:

an increased willingness to accept lower standards
a breakdown in instrument scanning patterns
mistakes made with familiar actions
decreased attention span
and especially, channelized attention with loss of situational
awareness.

In the process of becoming an outspoken safety advocate, Erik realized something else. He still longed to fly. So though he was climbing the ranks of a new career and driving trucks on the side, he began searching for a way back into the pilot's seat.

In the spring of 1989 Scott Deschamps stood amid the crush of humanity in Beijing's Tiananmen Square. It was hot, and sweat dampened his chest. To his left rose the massive columned facade of the Great Hall of the People, and in front of him, the Monument to the People's Heroes, a 38-metre-high carved stone plinth, pierced a pale blue sky. All around it, across the square's colossal expanse, were tens of thousands of people.

Since April 15, gatherings like this had been springing up in cities across China, sparked by the death of Hu Yaobang, a government official who'd been expelled from the Communist Party for his support of democratic reforms. In Beijing, students and workers had steadily streamed into Tiananmen Square until close to 100,000 were gathered. At first, there had been an almost concert-like atmosphere in the square. Music played and students strung colourful, painted banners from historic landmarks. But as the date of Hu's funeral approached, the demonstrations had taken on a decidedly harder edge.

Scott had studied Mandarin in Canada for two years leading up to his departure and now, after four months in China, was functionally fluent. Being able to speak Mandarin had heightened his enjoyment of the country's centuries-old history and exotic culture, and engendered curiosity and excitement from the people he'd met. For most of them, he'd been one of the first Mandarin-speaking Westerners they had ever encountered.

Here he stood, in the middle of the world's largest central city square, in the most populous nation on the planet, witnessing a sea change in that nation's history. He was thirty-three and considered himself completely different from the person he'd been at twenty-eight when he'd boarded that Wapiti flight. With singular and steadfast resolve over the past five years, he'd been ticking off items on his bucket list.

After the summer he'd lived with Erik and hiked the West Coast Trail, Scott had left White Rock for the resort town of Whistler so he could ski its stunning terrain for the winter. While there, he'd continued working on his undergraduate degree, taking courses through distance education and supporting himself working as a bouncer at a local bar. In the years that followed, he'd spent plenty of time in the outdoors, taken sailing lessons and sailed extensively, learned another language, and travelled to Australia, Europe and now China. None of his recent decisions had been motivated by things that had once seemed so important to him—image, money, possessions and career. Instead, Scott was driven by something far more important: a quest for understanding.

"I talked to psychiatrists, medical people, philosophers, priests," Scott told me in an interview years later. "One person I spoke with dealt with terminally ill hospital patients. He told me about his experiences with patients looking up to a corner of a room and seeing an angel. It was very similar to what I had experienced. He asked his patients: 'Why are you smiling when you're about to die?' I've researched angels, miracles, religion—all those things. Call it what you will, to me it was a spiritual presence and it gave me what I needed at the time. It was life altering."

Yet Scott still couldn't comprehend who or what he had witnessed that night, or why he'd been singled out. He only knew that when it happened, he hadn't felt frightened or alone. He had felt connected to something greater than himself. And despite all he'd accomplished since the crash, that sense of connectedness had eluded him.

In Tiananmen Square, the chants of the crowd intensified. Scott began moving toward the perimeter. As he jostled his way forward, faces came into focus. Hundreds of faces. People with whom he had no worldly connection.

In truth, other than his mother, Pauline, there weren't many people in his life with whom Scott had close connections. One of the goals he'd inked on his bucket list was having children, but he was glad he and Mary hadn't leaped into parenthood after the crash.

"It would have been a disaster," Scott later told me, "because I was too busy trying to figure out what I needed."

When it came to his dad's relatives, Scott had little contact, but he did have questions. Ever since he was young, Scott had heard whisperings of a family secret. Scott's father, Joe, had run an air force base in Zimbabwe during the Second World War; it was rumoured that he had married a woman there and had a child with her. After the war, Joe had apparently abandoned them when he returned to Canada. If the rumours about a second family were to be believed, Scott's father was not the man everyone said he'd been. It also meant that Scott had a half-sibling somewhere in Africa.

His father had been raised in Rossland, a picturesque town in the mountainous Kootenay region of southern British Columbia. The only one of his father's siblings still alive who might know something of his past was his sister, Jeanette, now in her eighties. He resolved to go see his aunt when he got back to Canada.

Shouts of protest filled the air as Scott walked the perimeter road flanking the west side of the square. A small white truck rolled slowly south, the non-stop drone of a female voice blaring from a loudspeaker. At first the words were drowned out by shouts from the crowd behind him. But as the truck drew nearer, Scott understood the woman's words perfectly: "Get off the Square," she urged. "Go back home."

No one has a clear picture of where Paul Archambault lived or how he survived in the years following his breakup with Sue, but accounts from people he was in contact with suggest that he drifted around northern Alberta. One of those people was reporter Byron Christopher, who'd covered the crash, Paul's subsequent court hearing, and the CASB inquiry in Grande Prairie. The two men became friends and saw each other on a number of occasions. During the brief time Paul lived in Edmonton, Byron invited him to dinner at his home in Spruce

Grove, a small town 20 kilometres west of the city. Byron and his wife, Hardis, had also invited two other people to join them that night—Vivian and Jack Murrell. The young couple had endured unimaginable torment. More than a decade earlier, their six-year-old daughter, Tania, had been abducted during her two-block walk home from school. She was never found.

"Later that night, Paul slipped his glass of Baileys liqueur down to our cocker spaniel, who eats anything except dog food," Byron recalled. "Well, the dog got so drunk she weaved her way out of the kitchen with a sort of pleasant look on her face. Paul howled with laugher. We all laughed so hard that tears ran down our cheeks. God, that was funny. The women came in from the living room saying, 'What's going on in here?' Paul said, 'That damn dog just stole my drink.'"

It was the most Byron had ever seen the Murrells laugh in the years he'd known them.

On another occasion, it was Paul's serious side the reporter remembered.

"One night Paul told Hardis and me about the time he had spent in prison. How he had hated prison. Paul talked for three hours, but it seemed like twenty minutes. That talk made quite an impression on me. Paul was the first guy I'd ever met who had spent any time in jail. Paul was basically a good guy and he made me realize there were probably thousands of Paul Archambaults behind bars. He changed the way I looked at prisoners."

Another person Paul made a lasting impression on was Irene Jorgensen, a cook with whom he worked at a drilling rig camp during the winter of 1989. The camp was located in the remote wilderness four hours' drive northwest of Grande Prairie. Irene clearly recalled the first time she laid eyes on Paul, who'd been hired as a camp helper.

"On the way to Milligan Hills, away out in no man's land, we stopped for a ten-minute lunch break. Paul ordered a coffee and my helper and myself each ordered a sandwich and soup. When the food arrived the portions were huge, but also there was something about Paul. Maybe the sadness in his eyes. I'm really not sure. Anyways, I just said: 'This is too much for me to eat in ten minutes.' So I gave him my huge bowl of soup and half my sandwich. He was no doubt very hungry, as it was gone in no time."

In her eighteen years working in camps, Jorgensen had met a lot of people, but Paul stood out in her memory.

"Paul was a good worker," she said, "always doing something. One day he peeled and sliced a half a box of apples. He didn't want them wasted, so asked me if I'd make pies out of them. It wasn't his job. He just did it."

Irene also spoke of Paul's loyalty. "If you treated him good, he'd die for you," she said, "but if you crossed him, look out." Like Byron Christopher, she had heard many of Paul's stories.

"When he felt like talking, he'd tell you about all sorts of things," Jorgensen recalled.

"He said if he spilled a glass of milk as a child he got a real beating. He could never please his stepdad. I don't know what it was about Paul Archambault," Irene said, "but once you met him, you would never forget him. I believe he had a heart of gold that had been badly damaged in his young life."

My father lost touch with Paul again after his second visit, and I know he fretted that he couldn't do more to help him. But Dad was preoccupied with challenges of his own. The province's economic climate hadn't improved, and his days were an endless barrage of long meetings and difficult decisions. The way the government was making those decisions had begun to trouble him. The style of politics, too, was changing. Honour, mutual respect, fairness and transparency—qualities that my father had heartily embraced—were giving way to partisanship and political quid pro quos.

"It wasn't long after the crash that what I was doing became a difficult thing," Dad told me. "I quit enjoying being in politics. A lot of it had to do with problems that were the same issues over and over and over again. People should have been looking after themselves, not expecting government to do it."

As the end of his fourth term in office approached, Dad wrestled with one of the most difficult decisions of his life: should he step down? Don Getty, after a single term as premier, had already announced his intention to retire. Suggestions surfaced that Dad run for the top job, but according to Lindsay Cherney, his executive assistant at the time, Dad felt the government needed new blood.

"If I really believe that," he told her, "why would I hang on?"

My brother Larry remembers similar sentiments.

"The biggest trap in politics," he recalls Dad saying, "is thinking it's about you. You do your job and are treated like a VIP. People roll out the red carpet for you. But the minute you start pretending that you're the reason and not your position, you're lost."

"He still wanted to contribute," Cherney said. "He told me 'I've only got so many more years when I can give something back to the community and if I stay here in government, I'll lose the opportunity to go back out and work in the private sector.'"

By the time the government set an election date for March 20, 1989, Dad decided that after sixteen years in politics, and at the apex of his career, he would call it quits. That election date was his birthday. He would be fifty-five.

There were offers of political appointments—plum posts in crown corporations and overseas political offices. True to his vow not to *hang on*, Dad turned them down and began thinking about a way to chart his own course. As Minister of Economic Development and Trade, he'd encountered many individuals with innovative products who lacked the necessary capital and management experience to make them work. He was excited about the prospect of helping these people and their ventures succeed, and was optimistic that his future in business would be robust.

Meanwhile, Scott's vow to pursue a life driven by dreams and accomplishments rather than money and possessions had hit a decidedly material snag. He was broke. When he returned from China, he'd rented an apartment near the ocean in Vancouver's diverse, densely populated west end. He still hadn't accomplished two of the most important things on his list. At thirty-four he was no closer to creating a family of his own. He also hadn't found his half-sister. However, in the late summer of 1990, someone found him.

Early one Sunday morning, Scott heard his apartment buzzer ring. "Who is it?" he answered on the intercom.

"Paul."

"Paul who?"

"Paul from Grande Prairie" came the reply.

Scott buzzed him in. When he opened the door, he was delighted to see his former prisoner and saviour standing on the threshold.

"He had found my name in the phone book," Scott explained. "He'd just gotten hired as a carnie with a local midway. He'd aged. He'd broken his leg in a zillion pieces in a car accident. He had this big, bad limp. He didn't have any clothes, but he didn't ask for anything from me."

Scott took his old friend out for a meal, and remembers Paul having the same devilish sense of humour that Scott had enjoyed that long day and night they'd spent together six years earlier. "He was a pleasure to be with; a little bit coarse and rude and stinky, but he was my friend."

Scott also remembers Paul being upset because he didn't have a pair of boots to wear—a requirement for his job on the midway. Scott took him out and bought him a pair of work boots and some work clothes. Later, the two men headed to a local bar where, according to Scott, "Paul told more of his stupid jokes. And then, away he went."

Scott laughed as he recalled that brief encounter. "I told him to look me up if he was in town. He said goodbye, and that was it."

It would be the last time Scott, or any of the survivors, would see or hear from Paul.

Andrew McNeil stands well over six feet tall and has the kind of rakish good looks that wouldn't seem out of place on the set of a Western movie. His thick, once-brown hair is cut short and shot with grey, and his eyes are a deep smoky blue. Dark stubble shadows his prominent jaw, and his lips, when in repose, draw a thin, stern line that seems to say: "Don't mess with me."

McNeil owns Alberta Pipefinders Inc., a small, thriving oil pipeline service company in Grande Prairie, and lives in a trim, cream and white bungalow that boasts the nicest lawn on the block. In the late 1980s and early 1990s, however, he was homeless.

At that time, the Wapiti Lodge was the closest Andrew McNeil came to having a permanent roof over his head. The dilapidated two-storey stucco building was a men's shelter just a few minutes' walk northeast of the city centre along the railroad tracks near the hospital. Built as a nurses' dormitory in the 1940s, the drab, flat-roofed lodge was also where Andrew first met Paul Archambault in the late summer of 1989. The men, who became drinking buddies, connected through a mutual friend who was a full-time resident in the shelter.

McNeil clearly remembers the first time he met Paul, introduced by his friend as a hero.

"What?" McNeil recalls asking.

"He's a hero," his friend told him. "You know, he saved those people in the plane crash."

McNeil did know. "I remember when it all went down in 1984," he said. "I thought Paul was amazing. He put his life on the line to save another man."

By the time he met Paul, others were calling him by his nickname, Hero, but most of them didn't share McNeil's sense of amazement.

"That name, Hero, started as something good. People were proud of him. But it switched. Suddenly when they called him 'Hero' it was like calling somebody 'nigger.' I think that ate at him, to be mocked by everybody."

He recalls Paul being a regular at the York and Park hotels, local taverns where friends would hook up every night to drink. These establishments smelled of cigarettes and stale beer, and their clientele were loggers, rig pigs and more than a few alcoholics. According to McNeil, drunks weren't uncommon in Grande Prairie at the time. He suspected several already suffered from wet brain, a layperson's term for a form of central nervous system damage common in long-time drinkers and manifested by a shuffling gait and often incoherent speech.

Paul wasn't one of those. Rather, he and McNeil were among the high-functioning homeless—men who typically worked during the day and headed to the bar every night. Corona Pizza had closed its doors by then and, for Paul, work would have been sporadic.

"Guys would come to the lodge at eight in the morning looking for day labourers to do odd jobs," McNeil recalled, "house painting, drywall, plumbing, electrical, construction. They paid cash and generally the same handful of people would put up their hands."

The tenor of their days was simple: work if you could, come back to the lodge for supper hour from 4:30 to 5:30, shower, and then go drinking. But there were rules. The shelter locked its doors at 11:00 p.m. and, unless a man was paying for his room at the Wapiti Lodge, his stay was temporary.

"They'd give you a few days at a time," said McNeil, "then the trustee would come and tell you: 'Today's your last day; off you go.'"

The men would have to find another place to sleep for several days before they could come back. Sometimes they would couch surf. Elpeda Palmer remembers a night Paul showed up very drunk at her dad's house, which was just up the street from the shelter. Teddy let him stay the night. At other times, the men would head to Muskoseepi Park, a long belt of greenway that bordered the city centre's western flank. There they would hook up with friends who hung out in the tent city on the far side of the river. The ramshackle collection of tarps and roughly hewn platforms was affectionately known as the Queen's Hotel and during summer it was as good a place as any to sleep. Often there was a warm fire crackling and enough cheap whiskey to make a man forget his troubles. The only problem was the cops. Every once in a while the RCMP would sweep through and clear everyone out. The men would scatter for a few days before setting up camp in a different stand of trees a little more removed from the paths that wound along the creek.

McNeil remembers seeing Paul at the park on more than one occasion. As for his troubles, they didn't seem the kind easily drowned in a bottle.

"He was tortured," McNeil said, adding that he couldn't imagine the levels of despair Paul battled.

"If something like that happened to me and I tried to use that as a springboard to change my entire life, and people rallied and raised money . . . and then if you didn't pull yourself up by your bootstraps, well . . . people would think you're just the scum of society. It wouldn't have mattered how many people or who they were who told Paul he was a good man, no amount of money, kudos or coverage was going to suffice because he didn't have enough self-worth to see his own goodness."

Grande Prairie wasn't a particularly kind place for a man without a permanent roof over his head during the final wintry months of 1990. Temperatures hovered between -10°C and -20°C , with the mercury sometimes dropping to as low as -40°C. More than 13 centimetres of snow fell on the city that November and December, and at times the winds gusted up to 55 kilometres an hour.

No one knows for certain what happened to Paul Archambault, but McNeil has a pretty good idea. He believes that Paul and a mutual friend went drinking together one evening and were walking back along the tracks to the lodge when they parted ways. It might have been that Paul had exceeded his quota of nights at the shelter. Or he may have decided to carry on drinking awhile longer, and returned to find the doors locked.

"Because the lodge catered to drunks," McNeil explained, "they were hard ass about it. They locked the doors at eleven o'clock and if you weren't in by then, you didn't get in. Most of the trustees who worked there were only a month or two into being sober, but they'd lord it over you like they'd never touched a drink in their lives."

Paul's younger brother Daniel Archambault, who lives in Ottawa, said he too doesn't know when or how Paul went missing. What Daniel did know was that Paul wasn't well toward the end of his life.

"The last time he came to visit, he had hepatitis and cirrhosis of the liver," Daniel said. Though his brother never stayed anywhere long, Daniel believes his health problems were the reason Paul took off back west.

"He always said that when he died, he wanted to be out in the bush the way Mother Nature meant man to die."

While the centre of Grande Prairie can hardly be considered the bush, there is a corridor of untamed land that runs along the train tracks east of where the Wapiti Lodge once stood. There the ground dips down into the gentle curve of a drainage gulch and snow lies in deep, soft folds along its edges. Sheltering the gulch is a dense thicket of willow trees, their branches a tangle of bare, gnarly brown. Spindly yellow sage grass curls around their feet. A stone's toss to the left, twin rails lie under a fresh layer of new snow, lines of frozen steel stretching north like an unending parallelogram.

On a cold night a man could make his way along the tracks unnoticed, his breath rising in translucent clouds before dissipating into blackness. His boots would crunch on the wind-packed snow and, in the distance, he might hear the hum of traffic or the clank of freight cars coupling and uncoupling in the railway yard a kilometre down the tracks. Above, if it were a typical northern winter night, the sky would glow with the twinkle of a million stars, and if he stared long enough into the abyss he could see the pale sweep of the Milky Way. Conceivably, if the man had had enough to drink, or didn't have a place to sleep, or was ill or just plain heartsick, he might set himself down on the edge of that quiet thicket. Perhaps as he lay back in the snow, oblivious as he'd always been to the cold, and gazed at the edge of his own galaxy, he might contemplate his place in the universe's vast wilderness. If he was feeling blue, he might reflect on his hard luck and how, despite his efforts, he had failed to turn things around—to create a life that he and others could be proud of. And though everyone knew the man to be a survivor, someone who would never give up, he might for a moment surrender to the weariness he felt, close his eyes, and let sleep carry him to a happier place.

In times of heavy snowfall along the railway lines that cut through northern Alberta, locomotives mounted with snowplows roar along the buried tracks. As they do, snow flies off the rails in great white geysers that arch skyward and then curl away from the rails in big C's. They leave snow piled thick and round in white bulging drifts running along either side of the tracks. Andrew McNeil believes that such a snowplow cleared the tracks through Grande Prairie the night Paul died, burying him in an icy grave.

Shortly after the spring melt in the following year, on May 7, 1991, a Canadian National Railways locomotive rolled slowly through the seldom-walked centre of Grande Prairie. It was after dark—10:30 at night according to the newspaper story published the next morning—when the train's headlights illuminated a body floating in a watery ditch about fifteen metres south of the tracks. The decomposition of the body suggested it had been there a long time. Later word would surface that a red poppy—commonly worn during the days leading up to Remembrance Day on November 11 to honour Canada's war veterans—was pinned to the lapel of the deceased's jean jacket. A battered old wallet was tucked into a back pocket. In it was the deceased's identification. He was Paul Richard Archambault, a man at one time lauded locally and nationally as a hero. He was thirty-three.

"Certainly when you have a body turn up, you don't rule out a suspicious death," RCMP Constable Ian Sanderson said at the time, "but so far there's been nothing to say it was foul play."

The body was later taken to the medical examiner in Edmonton to determine the cause of death. An autopsy concluded that he had died of exposure months earlier. No one had reported him missing.

Scott Deschamps learned of Paul's death from an Edmonton reporter who tracked him down for a comment. Still living in Vancouver, Scott was working for the Transit Police, and when he heard the news, terrible memories from his RCMP days in the unforgiving north came vividly to mind.

"In my five years in the Grande Prairie RCMP I saw lots of tangled wrecks of trucks and cars," he recalled. "I'd go into the bush and find these frozen remains."

Though terribly upset by the news, Scott wasn't surprised. "That would be the way he would go."

Others weren't as accepting. Elpeda remembers her mom, Donna Bougiridis, calling her in tears: "Paul's dead." Both women believed his death had to be the result of foul play.

"Paul was a survivor," Donna said. "If you ask me, someone bumped him on the head. I told the police that."

She was teary a quarter century later when she spoke of the crude promissory note found in Paul's wallet when his body was recovered.

"It said: 'To Donna, I owe you $50.'"

In Paul's wallet, police also found a piece of paper on which he'd scribbled another name: Sue Wink. She was still living in Saint John, New Brunswick, when the local RCMP knocked on her door. She hadn't heard from Paul since she'd left Grande Prairie almost four years earlier, and had seen him only once before she'd moved east. That was when she'd driven past Paul as he'd been hitchhiking along the highway.

In the weeks before he died, however, she'd tried to find him.

"In October 1990, my uncle passed away," Sue explained. "I came back to Grande Prairie for the funeral and was looking for Paul. I went into the hotel. I drove around the city. I was watching for him the whole time I was there."

She is haunted by a terrible conviction. "If I'd been able to find him he never would have died," she told me. "I still dream of him."

RETURN

On October 2, 2000, Erik Vogel sat in the co-pilot's seat of an airborne de Havilland DHC-6 Twin Otter. After a decade of effort, he'd clawed his way back into the aviation industry and now flew part-time for West Coast Air, a small float plane operation with scheduled passenger service between Vancouver's inner harbour and the surrounding islands. Erik looked out the cockpit window and took in the stunning view. The weather was clear and crisp, the Georgia Strait glittering below him in the late afternoon sun. Ahead, the Gulf Islands were strung out like a colony of giant green amoebae, their outlines alternately craggy with rock and smooth with sand.

Erik briefly removed his hands from the controls, easing the stiffness from his fingers, which had grown arthritic. They had been progressively worsening after they were mangled in the Wapiti crash. He noticed it most acutely when trucking long distances, as he often did when he wasn't working a shift at the fire hall. Or flying. But Erik didn't complain about his affliction. It was a small price to pay.

As the engine's vibration hummed through him, his chest swelled with emotion. In April he'd turned forty. He and Lee-Ann had married and had three children: a boy and two girls. He'd named his firstborn Duncan. One day he would tell the boy about his namesake, the pilot who had appeared at Erik's hospital bedside the day they brought him in.

Superficially, Erik Vogel's life seemed not unlike that of many other men who had attained a comfortable middle-class existence. He and his family lived on a modest acreage in Langley, a suburb forty-five minutes' drive east of Vancouver. Their house, a sprawling beige rancher, lay at the end of a narrow country lane along which was an understated sign, a small rectangle of metal with green block letters that read: *This Street Is Proudly Maintained by the Vogel Family.* Weathered fence posts and barbed wire lined one side of the road like rustic stanchions, and a grassy, water-filled ditch ran along the other.

At the entrance to the property was a second sign, large and hand painted, advertising pony rides. A gravel drive bisected a thin stand of trees, beyond which lay a sprawling lawn studded with a jungle gym, an enormous black trampoline and several picnic tables. In the distance at the end of the drive stood a little red barn. Every weekend from April through October, the Vogel property was overrun with birthday party participants. Erik had traded, bartered and built the place to entertain kids. He'd also constructed chicken coops that he'd populated not only with chickens, but several turkeys and a peacock. The main attraction, however, was Peaches, the Vogel's coffee-coloured pony. During birthday parties, Erik led Peaches and her excited riders one by one along a trail through the trees on the southeast corner of the property. The trail, which started by accident, had become a labour of love.

"I used to come in here to empty the buckets from the stall," Erik explained. "I stomped down some of the brush and just kept going farther and farther into the trees to dump them. Then, one day I'm walking in here and I realize that I've been making a trail. So I figured why not just keep going."

Erik could recall every storm that had blown across the property, the fences and trees they'd felled. He'd repaired or cleared away most of the damage, but one massive downed tree still remained, its enormous root system exposed to show the kids.

The trail was a wonderland of strange and interesting knickknacks and artifacts Erik had collected over the years. There were ceramic gnomes with floppy hats and bulbous noses, an old fire hose on a metal stand retrieved from a building before its demolition, an ancient, wooden wheelbarrow, and even a plastic pig wearing a polka-dot bikini.

What someone walking alongside Erik through his idyllic acreage might not understand was that he'd been working three jobs, even offering the pony parties, to make enough money to hang on to the farm. There was his primary job with the Burnaby Fire Department, and the second, driving a long-haul truck route every couple of weeks. But the third had been his first love—flying.

At first, Erik had simply kept up his pilot's certification and hours, begging, borrowing and—when absolutely necessary—paying for time in the cockpit, flying small planes at nearby airfields. Erik had shared with Scott his dream to fly again, and it was Scott who eventually connected Erik with his first paid flying position since the crash. Scott told him about a friend at Tundra Helicopters who was looking for a fixed wing pilot to shuttle chopper pilots and equipment to job sites. The company leased a Cessna 206, but had no one qualified to fly it. Erik flew sporadically for Tundra for a year, and then began volunteering with CASARA, Canada's Civil Air Search and Rescue Association.

"It was payback for me," Erik wrote of his five years with CASARA. "You find out fast that locating a small plane is nearly impossible in the bush if there is no ELT."

Though initially trained as a spotter on a Hercules, Erik later got permission from Tundra to use its C-206 to fly a four-man CASARA crew and their equipment on search-and-rescue missions. That privilege—deemed too costly by the company—would later end, as did shortly after, his job. His desire to spend time in the cockpit, however, only intensified. For a short time he flew as a crop duster, and finally, just before his thirty-eighth birthday, Erik had landed a co-pilot position with West Coast Air, a scheduled commercial carrier. Though small and relatively new, WCA was thriving on the brisk commuter traffic between the downtown harbours of Vancouver and Victoria, and to larger surrounding island communities. Erik loved it.

The opportunity had come his way through a former flying buddy who recommended him to the company's chief pilot. Though Erik was hired as a co-pilot, he and the pilot took turns at the controls. On the days he was scheduled to fly, Erik would leave the house early, driving across the Lower Mainland to downtown Vancouver's Coal Harbour, where the airline's modest terminal and docks were located. Dressed in a crisp white shirt and navy tie, he'd head down to the dock to greet his passengers. Often they were politicians travelling back and forth between Vancouver and the provincial Legislature in Victoria.

The days were long, sometimes lasting fourteen hours, and the pay was poor. On a typical shift, Erik might fly anywhere from three to eight legs and get paid a total of $135 a day. Erik didn't tell Lee-Ann about his rock-bottom wages. At the time, the two of them were struggling to make ends meet and Erik worried that if his wife knew how little he earned, she'd make him give up his co-pilot's position. For Erik, the job wasn't about money. It was about the joy of flying. In the remarks column of his pilot's logbook, Erik repeatedly wrote: "Great day!" It was also about being a safer, wiser pilot than the young man who'd succumbed to pressure, fatigue and fear. It was about making things right.

———

When it came to aviation safety, a lot had gone right since the Wapiti crash. On February 6, 1990, the Federal Court of Canada ruled in the case of *Swanson and Peever v. Canada*, finding that the Crown was one-third liable for the fatalities. In his forty-seven-page statement, Justice Allison Walsh wrote:

> Transport Canada was aware of serious deficiencies in the carrier's flight operations and maintenance practices and knew that Wapiti Aviation Ltd. had been repeatedly violating safety standards for at least a year and one-half prior to the accident date. Although Transport Canada had reasonable grounds to believe that Wapiti's operations were unsafe and that vigorous enforcement action was warranted, no effective action was initiated until after the accident to C-GXUC [the plane involved in the crash]. If Transport Canada had exercised its legislative responsibility with timely and effective action to correct the deficiencies in Wapiti Aviation's operations, the accident of C-GXUC most likely would have been averted.

The judgment set a legal precedent. It was the first time in the country's history that individuals had successfully sued the Canadian government for negligence in carrying out its regulatory duties and responsibilities.

For a while, Erik had high hopes. Wapiti had permanently closed its doors and Erik thought the judgment would usher in a new era of aviation safety. He'd joined West Coast Air filled with a renewed sense of optimism. When Erik had started his co-pilot's job two-and-a-half years earlier, training from the company had been excellent and the safety standards high.

Along the docks, he could see the hunger in the eyes of the young men who fuelled the planes; all of them licenced commercial pilots waiting for their chance to get into the cockpit.

And every few months, Erik heard or read about another small plane crash. In most, the details were eerily familiar: pilot fatigue, equipment failure, and pressure to fly in inclement weather. For years, Erik had run a one-man crusade to protect pilots by writing articles and letters, and talking to others about the industry's woeful lack of safety. But he'd grown disillusioned and lately had started to wonder if the risk and meagre pay of his flying job was worth it. Like the trail he'd inadvertently laid through the woods behind his home, Erik realized he had created something wonderful and worth fighting for in his life: a family he loved, and a satisfying career as a firefighter.

Erik laid his hands once more on the yoke. He'd already completed nine legs that day and felt good about his flying. The takeoffs and landings had gone smoothly. The rolling ocean swells of two days ago had flattened into calm waters; the winds were light, and the visibility limitless. He had so savoured the day that, rather than calling it quits after his eight scheduled legs, he'd offered to fly a final flight from Vancouver to one of the nearby islands and back. Now as he approached Vancouver Harbour for the last time, he took in the mountains around him and the glint of afternoon light reflecting off the windows of the downtown office towers. Erik gently pulled the power back and eased the yoke forward, bringing the plane toward the water. When he was ten feet above it, he held the controls steady and slowly pulled back on the throttle levers, allowing the aircraft to settle smoothly on the surface. Then he taxied toward the dock, shut the engine down, and stepped out onto the float. On the dock, an eager young future pilot waited to tie him up. When Erik had seen his passengers off the plane, he pulled out his hardcover blue pilot's logbook and flipped to the last page of entries. Taking a ballpoint pen from his dress shirt pocket, he entered the details of the flight: the month, day, type of aircraft and pilot's name. Under co-pilot he wrote *self.*

Then, under the column titled "Remarks," Erik entered his final notation: *Great last day!*

Around the time of Paul's death, Scott Deschamps began in earnest to search for his half-sister. By then, he had confirmation that the rumours of his father's first wife in South Africa, and the daughter they'd had together, were true.

His eighty-two-year-old aunt knew Scott's half-sister's name was Joanne, and that she lived in Bulawayo. But Scott's efforts to find a Joanne Deschamps in Bulawayo, Zimbabwe's second largest city, turned up nothing. However, as he struggled to find a meaningful connection halfway around the world, one arose unexpectedly under his nose. During a classical music appreciation course in Vancouver in 1996, he met Heidi Petrak, the woman with whom he would start a family of his own.

"She had travelled the world, loved to sail, had a pilot's licence, worked as a ski patroller," Scott said. "Marriage wasn't important to her, but she wanted a child."

The two moved in together and by 1997, Heidi was pregnant. That year, Scott took her to Rossland in search of his family's roots.

"When I arrived, I walked into the legion and found the oldest guy I could," Scott recalled. "I asked him, does he know anything about the Deschamps family?"

What happened next surprised Scott. All of the old-timers huddled together at a window and pointed to a house on a nearby hill. "That's the old place, up there," one of them told him, pointing to the house in which Scott's father and grandfather had lived.

Scott visited the town's museum. He remembers asking the museum's custodian, an older man named Jack McDonald, about Joe Deschamps. "I was Joe's best friend," he replied.

"He knew everything about my father," Scott said of McDonald, with whom he would form a close friendship. "The Deschamps were a founding family in Rossland. My grandfather was raised there and owned all the mills around." Scott later told me he'd discovered that he was twelfth-generation Canadian and that his family had come from Normandy in the 1500s.

While searching the archives at his mom's house, Scott found an old marriage certificate of his father's that also bore the name Rita Wren. By then Scott had not only reconnected with his dad's sister, Jeannette, but with her children, and grandchildren. With the help of a cousin who was a genealogist, Scott began to track down Rita Wren's daughter.

"Within a few days we had three possibilities," he recalled. "One of them was bang on. I wrote to her."

Several weeks later he received a letter from the woman, Joanne Deal. Scott had found his half-sister.

In September 1998 Scott and his cousins pooled their money and bought Joanne an airline ticket to Canada. Reuniting with his half-sister was the only unaccomplished item on his bucket list. At age forty-two, Scott had become a father. His daughter, Jozi, was still a baby when he and Heidi drove to the Vancouver International Airport to meet Joanne's flight. Scott vividly recalled the first moment he saw Joanne: "I looked at her and it was like looking into the face of my father, like I was looking straight at my dad. It was *unbelievable*! I hadn't seen my dad since he died when I was eleven and the similarity was striking. It was profound."

During that visit Scott took his sister to Rossland and showed her their father's old house and around the town where he'd grown up. "She was brave enough to come," Scott said of his sister. "She'd never left Africa in her life; never left Bulawayo, and she came here." Though separated by twelve years in age and entire continents, their relationship thrived. "It was grand," he said. "We got along fabulously and became very close."

Scott learned from Joanne that, though Joe had pleaded, her mother had refused to leave Africa, and that their father had faithfully paid child support until Joanne's eighteenth birthday. That knowledge dispelled the troubling questions about his dad's character that had plagued Scott for years. He also discovered a whole other family who would fully embrace their Canadian "brother."

"It's not about my relationship with Joanne," he would later reflect, "but the relationship of our extended families into the future. That's what it's about. It's the connectedness of that extended family. I never had that connectedness before."

The final piece in the puzzle of Scott's life would not fall as easily into place. Complete comprehension of the events on the night of the crash, including the presence of the Old Man, continued to elude him. In 1999 he completed a Master's Degree in Liberal Arts, during which he delved into the phenomena of miracles and angels. Though not religious, in a paper that would form the basis of his graduate thesis Scott wrote:

In the final analysis, interpretation and understanding of some events really does factor down to faith. For me, exploration into this most profound experience dances at the limits of both science and the supernatural. Was what I experienced a "miracle"? I'm not sure. The spontaneous ignition of the fire could have been just a gust of wind igniting an unseen ember. The opening of the clouds over the crash site could easily have been an isolated high pressure weather "eye." Some phenomena I may never fully understand or may never be permitted to understand. This does not mean it didn't occur. Nor does it mean that it wasn't a miracle—at least to me.

In the years since that experience, there had been only one occasion when Scott felt he might have revisited the realm of miracles. It happened one summer while sailing the remote inside passage of northern Vancouver Island. In 1992, he'd finally won the lawsuit he'd launched against Wapiti after the crash, and with the settlement, he'd purchased *Tanoo*, a twenty-eight-foot sailboat.

A gentle wind filled the sails. Scott sheeted in the main and jib and, with satisfaction, felt *Tanoo* heel and dig in. The rugged beauty of Blackfish Sound surrounded him: breathtaking snowcapped peaks and white-tipped blue waters. As his boat raced on the wind, Scott glanced astern. There, moving fast and directly toward him was the vertical six-foot-high dorsal fin of an orca. The whale's massive black blade sliced the water, drawing rapidly nearer until it was no more than ten feet astern. Then the fin submerged. Scott held his breath. A moment later, the orca surfaced three feet off the boat's port beam. For several long heartbeats the whale and Scott locked eyes. Then, with a huge wallop of its fluked tail, the orca dove, splashing Scott as it disappeared into the depths.

As Scott sat speechless, he couldn't shake the feeling that Old Man had just paid him a visit in the form of the orca. And why not? The West Coast First Nations spoke of the oneness of earth's creatures and believed that animals could supernaturally change their appearance at will to take on a human form and vice versa. All Scott knew for certain was that he was overcome with the same profound sense of peace and reassurance he had felt that long-ago winter night when life had begun anew.

My father's efforts to begin anew would not go as smoothly. True to his word, he'd severed his political ties and moved into a modest office west of Edmonton's city centre. Together with a few associates, he'd launched a consulting company and set out to do what he'd done so successfully in government: bring possibilities to life. From the outset, however, the business floundered.

"He felt let down with opportunities as a private citizen," said his former executive assistant, Lindsay Cherney, who kept in close contact with my dad after he left politics. "He tried to help others and to get ideas off the ground, but discovered that he couldn't do in business what he'd been able to as a Cabinet minister."

My brother Larry also recalls that period of struggle. "His focus was on creating value rather than making money," he said, adding that our father's values often put him at odds with others involved in his business ventures. "When he connected with someone, his commitment was unwavering. If things got difficult, he persevered, and when others didn't follow through, he was disappointed."

Within a few years, many of those upon whom my father thought he could rely had failed him, and the supporters and acquaintances who'd once clamoured for his attention had moved on. I remember visiting him once in his modest, off-the-beaten-track office. It contained a cheap-looking desk, a couple of metal and leather straight-backed office chairs, a bookshelf, a filing cabinet and a stack of unsightly cardboard boxes. The walls were depressingly unadorned. When the phone rang, he answered it himself: "Shaben World Enterprises." He didn't have a computer at the time, and penned his letters in a wobbly script—the result of a pronounced tremor he had developed—then faxed his correspondence to a typist who worked from home. It was crushing to witness.

The year was 1994 and my dad was financially strapped and, though he'd never admit it, deeply disillusioned. It was around that time, according to Cherney, that he began to unpack the boxes he'd brought with him when he'd left the Legislature six years earlier. Inside were old files, memorabilia from his sixteen years in politics, and pictures of his family. As he opened the boxes and started sifting through their contents, my father also began taking stock of his life.

He reflected on the decade he'd lived since the crash. What had he done to repay God for the gift of life? Among the items he pulled from the boxes were photographs of his wife and children, and his father, Albert, who had come to Canada almost a century earlier as an immigrant Muslim boy. Albert, though he couldn't speak English when he immigrated, had gone on to become a leader in his community. Dad realized that the values his father had instilled in him, and that still guided him—charity, tolerance, seeking consensus in decision making, even his reluctance to charge interest on money others borrowed from him—were deeply rooted in his faith. His religion, his family and his roots in the Arab community were an essential part of him. Why then, he wondered, had he put them all aside?

On a Friday afternoon not long after that day, I recall my dad telling me he'd attended Friday prayers at Edmonton's Al-Rashid Mosque. I was shocked, as I couldn't remember the last time he'd done so. The mosque he visited wasn't the understated red brick building where he'd spent his youth celebrating holy days and learning how to dance the *dabke* in the basement. This was a gleaming modern structure with a soaring white minaret and clean, modern lines. In the time Dad had been living in High Prairie and then immersed in his political career, the Edmonton Muslim community had grown from a handful of largely Lebanese families to more than twenty thousand diverse members. There were many faces my father didn't recognize. But many members recognized him as he entered the large open prayer area and knelt on the carpet. Sunlight filtered through the high surrounding windows and the melodious chant of the imam's voice filled the air as my father, shoulder to shoulder with others, bent to pray. When prayers ended, many in the room came to say hello. A quiet buzz about his presence filled the mosque. Men shook his hand, welcomed him and sought his counsel. My father felt as if he'd come home.

Over the next few years, he would continue to attend Friday prayers, even complete the Haj—Islam's sacred pilgrimage to the holy city of Mecca, Saudi Arabia—and to reflect deeply about his purpose in life. But it would be external events, rather than his religious devotion and quiet musings that would set him on his final path.

At two in the morning on Halloween night, 2000, Sol Rolingher, the incoming president of Edmonton's Beth Shalom Synagogue, received a phone call from police. Their news was unsettling: a fire was burning inside Edmonton's largest synagogue. Rolingher dressed quickly and rushed to the building.

"Kids were running up and down the streets in costumes. There was a lot of yelling and partying going on," he recalled.

The fire department had doused the fire by the time he arrived and Rolingher was content to dismiss the incident as a random act by Halloween hooligans until police discovered an unlit Molotov cocktail on the ground outside the building. The perpetrator clearly had intended to throw a second incendiary device when something had gone wrong.

Following a hunch, the police began to search local hospital emergency departments. At one of them, they found a youthful, dark-haired man with a badly burned arm. The young Arab, who spoke little English, had recently arrived in Canada from the Middle East. Police charged him and he was released on bail. He subsequently disappeared.

"All hell broke loose in the Jewish community," Rolingher said. He went to the police who reassured him that the accused had probably fled the country, but the community was not mollified. A lawyer by profession, Rolingher was accustomed to solving problems. This time, however, he was at a loss.

"I didn't know Edmonton's Muslim community," he said, "but I did know Larry Shaben." The two men had met at various political functions. Rolingher picked up the phone. "I don't know where to turn," he told my dad.

"I'll see what I can find out," Dad promised. What my father ended up finding the following year, inside a small mosque in the city's north, was the accused himself. Dad and other members of the Muslim community brought him to a meeting with Rolingher in June 2001. Rolingher remembers my father saying to the young man, who had grown up amid the violence and hatred in Israel and the Occupied Palestinian Territories, "That may be the way they do things there, but it's not the way we do things in Canada." The twenty-one-year-old later apologized to the Jewish community, paid for the damages and faced charges.

"My community owes you a debt of gratitude," Rolingher told my dad after that meeting. "You can count on me."

Three months later, Dad would.

On September 11, 2001, two jetliners slammed into New York's World Trade Center. My father immediately knew that the backlash against the Muslim community would be swift and devastating. As it was, the media often portrayed Muslims in a negative light and the actions of a radical few, like the misguided youth Dad had helped bring to justice, hadn't helped. Now with a Muslim terrorist group identified as the perpetrator of an unspeakable atrocity, my father feared the worst.

Rolingher was quick to understand the repercussions.

"I can't imagine what you're about to go through," he told Dad that afternoon. The two men agreed to draft a statement to release to the media the next day. To their surprise, every media outlet in the city was interested in their announcement, which condemned the attacks and offered sympathy to the victims. In addition, the Jewish and Muslim leaders pledged to "respect each other's faiths, traditions and institutions and continue to work together." It concluded: "To this end those present have reached an accord to meet on a regular basis to continue a dialogue of mutual support and peace." The news release was signed by the presidents of both Edmonton synagogues, the president of its largest mosque, and by one private citizen, Larry Shaben. As a result of these actions, Edmonton would become one of the only major cities in Canada after 9/11 where there was no significant backlash against Muslims. My father would also discover a way to put his values into action and to fulfill his commitment to make a positive difference with the years he'd been given.

The dialogue that my father and Sol Rolingher began between their communities would rapidly spread to include the Edmonton Police Service Hate Crime Unit as well as the city's Catholic community. The four parties soon formed the Phoenix Multi-Faith Society whose goal was fostering understanding and respect for all faiths and eliminating negative stereotypes, bias and prejudice. The initiative would be widely lauded, eventually garnering attention from the International Police Service, who later presented Edmonton's police department with an award for its commitment to civil rights.

While interfaith dialogue was important to my father, he knew that serious dialogue was also needed within his community. From a handful of Lebanese families and a single, tiny mosque that had welcomed everyone, including Greeks, Jews and other minorities, Edmonton's Muslim community now worshipped in half a dozen mosques across the city. Its followers, comprised of more than fifty diverse ethnic backgrounds, belonged to different sects that were at times openly hostile to one another.

My father understood that if he were to fight racism and stereotypes against Muslims, he would first have to bring his fractured community together. In late 2001, he invited the leaders of Edmonton's various mosques and Muslim communities to a meeting that has since become legendary. It is likely that a man of lesser stature would not have succeeded in bringing such a group of Muslims together. And it is almost certain that no one else could have gotten away with the ground rules my father imposed on the participants that day.

"Park your ego at the door," he told them. "Treat each other with utmost respect and resist the temptation to lecture."

That conversation marked the start of what would become the Edmonton Council of Muslim Communities, an umbrella organization of Muslim groups, mosques and communities whose mission was to eliminate acts of racism against Muslims and promote a deeper understanding of Islam. Its values embodied the dream of a better society—one that embraced humility, respect, non-violence, honour, diversity, integrity, honesty, fairness, teamwork and collaboration.

These values were grounded in Islam itself and guided by the hand of a man who understood what was possible when people set aside their differences and worked collectively. It was a lesson my father had learned from his family, his faith and his fellow survivors.

EPILOGUE: SURVIVORS

n October 2004, Larry Shaben descended on an escalator to the arrivals area of the Vancouver International Airport. Tucked inside his shirt pocket was a folded copy of an e-mail he'd received from Erik Vogel a week earlier. Don't worry about recognizing us, it said, we'll be the ones grinning like idiots.

Almost twenty years to the day after the crash of Wapiti Aviation Flight 402, Larry arranged one of the most significant meetings of his life: a reunion of the survivors.

"It felt like something that needed to be done," he said.

He was just shy of his seventieth birthday and sported a fringe of gray hair around his balding head. His face had softened into a kind, fleshy roundness and his olive skin was speckled with age spots. His brown eyes appeared enormous behind thick glasses and his smile was warm and easy. Larry seemed to have grown into the nickname Paul Archambault had privately given him so many years before: Mr. Magoo.

He was dressed in faded jeans and a pale blue cotton shirt, a far cry from the power suits of his days as a high-profile politician. A bulge of stomach protruded over his cinched brown belt, testimony to his wife's good cooking. Larry stepped gingerly from the escalator and walked toward the automatic doors that opened to the baggage claim area.

"Larry!" a voice boomed from the other side as the frosted glass doors slid open. Then he saw them—Erik Vogel and Scott Deschamps, the only other remaining survivors of that long-ago tragic night. The pilot, whom Larry remembered as being little more than a boy, was tall and still handsome. He'd filled out since those days, and the haunted look that Larry remembered was nowhere to be seen on his smiling face. He looked like a man you could trust your life to. He wore black jeans and a green polo shirt with the insignia of the Burnaby Fire Department clearly visible on his broad chest. His brown hair was cut short and he continued to sport a bushy moustache.

Standing next to him, and a full head shorter, was Scott Deschamps. Erik had picked him up at the ferry terminal earlier that day and together they had driven to the airport to meet Larry's flight. Scott and Erik had kept in touch over the years. Not long before Scott moved away from the city, he'd called on his friend for a last-minute favour.

"I'm putting together a birthday party for my daughter and I need a pony," Scott told him.

"When?" Erik asked.

"Tomorrow."

The former pilot hadn't missed a beat. "What time?"

"Eleven-thirty."

The next day, according to Scott, Erik had pulled up at his house with a trailer carrying his pony, Peaches.

On the day of the reunion, Scott wore beige chinos and a button-down dark green shirt. Though less the Adonis than Larry remembered, at forty-eight Scott still appeared fit and youthful. His thick auburn hair was shot through with gray and his eyes were sparkling. As promised, both men were grinning like idiots.

They approached Larry as if two days rather than two decades had passed. "There was not a trace of awkwardness," Larry remembered.

Without hesitation, the men traded hugs instead of handshakes. Larry's suitcase slid down the ramp and Erik plucked it deftly from the carousel. Conversation flowed easily as they made their way outside to Erik's car. They drove to a nearby restaurant where they settled knee-to-knee around a small table. As they ordered drinks and waited for lunch, they joked about the changes time had wrought in their appearances and their lives.

"Each of us was interested in what the others had gone through and each had completely different experiences," Larry would later recall.

By then Erik had eighteen years of firefighting under his belt and had recently achieved the rank of lieutenant with the Burnaby Fire Department. He pulled out a small, bugle-shaped brass lapel pin and gave it to Larry. It was the pin the department had given to Erik when he'd received his promotion. The gesture moved Larry greatly.

"I've become 'Mr. Safety' at the fire station," Erik said, lightening the mood. "Most of the guys think I'm totally anal."

He'd achieved the highest levels possible in Industrial First Aid and as a First Responder, was a certified CPR instructor with both St. John Ambulance and the Red Cross, and had trained with the Coast Guard and the Vancouver Fire Department's fire boat program. He'd also trained in high-angle rescue, which equipped him to extricate injured or trapped victims in environments ranging from tower cranes and bridges to building shafts and steep slopes. In his off hours, Erik still drove eighteen-wheelers.

"I'm certified to drive, fly or boat anything now," he quipped, adding, "it never seems like enough."

Scott had returned to law enforcement and was working with the criminal justice department. "I still do what I used to do," he explained, "because that's what I was trained for. But I do it differently. I'm not the black-and-white, rigid, career-driven, typical kick-down-the-door cop that I was."

In 2002, Scott and his family had abandoned the hectic crush of the city for the quiet coast of Vancouver Island. "I'm not grinding it out in Vancouver," he said, describing his life as peaceful.

Scott had grown close to his half-sister over the years and the two had spoken by phone every two weeks. Not long after Joanne's first visit to Canada, Scott had travelled to Bulawayo where he'd met his nieces and Joanne's four half-brothers, who had taken him hunting on the African savannah. He'd since become very close to Joanne's daughters, with whom he corresponded regularly.

A year after the survivors' reunion, Joanne fell ill. One of her daughters called Scott and he returned to Africa, this time to be at his sister's bedside during her final days. "I had her for five years," he said, his voice full of gratitude. "Even better than the relationship I had with her is the relationship I have with her daughters and granddaughters. I have little grandnieces that are the same age as my own children."

Larry had continued to dedicate himself to philanthropic and volunteer work. He was now a pillar of the Muslim community, a voice for interfaith tolerance and understanding, and a tireless champion for future generations of Muslims. He had helped raise money to build an Islamic school in Edmonton, and would later be instrumental in establishing Canada's first academic chair in Islamic studies at the University of Alberta—a post intended to increase knowledge of Islam's rich intellectual and cultural heritage and its relationship with other societies and faiths. Through his work with the Edmonton Council of Muslim Communities, he also established an annual dinner held after Ramadan—the month of the Islamic calendar during which Muslims the world over refrain from eating and drinking during daylight hours, and focus on increasing charitable contributions to others. The dinner was not intended to feed members of the Muslim community, but instead to provide a free, family-style meal to one thousand needy residents of Edmonton's inner city.

Larry did not limit his volunteerism to his own community. He served on the boards of numerous non-profit societies working to improve the lives of the less fortunate. One of those non-profits was Homeward Trust, an organization with a mandate particularly close to his heart: ending homelessness. So instrumental were Larry's efforts to create safe, secure and affordable housing for Alberta's homeless that the organization would later create an award in his memory. Called the Larry Shaben Award for Outstanding Leadership in the Housing Sector, the annual award now recognizes individuals "highly committed to working in the housing sector, who promote or develop housing or related services and who are passionate about what they do."

By the time the food arrived, talk at the reunion had turned from the present to the long night the men had shared two decades earlier.

"You never sat down the whole time," Erik asked Larry. "Why?"

"My tailbone was sore." Larry did not say broken, as if such specifics were somehow trivial.

Erik and Scott reminded him of how he'd wanted to walk out of the bush that night, and how it had taken Paul's physical restraint and every bit of persuasion they possessed to stop him. They could now laugh at the fact that Larry wouldn't have had a hope of surviving if he'd left the crash site that night.

Scott recalled the stream of colourful jokes Paul had rattled off to entertain them during their ordeal. Though they did not speak of his death, the tragic end of the man who had helped keep them all alive hovered on the edge of the reunion. Paul was the one who had the shortest distance to fall and the farthest to climb. His spectacular rise to heroism had given each of them hope during the difficult years in which they all struggled; proof that something truly good could come of a terrible tragedy. Now the survivors knew that each of their lives was both a journey of discovery and privilege. Between them there was also an unspoken understanding of the lucky fact that they sat here together.

Toward the end of the meal, Larry reminded Erik and Scott of the question he'd asked in the darkest hour of the night, when the survivors thought the rescue planes had abandoned them: "What would you wish for if you could have anything in the world right now?"

For Erik, it had been a cold drink, for Larry, a hot bath. He recalled that Paul had wanted a joint. That recollection made them laugh.

Scott didn't remember his wish that night, but Larry recalled it for him. "You said, 'I would like to take my wife in my arms and apologize to her and tell her yes, we can have a child.'"

Scott, who now had two children who were more important to him than anything else in the world, knew that the night of the crash had been a rebirth. "My whole life changed in an instant," he said. "When I get unfocused, or fuzzy in my priorities, or stressed, disappointed or out of sorts, I just have to take my mind back to that time and things become clear. Clarity of thought comes when you're lying on a mountain, dying. That's when you're honest, authentically pure in your thoughts. Not too many people have that experience."

Erik and Larry understood. In their own ways, they had both continued to honour the experience. Every October 19, Erik would take the day off work. Larry would send an e-mail to his fellow survivors letting them know he was thinking about them and reminding them how lucky they were to be alive.

"Every year on that day I wonder what good I've accomplished in the extra years I've been given," Larry said.

For each survivor this was the indelible mark of that night—not one to be found in the groove of scars on Larry's shins where the metal of the seat had cut into his flesh, or the bump on Scott's head that never went away, or Erik's arthritic hands. The true mark of that tragedy was who they had become and how they lived their lives each and every day.

Conversation dropped off as the waitress arrived to clear the dishes. Larry's coffee cup clattered against the table as his now unsteady hands set it down.

"This was a good idea," he said. "We should do it again."

Erik seconded the suggestion. Although he didn't admit it at the time, he'd been nervous about the reunion. "It was much more comfortable talking about it than I imagined it would be," he wrote in an e-mail to Larry two days later.

The twenty-year reunion of the plane crash would be the last time the three men would meet. Four years later, before they had an opportunity to make good on their promise to reunite, Larry Shaben, at the age of seventy-three, died of cancer. Two days before his death, Erik wrote him a final e-mail:

> *To Larry,*
> *I am writing this with a heavy heart from my new "desk job." The only reason that I looked forward to October 19th was because I would get a note from you reminding us that we were lucky to be alive and how great life was going. It always made me smile . . . You have been a hero in my "new" life,*

Larry, and I have tried to make you proud with our new lease on this life.
I was hoping to give you a new tiepin to go with your bugle that I gave you.
This one is my new Captain's bugle that came with my promotion. I know it
is just a job, but this job helped me redeem myself to you and many others.
I will miss you, my friend. And now, I have to explain to my chief across the
room why a 6'3" Fire Captain is crying at his desk.

Every October 19, on the anniversary of the crash of Wapiti
Aviation Flight 402, Erik Vogel continues to take the day off work.
He e-mails Scott Deschamps and, if the day is warm and sunny, he
thinks not just of the tragedy, but also of its survivors, their transfigured lives, and that memorable reunion twenty years later. That late-
autumn day, when Erik, Larry and Scott finally emerged from the
restaurant, the sky was a bright, brittle blue, and the sunlight was
warm on their faces. Just out of sight and not far to the west was the
Vancouver airport. Above the hum of city traffic, Erik could just
make out the distinct pitch of powerful engines starting up. Slowly
they revved to life, the sound growing from a whisper to a whine,
and finally to a roar as an airplane thundered down the runway, lifted
from the ground and took flight.

NOTES

EPIGRAPH

Diane K. Osbon, *Reflections on the Art of Living: A Joseph Campbell Companion*, New York: HarperCollins, 1991, 24.

INTRODUCTION

4   "In the words of Campbell": Diane K. Osbon, *Reflections on the Art of Living: A Joseph Campbell Companion*, New York: HarperCollins, 1991, 22.

6   "A major investigative report on Canadian aviation incidents between 2000 and 2005": Robert Cribb, Fred Vallance-Jones, Tamsin McMahon, "Collision Course," *Toronto Star*, June 3, 2006.

PART I

Epigraph: Lucius Annaeus Seneca, as translated from *Epistolae Morales ad Lucilum, (Moral Letters or Epistles to Lucilius)*, letter 70, number 14.

1. DEPARTURE

13   "any passengers headed for High Prairie": Interview with Larry Shaben, October 10, 2004.

15   "I'll tell you what . . . if we can't land": Ibid.

16   "Gordon had planned to take the bus": Interview with Bob Nazar, June

11, 2012. Nazar drove Gordon Peever to Edmonton the day of the crash.

17   "Watch me": Interview with Scott Deschamps, December 5, 2007.

18   "if there is any trouble, the full force of the RCMP will be on you": Ibid.

22   "'Wapiti 402,' a voice squawked into his headset": D. L. Abbott, Aviation Safety Bureau, Investigation Division, Edmonton Municipal Air Traffic Control tower tape recording, November 6, 1984, 2.

22   "Erik felt pressured to get into his destinations": In a 1990 Federal Court of Canada judgment, Justice Allison Walsh concluded: "There was considerable evidence to establish that Wapiti Aviation Ltd. exerted considerable pressure on its pilots to induce them to fly in marginal weather conditions, flying under VFR (Visual Flight Rules) at night when weather conditions required that the flights be undertaken under IFR (Instrument Flight Rules) which require a second pilot or at least an auto-pilot in good working condition." Judgment in Court Action No. T-1637-85 between Sally Margaret Swanson and Her Majesty the Queen, February 6, 1990, 13.

25   "Unfortunately, only one of the plane's two ADFs was serviceable": Canadian Aviation Safety Board Civil Aviation Occurrence Report Number 84-H40006, *Wapiti Aviation Ltd. Piper Navajo Chieftain PA-31-350 C-GXUC*, December 18, 1986, 21.

26   "You can remain on this frequency": D. L. Abbott, ATC tower tape recording, 3.

26   "On that flight, the plane had broken through the clouds 2000 feet above the airport": Canadian Aviation Safety Board, *Wapiti Aviation Ltd. Inquiry Proceedings, H40006*, Grande Prairie, Alberta, February 26–March 1, 1985, 54.

27   "Dale would ask what altitude he had tried": Ibid., 128.

29   "I just got the call that Wapiti had room for me": Larry Shaben interview, October 10, 2004.

30   "I am lucky to be alive": John Geiger, "Bizarre Omen Before Crash: Notley Killed Elk 2 Months to the Day of His Death," *Edmonton Sun*, October 22, 1984, 13.

30   "Wapiti four zero two is inbound from the southeast on descent": Whitecourt Flight Service Station tape transcript, Edmonton Municipal Tower, November 6, 1984, 2.

31   *"Why isn't the needle swinging?"*: Interview with Erik Vogel, October 21, 2003.

2. IMPACT

33   "The plane finally came to rest upside down 684 feet from where it had first hit the trees": Canadian Aviation Safety Board Civil Aviation Occurrence Report Number 84-H40006, 8.

33   *"I'm going to die"*: Paul Archambault, "They Called Me a Hero," unpublished manuscript, 1985, 21.

34   "You dumb, fucking asshole!": Larry Shaben interview, October 10, 2004.

35   "One end was wet, so he tore it off": Archambault, "They Called Me a Hero," 34.

PART II

Epigraph: Leonardo Da Vinci, *Codex Forster III, 66v.*

3. FLIGHT

48   "if you survived a summer at La Ronge, then you must be okay": Author correspondence with Vogel, September 20, 2007.

50   "Bush pilots have the highest mortality rate of any commercial pilots": CNN Money, "America's Most Dangerous Jobs," August 26, 2011, http://money.cnn.com/galleries/2011/pf/jobs/1108/gallery.dangerous_jobs/4.html.

51   "Tell him to go away": Vogel interview, November 8, 2011.

55   "we'd never stay in business": Ted Grant recalls his former partner, Paul Jones—a long-time bush pilot—expressing similar sentiments. Interview with Ted Grant, June 21, 2012.

4. WAPITI

60   "Dale Wells would get in the airplane and make him do the flight again": The Canadian Broadcasting Corporation, *the fifth estate,* 1985–1986, episode 20: "Dead Reckoning."

60   "Fourteen pilots had quit or been fired from the airline in the previous six months": Judgment in Court Action No. T-1637-85 between Sally Margaret Swanson and Her Majesty the Queen, February 6, 1990, 15.

61   "failed to conduct the mandatory airworthiness inspections": Transport Canada notices of aircraft conditions for Wapiti Aviation Ltd., October 2, 1984. Courtesy of Dale Wells.

61   "It didn't strike me as a place I wanted to stay a long time": Canadian Aviation Safety Board, *Wapiti Aviation Ltd. Inquiry Proceedings, H40006,* 141–42.

62   "take this flight or you won't be taking any": Judgment in Court Action
      No. T-1637-85 between Sally Margaret Swanson and Her Majesty the
      Queen, February 6, 1990, 15.

65   "I've got a flight to McMurray and I really could use a co-pilot": Vogel
      interview, October 21, 2003.

65   "pilots who broke the rules": Department of Transport telephone record
      of discussion between Jim Powell and Dave McCracken, October 15,
      1984. Courtesy of Dale Wells.

66   "engaged the autopilot on his plane and it responded erratically": Vogel
      interview, October 21, 2003.

66   "practice of terminating pilots before their ninetieth day of employment
      to avoid having to provide two weeks' notice and holiday pay":
      Judgment in Court Action No. T-1637-85 between Sally Margaret
      Swanson and Her Majesty the Queen, February 6, 1990, 14.

68   "Pretty ugly icing up there": Vogel interview, October 21, 2003.

70   "I barely made it off": Vogel interview, May 12, 2009.

70   "*Ceiling 1,000 ft broken, 2,000 ft overcast*": Canadian Aviation Safety Board
      Civil Aviation Occurrence Report Number 84-H40006, 5.

73   "support be given to Wapiti Aviation, for the establishment of a regularly
      scheduled air service, whereby the Carrier could overfly localities in the event
      that there was no confirmed traffic": Minutes of a meeting held at the Town
      of Fairview Provincial Building to discuss the feasibility of establishing a
      scheduled air service from Grande Prairie to Edmonton via Fairview–Peace
      River–High Prairie–Slave Lake, March 2, 1982. Courtesy of Dale Wells.

74   "I am in complete support of the entire concept": Larry Shaben, Alberta
      Minister of Utilities and Telephones, correspondence with Ike Lawrence,
      chairman, High Prairie Airport Commission, April 1, 1982. Courtesy of
      Dale Wells.

74–75 "RCMP had written Dale a letter alleging violations of regulations":
      Royal Canadian Mounted Police, Memorandum 1413-83, February 1,
      1983. Courtesy of Dale Wells.

75   "This nonsense has got to stop": Carol Picard, "Pilot Admits Flight
      Unsafe," *Edmonton Sun*, December 17, 1985.

PART III

      Epigraph: "Dark Night of the Soul" by Saint John of the Cross: A. Z. Foreman,
      "Poems Found in Translation," http://poemsintranslation.blogspot.com.

5. THRESHOLD

79 "There was a long, ear-splitting *grrrrrrrr*": "Terrible Crack Signaled Disaster," *Calgary Herald*, October 22, 1984.

6. BURIED

84–85 "The world around him was a mixture of muted white and dim shadow": Scott Deschamps, "Once Upon an Angel: The Story of Flight 418," Simon Fraser University, Master of Arts in Liberal Studies essay, 2009, 1.

86 *"Why can't I find the windows?"*: Vogel interview, October 21, 2003.

87 "I have to get out of here now. I can't breathe!": Canadian Aviation Safety Board, *Wapiti Aviation Ltd. Inquiry Proceedings*, H40006, 229.

88 "The person's jaw was crushed. It felt to Paul like mush or rubber": Archambault, "They Called Me a Hero," 23.

7. FIRE

90 "It seemed to Paul that Larry and Erik had no mind or that they were really dazed": Archambault, "They Called Me a Hero," 25.

91 "I'm happy you're here": Ibid., 26.

92 "Where's your friend?": Vogel interview, October 21, 2003.

94 "Paul moved around touching everyone he could, but they were all dead.": Archambault, "They Called Me a Hero," 26.

94 "His right arm was stuffed into the pilot's flight bag": Ibid.

8. MISSING

97 "Over the past few days the weather had truly been a concern": Luella Wood, personal diary, October 21, 1984.

97 "Edie, anybody call?": Interview with Luella Wood, July 20, 2011.

98 "She couldn't explain it, but things just didn't seem right": Wood diary, October 21, 1984. Wood later noted that there was "hardly a Wapiti pilot who came through High Prairie who wasn't worried" when it came to mechanical issues or a potential accident: Wood interview, June 25, 2012.

98 "Pacific Western Airlines Flight 594": Canadian Aviation Safety Board Civil Aviation Occurrence Report Number 84-H40006, 9.

99 "It can't be": Wells interview, December 22, 2007.

100   "RCMP is here and the military has launched a search": Wood diary, October 21, 1984.

101   "find out if any other government members from the north are on that plane": Interview with Bob Giffin, June 2, 2011.

102   "Grant had stayed over in Edmonton because the Wapiti flight had been fully booked": Ibid.

103   "Grant had caught a flight out of Edmonton": Peter Stockland, "Notley Kids Broke News," *Edmonton Sun*, October 22, 1984.

104   "Del had not wanted to get on a plane since": Wells interview, December 22, 2007.

104   "had demonstrated strong airmanship, the ability to think on his feet, and a good awareness of what was going on around him": Canadian Aviation Safety Board, *Wapiti Aviation Ltd. Inquiry Proceedings*, H40006, 315.

104   "During passenger check-in Dale had briefly considered taking the flight himself": Wells interview, December 22, 2007.

105   "prima donna pilots who'd come and gone over the years": Ibid.

105   "They wanted everything handed to them on a platter": Ibid.

105   "I'm in the vicinity and I'm going to try to locate the ELT signal": Wood diary, October 21, 1984.

106   "All hell's breaking loose": Interview with Marvin Hopkins, June 14, 2011.

107   *"Don't crash"*: Interview with Dave Heggie, June 13, 2011.

9. CONFESSION

110   "He'd diagnosed his own condition as a flail chest": Deschamps interview, December 5, 2007.

111   "there are four chocolate chip cookies in that bag": Vogel interview, October 21, 2003.

112   *"He's going to kill me for crashing the plane"*: Ibid.

112   "we're not leaving you. Rescue is coming soon": Archambault, "They Called Me a Hero," 27.

114   "Does the government consider there is, if not a legal obligation, a moral obligation for restitution?": Alberta Hansard, Legislative Assembly of Alberta, October 19, 1984, 1219.

114   "I could tell he was hurting physically and emotionally": Larry Shaben interview, October 10, 2004.

10. SEARCH

117 "ceiling of zero feet and one-eighth of a mile visibility": Search and Rescue Mission Report 8400448, SAR Vogel, October 19–20, 1984. Obtained through Access to Information Request A-2011-00242, Library and Archives Canada.

117 "Paul commented on how beautiful they were, busted up and covered in blood": Archambault, "They Called Me a Hero," 27.

117 "Any time you can walk away from an airplane, you're lucky": Peter Stockland, "Shaben Describes Nightmare," *Edmonton Sun*, October 23, 1984.

121 "the signal was weak and distorted, often fading in and out as if obscured by something unseen below": Rescuers later discovered that the cause was the plane's upturned position, which had partially buried the ELT antennae in the snow.

122 "he was sure it had been the man's soul leaving his body": Interview with Daniel Archambault, April 1, 2009.

123 "*Airport '77*": Archambault, "They Called Me a Hero," 11.

123 "What kind of chance would I have to become a cop?": Ibid., 14.

123 "they'd turned him down because he had only one kidney": Daniel Archambault interview, April 1, 2009.

11. ABORT

128 "We're outta here": Vogel interview, October 21, 2003.

129 "*Why would they drop it over there?*": Ibid.

130 "'Is it on?' Paul asked, a note of sarcasm in his voice": Deschamps, "Once Upon an Angel," 5.

131 "decided to shut down the faltering No. 2 engine to conserve fuel": Interview with Everett Hale, June 10, 2011.

12. CRIMINAL

134 "It's too quiet . . . I don't like it": Deschamps, "Once Upon an Angel," 6.

134 "If it's not working, we'll try to fix it": Archambault, "They Called Me a Hero," 33.

134 "Watch out where the huskies go, and don't you eat that yellow snow": Frank Zappa, "Don't Eat the Yellow Snow," © 1974 Munchkin Music. Grateful acknowledgement is made to Gail Zappa and the Zappa Family Trust.

135   "loss of situational awareness is responsible for up to 15 percent of fatal crashes": Richard Leland, "Night VFR: An Oxymoron?" *Journal of Aviation/Aerospace Education and Research*, Vol. 9, No. 1 (Fall 1999), 13–15, Embry-Riddle Aeronautical University.

137   "Fatigue is by far the most common physiological factor contributing to aviation mishaps": Ibid.

137   "I'm going to pass out": Archambault, "They Called Me a Hero," 34.

138   *"The little bugger's a chain-smoker"*: Larry Shaben interview, October 10, 2004.

140   "a B and E occurred and $10,000 was stolen from the club": Jack Aubry, "Quebec Court Gives Hero Probation for Break and Enter," *Ottawa Citizen*, January 9, 1985.

140   "turned down the idles on every cop car that came in for repair": Daniel Archambault interview, April 1, 2009.

142   "Paul was locked up inside a windowless concrete room where he slept on the floor": Archambault, "They Called Me a Hero," 4.

143   "I'm a human being just like you": Ibid.

13. ICE

145   "He closed his eyes and tried to conjure some long-forgotten God": Deschamps, "Once Upon an Angel," 8.

146   "he was not going to get out of here alive": Ibid., 9.

147   "having kids as nothing more than an outdated biological urge": Ibid., 10.

148   "Scott knew with utter certainty that he was looking into the face of an otherworldly presence: God, an angel or a benevolent spirit": Ibid., 11.

148   "Larry stepped behind him and embraced Paul in a firm bear hug": Archambault, "They Called Me a Hero," 31.

148   "Even as a child, he had felt his dad's constant disapproval": Daniel Archambault interview, April 1, 2009.

149   "had talked her doctor into letting her go home early to be with her husband and children": Tom Barrett, "Father and 14 Children Fear Future," *Edmonton Journal*, October 23, 1984, 1.

151–52   "someone below had to be alive and cycling the switch": Interview with Hazen Codner, June 28, 2011.

152–53   "Vivid in his mind were the images of corpses lying frozen and lifeless in the car wrecks he'd responded to during his time as an RCMP officer in northern Alberta": Deschamps, "Once Upon an Angel," 7.

153   "fire off a couple of shots and bring the planes circling back": Archambault, "They Called Me a Hero," 37.

153   "afraid that the fire might spread and gut the fuselage": Ibid., 33.

153   *"We're alive! We're here!"*: Ibid., 31.

153   "My wallet. It's still in the plane": Larry Shaben interview, October 10, 2004.

154   "If you had one wish you could have fulfilled right now": Ibid.

154   "I'd tell my wife I'm sorry": Ibid.

154   "When this is all over we're going to get together and have a few drinks": Archambault, "They Called Me a Hero," 35–36.

155   "Scott, do you know that you're a sniveller?": Ibid., 36.

156   "Campfire on the ground!": Codner interview, June 28, 2011.

14. RESCUE

158   "In daylight, he saw everything in gruesome detail": Archambault, "They Called Me a Hero," 38.

158   "An orb of ice the size of a racket ball hung from his mouth": Ibid.

159   "Larry, wake up!": Deschamps, "Once Upon An Angel," 13.

160   "You must be stoned or something": Archambault, "They Called Me a Hero," 38.

160   "We're going to be found here, so we stay together": Ibid., 35.

160   "We're not going to last much longer": Deschamps, "Once Upon an Angel," 15.

162   *"That's strange.* He was trying to figure out why on earth a canoe would be in the middle of the wilderness": Interview with Bill Burton, September 23, 2011.

164   "The guys on the ground need your help": Interview with Brian Dunham, July 19, 2011.

164   "You don't by any chance have a Thermos of coffee in your pack?": Archambault, "They Called Me a Hero," 39.

165   "I was just so sure Grant was one of the survivors": Peter Stockland, "Notley Kids Broke News," *Edmonton Sun*, October 22, 1984, 12.

166   "I think she suspected because the Mounties had turned off the radio": Allan Kellog, "Knocking on the Door of the Dome," *Edmonton Journal*, April 14, 2007.

166   "What are you doing with that knife? Get rid of it": Archambault, "They Called Me a Hero," 30.

166   "He can't forget this because his gun and handcuffs are inside": Ibid., 57.

167   "It was the greatest feeling in the world": Ibid., 40.

PART IV

15. HERO

172   "He saved my life": John Colebourn, "Prisoner Saves Officer," *Edmonton Sun*, October 21, 1984, 21.

172   "Larry wanted to step down from the plane under his own steam": Giffin interview, June 2, 2011.

174   "The memory of the two girls running by me crying is locked in my mind as though it happened yesterday": Interview with Byron Christopher, October 8, 2011.

175   "Was he killed or wasn't he?": Hopkins interview, June 14, 2011.

175   "Grant's gone": Ibid.

177   "I had to be chained to my bed like an animal": Archambault, "They Called Me a Hero," 44–45.

177   "He saved Deschamps' life": Larry Shaben, October 10, 2004.

179   "Duncan took Erik's hand and held it so long that Erik felt uncomfortable": Vogel interview, October 21, 2003.

180   "I'm not a rapist or a rat, so why the isolation?": Archambault, "They Called Me a Hero," 48.

181   "Paul Archambault did an outstanding job": Tom Barrett, "Shaben Thankful Number Not Called," *Edmonton Journal*, October 22, 1984, 1.

181   "I just did what I thought had to be done": Gary Poignant, "Prisoner Downplays 'Hero' Role," *Edmonton Sun*, October 22, 1984, 21.

181   "He lasted hours": Darcy Henton, "Dying Man's Moans Haunt Air Crash Hero," *Edmonton Journal*, October 23, 1984.

183   "He was quiet and respectful": Interview with Kenneth Staples, October 14, 2011.

183 "The judge then excused him from the courtroom": Canadian Press, "Charges Dismissed, Crash Hero Freed," *The Globe and Mail*, October 23, 1984.

183 "They smelled something fierce of fire": Archambault, "They Called Me a Hero," 51.

184 "didn't even have the coins to wash his smoke-smelling clothes": Canadian Press, "Charges Dismissed, Crash Hero Freed," *The Globe and Mail*, October 23, 1984.

184 "'That way my feet are on the ground and I like the view": Gary Poignant, "Prisoner Downplays 'Hero' Role", *Edmonton Sun*, October 22, 1984, 21.

184 "Like, one minute they couldn't give a shit who I was and then the next minute I'm something great": Havard Gould, "Archambault Here," CBC Newsday, television footage, Ottawa, January 4, 1985.

184 "I didn't do anything different than a whole lot of other people would have done in that situation": Citizen Staff and News Services, "Hero of Crash Wants to Be Left Alone," *Ottawa Citizen*, October 23, 1984.

185 "I don't want to get hounded": Ibid.

185-86 "he hoped Albertans who wanted to contribute to a fund for him 'won't go crazy'": Agnes Buttner, "Brighter Prospects for Hero," *Edmonton Journal*, October 26, 1984, A12.

16. INQUEST

187 "What the hell were you thinking?": Vogel interview, October 21, 2003.

188 "They're going to use any statement you make to press criminal charges": Ibid.

189 "If they persist in this matter of operation for a much longer period we are virtually certain to be faced with a fatality": Memorandum from Inspector Griffiths, re: Wapiti Aviation Ltd, August 17, 1984. Courtesy of Dale Wells.

191 "the Company failed to meet a regular maintenance check on part of its fleet": Canadian Air Transportation Administration, media statement, October 22, 1984. Courtesy of Dale Wells.

191 "he was considered conscientious and a careful pilot": Record of telephone conversation between Dave Klippenstein and Dale Wells, Oct. 22, 1984. Courtesy of Dale Wells.

191 "lawsuit against Wapiti alleging 'wanton or reckless operations'": Letter

from Leighton Decore, Decore and Company, November 17, 1984. Courtesy of Dale Wells.

192   "Dale would also lose his status as chief engineer": Letter to Wapiti Aviation Ltd. from D.A. Davidson, Regional Director, Aviation Regulations for Ministers of Transport, December 18, 1984. Courtesy of Dale Wells.

192   "lacked sufficient knowledge of the intricacies of the present operations to permit him to competently discharge his duties as operations manager": Letter to Wapiti Aviation Ltd. from L.A. Klein, Regional Manager, Air Carrier Operations, Transport Canada, December 19, 1984. Courtesy of Dale Wells. In a 1990 Federal Court of Canada judgment, Justice Allison Walsh noted: "Unlike the case of Delbert Wells, all the witnesses speak highly of the work and ability of his son, Dale Wells. He was carrying on several jobs as Chief Pilot, Chief Maintenance Engineer, Chief Flying Instructor and Designated Flight Test Examiner. In March and April 1983, the Department of Transport, through its regional superintendent Aeronautical Engineering and regional superintendent Air Carriers approved forms in which Delbert Wells was formally designated as Director of Flight Operations and Dale Wells as Director of Maintenance, Chief Pilot and Chief Flying Instructor. While Dale Wells was qualified for the positions he occupied as the airline grew he had too many different duties for one person to accomplish. Delbert Wells' qualifications to act as operations manager (Director of Flight Operations) were never thoroughly checked." Judgment in Court Action No. T-1637-85 between Sally Margaret Swanson and Her Majesty the Queen, February 6, 1990, 16–17.

194   "I feel it could turn my life around. I want to put the past behind me, starting today": Jack Aubry, "Quebec Court Gives Hero Probation for Break and Enter," *Edmonton Journal*, January 9, 1985, B1.

195   "We will not point an accusing finger at anybody": Canadian Aviation Safety Board, *Wapiti Aviation Ltd. Inquiry Proceedings*, H40006, 3.

196   "Did you have an opportunity to sleep?": Ibid., 149.

198   "They thanked him for telling the truth": Vogel interview, October 21, 2003.

198   "I burned it in the fire": Canadian Aviation Safety Board, *Wapiti Aviation Ltd. Inquiry Proceedings*, H40006, 163.

202   "I believed I was farther ahead than I was": Ibid., 201.

202   "has the operations manager ever rejected a request by a pilot for a co-pilot?": Canadian Aviation Safety Board, *Wapiti Aviation Ltd. Inquiry*

Proceedings, H40006, 262. Delbert Wells did not testify at the inquiry. A medical report submitted at the opening of proceedings stated that he should not be submitted in his present medical condition due to the possible difficulties of testifying. *Wapiti Aviation Ltd. Inquiry Proceedings, H40006*,16.

203 "I had never at any time told any pilot to go take a look and go down to 800 feet": Ibid., 305.

204 "I could see no reason whatsoever for any lack of sleep": Ibid., 330.

205 "I only did what I had to do": Douglas Sweet, "Plane Crash Hero 'Did What I Had to Do,'" *Edmonton Journal*, March 2, 1985.

206 "Maybe now he'll be proud of me": Christopher interview, September 30, 2011.

206 "he'd grown up a lot": "Crash Hero," *Midday*, segment D, CBC television footage, April 16, 1985.

17. AFTERLIFE

208 "That experience definitely changed my outlook in the sense that I now have a greater appreciation of life": Maureen Buchholz, "Survivor Changed," *The Peace Arch News*, December 1, 1984.

209 "So if you haven't done the things that you've always wanted to do, it's time to do them": "Deschamps Quits," CBC television footage, *Edmonton Newsday*, February 27, 1985.

209 *"What am I doing wasting my time here?"*: Deschamps interview, December 5, 2007.

212 "a wrecked ship for every mile of coast along the Graveyard of the Pacific": Graveyard of the Pacific, Virtual Museum of Canada, www. museevirtuel-virtualmuseum.ca.

214 "This is the pilot who flew the plane": Vogel interview, October 14, 2011.

214 "Never touch me when I'm sleeping or I'll take a swing at you": Author correspondence with Vogel, November 9, 2011.

215 *"your services will be required until approximately October 11, 1985"*: Erik Vogel, personal files.

216 "Corona Mafia": Warren Michaels, "Archambault Pizza," CBC television footage, *Edmonton Newsday*, July 2, 1985.

217 "He looked like Grizzly Adams": Interview with Elpeda Palmer, November 19, 2011.

217   "Paul was close to everyone and he was very loyal": Interview with
        Donna Bougiridis, November 11, 2011.

218   "I'm striving to be better for myself—mentally, physically, morally—and
        I'm not doing too bad": Warren Michaels, "Archambault Pizza," CBC
        television footage, *Edmonton Newsday*, July 2, 1985.

218   "Ed Sullivan had appeared on the show": Paul appeared on CBC
        television's *Front Page Challenge*, May 4, 1985.

219   "that's how I get around": Interview with Sue Wink, October 20, 2011.

220   "Do you consider yourself a brave man?": *Front Page Challenge*, CBC
        television footage, May 4, 1985.

223   "He's just a good friend": Wink interview, October 20, 2011.

223   "I can't go a day without thinking about it": Canadian Press, "Pilot to
        Tell Story at Fatality Inquiry," *Edmonton Sun*, November 9, 1985.

224   "do you have any issues with the law?": Author correspondence with
        Vogel, October 27, 2011.

224   "I just did it": *Herald* Staff Writer, "Pilot to Tell Story at Fatality Inquiry,"
        Daily Herald Tribune, Grande Prairie, November 9, 1985.

18. FATE

227   "He couldn't bring himself to examine the contents of that box":
        Interview with Randy Wright, January 6, 2011.

227   "I had to prove to myself that I hadn't lost my nerve": Ibid.

230   "Not many people had that kind of one-on-one access": Ibid.

231   "What do you think I can do to solve this problem?": Interview with
        Lindsay Cherney, December 8, 2010.

232   "in order to be an effective government, he needed to include people":
        Jim McQuarrie, producer, "Generations: A Hundred Years in Alberta,"
        CBC documentary on Muslim families in Alberta, December 28, 2005.

233   "You put those together and you get an exceptional minister": Keith
        Gerein, "Cancer Claims Larry Shaben," *Edmonton Journal*, September 7,
        2008, A3.

235   "I got to make tips": Wink interview, December 4, 2006.

236   "He wanted to come home": Wink interview, October 20, 2011.

237   "When he told her it was Demerol, she got mad": Ibid.

240 "He needed somebody to appreciate his worth as a human being": Larry Shaben interview, October 10, 2004.

241 "The airline had immediately launched a lawsuit against Transport Canada for damages, challenging the legality of the decision in court": Wapiti's lawsuit against Transport Canada never made it to trial.

241 "We saw a car's lights go off and on a couple of times and from the angle of the lights, it was in the ditch": Randy Hardisty, "Robbers Attack Shaben," *Calgary Herald*, December 8, 1986.

241 "Stop the car. They need help": Alma Shaben interview, December 8, 2010.

242 "turned to open the back door to let him in": Hardisty, "Robbers Attack Shaben."

242 "Don't pay any attention to her. She's drunk": Alma Shaben interview, December 8, 2010.

19. ATONEMENT

245 "*Hi Erik, Just a short note to let you know that I am still behind you in every way*": Correspondence between Erik Vogel and Carla Blaskovits, May 1986. Courtesy of Erik Vogel.

246 "defamation lawsuit by Wapiti Aviation against the CBC for a documentary on the crash in which Erik, along with several other former Wapiti pilots, had participated": The lawsuit never made it to trial.

248 "channelized attention with loss of situational awareness": Erik Vogel, "It Won't Happen to Me," Helicopter Professional Pilots Safety Program newsletter, Volume 7, No. 1, 1995.

250 "It was life altering": Deschamps interview, December 5, 2007.

250 "'It would have been a disaster,' Scott later told me, 'because I was too busy trying to figure out what I needed'": Ibid.

252 "'That damn dog just stole my drink'": Letter from Byron Christopher to Gayle Archambault following Paul's death, May 14, 1991.

252 "He changed the way I looked at prisoners": Ibid. Byron Christopher went on to become a crime reporter and eventually began a long-term correspondence with Richard Lee McNair, one of America's most wanted prisoners. That correspondence resulted in an award-winning newspaper series and formed the basis of a biography, which Christopher is currently writing on McNair.

253 "He was no doubt very hungry, as it was gone in no time": Author correspondence with Irene Jorgensen, December 2006.

253   "It wasn't his job. He just did it": Interview with Irene Jorgensen, December 10, 2006.

253   "I believe he had a heart of gold that had been badly damaged in his young life": Ibid.

254   "People should have been looking after themselves, not expecting government to do it": Larry Shaben interview, October 10, 2004.

254   "the minute you start pretending that you're the reason and not your position, you're lost": Interview with Larry Shaben, Jr., November 29, 2011.

254   "I'll lose the opportunity to go back out and work in the private sector": Cherney interview, December 8, 2010.

255   "he didn't ask for anything from me": Deschamps interview, December 5, 2007.

256   "He said goodbye, and that was it": Ibid.

257   "He put his life on the line to save another man": Interview with Andrew McNeil, December 5, 2010.

257   "I think that ate at him, to be mocked by everybody": Ibid.

260   "he wanted to be out in the bush the way Mother Nature meant man to die": Daniel Archambault interview, April 1, 2009.

261   "there's been nothing to say it was foul play": John Ludwick, "Police Investigate Man's Death," *Daily Herald Tribune*, May 8, 1991, 1.

262   "I'd go into the bush and find these frozen remains": Deschamps interview, December 5, 2007.

262   "If you ask me, someone bumped him on the head. I told the police that": Bougiridis interview, November 11, 2011.

263   "I still dream of him": Wink interview, October 20, 2011.

20. RETURN

265–66   "I realize that I've been making a trail. So I figured why not just keep going": Vogel interview, October 21, 2003.

266   "locating a small plane is nearly impossible in the bush if there is no ELT": Author correspondence with Vogel, October 27, 2011.

268   "the accident of C-GXUC most likely would have been averted": Federal Court of Canada Judgment in Court Action No. T-1637-85 between Sally Margaret Swanson and Her Majesty the Queen, February 6, 1990, 25. Justice Walsh quotes expert aviation witness Walter Gadzos, formerly of

the Department of Transport, who assisted Justice Charles Dubin in the 1979 Commission of Inquiry on Aviation Safety.

270   "His eighty-two-year-old aunt knew Scott's half-sister's name was Joanne, and that she lived in Bulawayo": Deschamps interview, December 5, 2007.

270   "I asked him, does he know anything about the Deschamps family?": Ibid.

272   "I never had that connectedness before": Ibid.

272   "Nor does it mean that it wasn't a miracle—at least to me": Deschamps, "Once Upon an Angel," 17.

274   "he couldn't do in business what he'd been able to as a Cabinet minister": Cherney interview, December 8, 2010.

274   "If things got difficult, he persevered, and when others didn't follow through, he was disappointed": Larry Shaben, Jr. interview, November 29, 2011.

275   "reluctance to charge interest on money others borrowed from him— were deeply rooted in his faith": In Islam, profit is permitted, but interest is forbidden.

275   "dance the *dabke* in the basement": The *dabke* is a traditional Middle Eastern line dance.

276   "There was a lot of yelling and partying going on": Interview with Sol Rolingher, November 29, 2011.

278   "continue a dialogue of mutual support and peace": Edmonton Jewish and Muslim communities media release, September 12, 2001. Courtesy of Sol Rolingher.

279   "Treat each other with utmost respect and resist the temptation to lecture": Edmonton Council of Muslim Communities, "Larry Shaben: An Embodiment of a True Leader," September 10, 2008.

EPILOGUE—SURVIVORS

280   "Don't worry about recognizing us, it said, we'll be the ones grinning like idiots": Author correspondence with Vogel, October 23, 2006.

282   "it never seems like enough": Ibid.

283   "I'm not the black-and-white, rigid, career-driven, typical kick-down-the-door cop that I was": Deschamps interview, December 5, 2007.

284   "who promote or develop housing or related services and who are passionate about what they do": Homeward Trust Edmonton website,

http://www.homewardtrust.ca/programs/rooph-awards.php.

285   "I would like to take my wife in my arms and apologize to her and tell her yes, we can have a child": Larry Shaben interview, October 10, 2004.

285   "Not too many people have that experience": Deschamps interview, December 5, 2007.

286–87   *"why a 6'3" Fire Captain is crying at his desk"*: E-mail correspondence from Erik Vogel to Larry Shaben, September 4, 2008.

IMAGE CREDITS

Page i (top) Erik Vogel; (bottom) Alma Shaben
Page ii Alma Shaben
Page iii *Edmonton Journal*
Page iv (top) Erik Vogel; (bottom) *Edmonton Journal*
Page v Paul Archambault, "They Called Me a Hero" (1985), 28
Page vi (all) *Edmonton Journal*
Page vii (all) QMI Agency
Page viii (top) QMI Agency; (bottom) *Edmonton Journal*
Page ix (top) *Edmonton Journal*; (bottom) Ken Archambault
Page x (all) Scott Deschamps
Page xi (all) Erik Vogel
Page xii Courtesy of the author

SELECTED BIBLIOGRAPHY

Bach, Richard. *A Gift of Wings*. New York: Dell Publishing, 1974.

———. *Illusions: The Adventures of a Reluctant Messiah*. New York: Dell Publishing Co. Inc., 1977.

Bauer, Harry. *The Flying Mystique: Exploring Reality and Self in the Sky*. New York: Delacorte Press, 1980.

Boer, Peter. *Bush Pilots: Canada's Wilderness Daredevils*. Edmonton: Folklore Publishing, 2004.

Cobb, Roger W. and David M. Primo. *The Plane Truth: Airline Crashes, the Media and Transportation Policy*. Washington: Brookings Institution Press, 2003.

Collins, Richard L. *Air Crashes: What Went Wrong, Why and What Can Be Done About It*. Charlottesville: Thomasson-Grant, 1986.

Dickens, C.H. *From the Ground Up*. Ottawa: Aviation Publishers Company Ltd., 1984.

Flying Magazine eds. *Pilot Error: Anatomies of Aircraft Accidents*. New York: Van Nostrand Reinhold Co., 1977.

Gann, Ernest K. *Fate Is the Hunter*. New York: Simon and Schuster, 1961.

Langewiesche, Wolfgang. *Stick and Rudder: An Explanation of the Art of Flying*. New York: McGraw-Hill Inc., 1944.

Marshall, David and Bruce Harris. *Wild About Flying: Dreamers, Doers & Daredevils*. Toronto and Buffalo: Firefly Books, 2003.

Montgomery, M. R. and Gerald L. Foster. *A Field Guide to Airplanes: How to Identify Over 300 Airplanes of North America: Illustrations, Descriptions and Specifications*. Boston: Houghton Mifflin, 1984.

Obson, Diane K., ed. *Reflections on the Art of Living: A Joseph Campbell Companion*. New York: HarperCollins, 1991.

Reid, Piers Paul. *Alive: The Story of the Andes Survivors*. New York: Avon Books, 1974.

Saint-Exupéry, Antoine de. *Airman's Odyssey*. New York: Harcourt Brace & Company, 1939.

Schiavo, Mary. *Flying Blind, Flying Safe*. New York: Avon Books, 1997.

Sherwood, Ben. *The Survivors Club: The Secrets and Science That Could Save Your Life*. New York: Grand Central Publishing, 2009.

Smith, Patrick. *Ask the Pilot: Everything You Need to Know About Air Travel*. New York: Riverhead Books, 2004.

Taylor, John W. R., ed. *Jane's Pocket Book of Commercial Transport Aircraft*. New York: Collier Books, 1973.

Transport Canada. *Flight Training Manual*. Toronto: Gage Publishing Ltd., 1986.

ACKNOWLEDGEMENTS

This book took flight the day I met my agent, Jackie Kaiser. Months earlier, MFA classmate and fellow writer Rob Weston had recommended Jackie to me, but I'd been reluctant to contact her. I was still smarting from unsuccessful efforts to interest others in the book. I had shelved my business career to write, and had all but given up on my dream when an article I'd written on aviation safety for *The Walrus* (under the gifted stewardship of editor Jeremy Keehn) garnered a trio of National Magazine Award nominations.

Just after midnight on the day I was scheduled to fly across the country for the awards ceremony, I mustered the nerve to send Jackie a brief e-mail sketching an outline of the book and requesting a few minutes of her time. Her response was instantaneous. By the end of our two-hour meeting the next day I knew that I had found not only a remarkable champion, but also the makings of an enduring friendship.

I've often discovered that individuals of exemplary character and unbridled enthusiasm surround themselves with like-minded souls. To my great fortune, one such person in Jackie's orbit was my editor, Anne Collins, publisher at the Knopf Random Canada Publishing Group. Within hours of receiving the proposal, she called Jackie with an offer. Anne's commitment to and support for this book has since been unwavering. Her extraordinary talent and vision as an editor is etched into every page. Anne, it has been a joy, inspiration and privilege to work with you.

I've also been fortunate to work with Amanda Lewis, associate editor, Knopf Random Canada. Not only is Amanda a skilled and sharp-eyed editor, she hails from the west coast and a firefighting family, both of which added to her impressive attention to, and understanding of, the characters, setting and subject matter.

Outside Canada, I've been blessed with two brilliant editors who worked seamlessly with Anne to help me create a far better book. My profound thanks extend to Jon Butler at Macmillan Publishers in London and Helen Atsma at Grand Central Publishing in New York for their insight, guidance and enthusiasm.

There is incredible trust involved in letting another person tell your story, especially one with such tragic and devastating personal consequences. Erik Vogel bestowed that trust upon me, and breathed life into this book the day he invited me to our first meeting at his home in the fall of 2003. He has since remained an honest and generous steward. My thanks go to Erik for his belief, patience and Herculean efforts to respond to my incessant inquiries and stay with me on this extraordinarily long journey. I am similarly thankful to Scott Deschamps, the other living survivor of this story, for trusting me to tread the tender and very personal territory of his remarkable life, and to Heidi Petrak, who helped me keep the faith. My gratitude also goes to Paul Archambault's siblings: Ken, Daniel and Angele, for sharing Paul's unpublished manuscript and the details of his life; to Sue Wink for her unstinting honesty; and to his aunt Myrna Quesnel and friend Andrew McNeil, for responding to the tiny, obscure ads I placed in their local newspapers. Paul was always a hero to me, and I hope I have done justice to his noble spirit.

When it came to chronicling a life, none was more difficult than that of my father, Larry Shaben. I knew him in the loving but limited way that an adoring daughter knows a dad. Delving into the messy emotional terrain of his years of struggle was both terrifying and gratifying: terrifying because I didn't know what I would find or how it might change my memory of him; gratifying because it allowed me to discover in my father a man of exceptional character who I never fully appreciated while he was alive. For helping me complete the picture, love and gratitude are due to my siblings, Larry, James and Joan, and to my sister Linda for also being my muse, escape hatch and personal chef when I was far too close to the edge.

To my mother, Alma, I owe immeasurably more than love and gratitude: I owe who I am. You are grace and generosity personified, Mom, and your love has seen me through so much more than this book.

The family I was born to is not my only family. Love and thanks go to Sharon, Baha and Yasmeen Abu-Laban for their unwavering faith and devotion. Nor could I have written this book without the incredible support of my community of friends, particularly the moms and dads of Dunbar who helped care for my boys and cheer me along. Among them, I'd particularly like to acknowledge Sue Climie for many inspiring talks and walks; Stacey Shaw for being an irrepressible friend and fan; Liz O'Malley for her non-stop encouragement and 6:00 a.m. smile as I sat bleary-eyed and exhausted on a spin bike; and Annette O'Shea, for dragging me from my desk for pho and joining me in the soul-restoring therapy of putting our hands in the earth.

Writing can be a lonely pursuit and I am indebted to those who have shared the journey with me over the past decade, in particular my dear friend Cori Howard and my writing group, The Lyin' Bastards: Nancy Lee, John Vigna, Denise Ryan, Dina Del Bucchia, Keri Korteling, Judy McFarlane and Sally Breen. Thanks for holding me up and pushing me forward and, of course, for the finely observed critiques, cheap wine and good eats. I also wish to thank the extraordinarily wise and wonderful Andreas Schroeder, and the many other talented writers and professors in the University of British Columbia's Creative Writing Program who gave me my start. In addition, acknowledgement is due to the incomparable Geoff Le Boutillier for first igniting a small flame that would grow to a roaring fire.

Along the complex and difficult road of researching and reconstructing the events of a decades-old crash and its aftermath, I owe thanks to a plethora of people including Rosemary Richards, librarian extraordinaire at the Transportation Safety Board of Canada; Captain Lisa Evong, chief of the air staff, Air Force Public Affairs, Department of National Defence Canada; Diane Sweet, CBC Edmonton's senior media librarian;

Jean-François Coulombe, senior analyst at the Library and Archives Canada; Debra Dittrick, library assistant at the *Edmonton Journal*; and Diana Rinne, news and assignment editor for Grande Prairie's *Daily Herald Tribune*. From my hometown of High Prairie, I am indebted to Luella Wood for sharing her sharp recollections and meticulously documented personal papers, and Kevin Cox and Charlie Goutier of Cox Contracting Ltd., for helping to clarify and recreate details of the overland rescue route.

For the opportunity to fly, and their trust in letting me take the controls of their small plane, I give my heartfelt thanks to Lisa Shemko and David Speirs, pilots, friends and fellow Fastlane swim club compatriots. Particular appreciation goes to Dave for his impeccable attention to detail in reviewing and editing the technical aviation sections of the book.

I owe to-the-moon-and-back love to my son, Max, who let me disappear into my office for hours, even days on end, allowed me to miss countless school field trips and soccer and hockey games, and weathered the emotional rollercoaster of this project with such maturity and strength. Max, you inspire me every day. In you, I see the wisdom, character and generosity of your grandfather and know that the best part of him lives on in you.

Finally, to my husband, Riyad: words can't begin to express my gratitude. This book exists because of your faith, editorial acumen, Sherpa-esque endurance, patience and love. Thank you for being my partner in crime and all things of the heart.

C.N.S.
Vancouver, Canada
July 6, 2012

NT Photo

CAROL SHABEN was nominated for three National Magazine Awards, including Best New Magazine Writer, and won two of them, a Gold Medal for Investigative Reporting and a Silver Medal for Politics and Public Interest. A former international trade consultant and CBC writer/broadcaster, Shaben was twenty-two, living and working as a journalist in the Middle East, when the crash occurred. She learned of the event, and her father's survival, reading a local newspaper.